Multilevel Protection of the Principle of Legality in Criminal Law

Mercedes Pérez Manzano •
Juan Antonio Lascuraín Sánchez •
Marina Mínguez Rosique
Editors

Multilevel Protection of the Principle of Legality in Criminal Law

Springer

Editors
Mercedes Pérez Manzano
Faculty of Law
Universidad Autónoma de Madrid
Madrid, Spain

Juan Antonio Lascuraín Sánchez
Faculty of Law
Universidad Autónoma de Madrid
Madrid, Spain

Marina Mínguez Rosique
Faculty of Law
Universidad Autónoma de Madrid
Madrid, Spain

ISBN 978-3-319-63864-5 ISBN 978-3-319-63865-2 (eBook)
DOI 10.1007/978-3-319-63865-2

Library of Congress Control Number: 2017954355

Printed on acid-free paper

This Springer imprint is published by Springer Nature
The registered company is Springer International Publishing AG
The registered company address is: Gewerbestrasse 11, 6330 Cham, Switzerland

To the memory of Susana Huerta

Preface

Fundamental rights are recognized and protected through a multiplicity of national and international norms and jurisdictions. This situation of concurrency of norms and courts has created a model of multi-level protection of fundamental rights, raising several relevant legal problems. The practical effects of these problems deserve to be the object of in-depth study, due to their complexity, novelty and importance. In particular, this model allows a varied content and scope to be assigned to fundamental rights in different States and under different jurisdictions. Within the framework of the federal or pluralist constitution, it hardly appears to prompt special reservations, as it constitutes a means of maintaining and respecting the different national sensitivities. The inverse should not, however, be forgotten (the shadow side of this model of multi-level protection in such a peculiar yet essential matter): on the one hand, it clashes with the universal character of fundamental rights, and, on the other, it generates legal insecurity and inequality in the juridical-constitutional status of national citizens according to the State or jurisdiction that may apply these rights.

This situation of concurrency of norms and jurisdictions affects Spain in a special way, and it is especially relevant for criminal law. It especially affects Spain, in the first place, because of its constitutional openness to international human rights law, as international conventions for the protection of human are integrated in the internal order and constitute a parameter for the interpretation of the content of the rights recognized in the Spanish Constitution (Art. 10.2 SC). In the second place, it impacts peculiarly on the Spanish legal order, because of the accession of Spain to a supranational institution: the European Union. Even though the Union originally lacked competence in matters of fundamental rights, these rights have gradually been included in its normative system—which has primacy over the national—firstly as general principles and more recently through the constitutionalization of the Charter of Fundamental Rights of the European Union.

This model of multi-level protection is of special theoretical importance for criminal law, because, on the one hand, the essential function of the latter is precisely the protection of fundamental social rights and values; on the other, it fulfils this function precisely through the restriction of the fundamental rights of the accused and the convicted person; and, finally, it can only achieve this mission in a legitimate way in the framework of respect for specific principles and constitutional guarantees, which protect the citizen against the risks of excessive or arbitrary use of *ius puniendi* by the State. Therefore, the determination of the content and scope of each fundamental criminal right, principle or guarantee is an essential task for the delimitation of the legitimacy of criminal law. However moreover, the situation of multi-level protection of fundamental rights has, moreover, acquired an important practical relevance for the application of criminal law, because, in a strongly globalized world, the crimes and the criminals continually trespass national borders. So, their effective prosecution and sanctioning require permanent cooperation between the jurisdictions of courts from different States. This situation presupposes the recognition—not always constitutionally possible—in Spain of the judicial decisions of other States with different legal orders and with different standards with regard to their principles and guarantees in criminal law.

It is not by chance that two of the most relevant and well-known cases in which these problems of fundamental legal interaction emerge have been cases arising in the criminal jurisdiction. Indeed, the Melloni case, which resulted in the decision of the Spanish Constitutional Court ATC 86/2011 of 9 June 2011; the ECJ (GC) Judgment of 26 February 2013, Melloni (C-399/11); and the Constitutional Court Judgment STC 26/2014 of 13 February 2014, is a paradigmatic example of the problems presented by the disparity of standards of protection within the framework of the European Union, specifically when the standard of national protection offers greater guarantees than the international standard. And the so-called Parot case (STS 197/2006 of 28 February 2006), which gave rise to the series of judgements of the Constitutional Court initiated with STC 39/2012 of 29 March 2012 and the ECtHR Judgment of 21 October 2013, in the case of Del Río Prada, is a further significant example of this lack of uniformity of standards for inverse reasons: this time the internal standard offered fewer guarantees than the international one.

The book that we are now presenting, substantially, includes the result of a multidisciplinary seminary that was held at the Faculty of Law of the *Universidad Autónoma de Madrid* on 27 and 28 November 2014, in the framework of research project DER2012-33935 "La tutela multinivel de los principios y garantías penales" [Multi-level protection of principles and guarantees in Criminal Law], directed by Mercedes Pérez Manzano, in which Enric Fossas Espadaler, Susana Huerta Tocildo, Cristina Izquierdo Sans, Juan Antonio Lascuraín Sánchez, Marina Mínguez Rosique, Teresa Rodríguez Montañés and Ignacio Villaverde Menéndez all participated. The project had as its central objective both the identification of the similarities and the differences in the standards of protection applied by the different competent national and international courts with respect to principles and guarantees in criminal law and, whenever that was not possible, the proposal of common standards and criteria for their interconnection.

This book is of a more limited scope as its objective is merely to analyse the state of the question with regard to one of the principles, the principle of legality in criminal law. It concerns the most relevant of all the principles, and, probably, it is also the principle with the most extensive content, integrating a broad set of guarantees for the citizen. For this reason and because the decision by the ECtHR in the case of Del Río Prada, relating to the so-called Parot doctrine, constitutes, without doubt, a *leading case* that has aroused intense debate, we decided to organize a specific seminar at which to present the partial results of our research and to discuss those results with specialists in criminal law, constitutional law, the philosophy of law and international public law.

"Multilevel protection of the principle of legality in Criminal Law" is an abridged version in English of the publication "La tutela multinivel del principio de legalidad penal" (editorial Marcial Pons, 2016) in Spanish. References to the Spanish legal order have been removed, so as not to distract the reader's attention from the global debate regarding the challenges raised by the simultaneous recognition and defence of fundamental rights by different courts.

The book has three separate parts. The first, composed of the contributions from Enric Fossas and Cristina Izquierdo, addresses some general questions: the analysis of little-known pronouncements by the European Court of Human Rights regarding the conventional limits (of the European Convention of Human Rights) on the national legislator (Enric Fossas) and the progress of the Melloni case both within and outside Spain, with the purpose of situating the problems of multi-level protection in the framework of the European Union (Cristina Izquierdo).

The second part centres on the examination of the principal guarantees tied to the principle of legality, so as to expound the concordances and discrepancies of national and international standards. Ignacio Villaverde analyses the mandate of determination; Juan Antonio Lascuraín deals with the strict subjection of the judge to legal definitions of offences and penalties; Mercedes Pérez Manzano examines the prohibitions on *bis in idem*, given that the Spanish Constitutional Court has situated material *bis in idem* under Art. 25.1 of the Spanish Constitution; and Marina Mínguez Rosique accompanies us on a tour through the case law of the Inter-American Court of Human Rights to present us with a panorama of the pronouncements of this Court on the principle of legality.

The third part is dedicated to the analysis of the judgements linked to the Parot doctrine. Fernando Molina occupies himself with the analysis of the judgement of the Spanish Supreme Court, analysing consistency in the interpretation of the norms of the Penal Code strictly from the perspective of the penal order. Susana Huerta and Teresa Rodríguez Montañés examine the internal judgements of both the Supreme Court and the Constitutional Court, from the viewpoint of the Spanish Constitution, on the principle of legality in criminal law (Art. 25.1 SC and 7 ECHR) and the right to liberty (Art. 17.1 SC and 5 ECHR). Juan Antonio García Amado centres his analysis on the question of the retroactivity of case law when this is favourable to the offender. And, finally, Argelia Queralt and Carlos Ruiz Miguel examine the problems of internal enforcement of the judgements of the European Court of Human Rights, in the wake of the Judgment of the European Court in the Del Río Prada case and the manner in which the Spanish Supreme Court decided to apply that decision in this and in other cases.

Any well-advised reader will be aware of an important gap in this book, as it contains no analysis of the principle of the nonretroactivity of unfavourable criminal norms, in the part dedicated to describing and analysing the national and international standard. It is not out of forgetfulness. Neither was it a decision taken because of abundant indirect analysis of the topic owing to the scrutiny of the Parot doctrine.

The gap is owing to the misfortune of the death of our beloved colleague, coresearcher and friend Susana Huerta, who was in charge of the task. Susana, not only the director but the heart and soul of the first research project on which we embarked, a group of professors of criminal and constitutional law, linked together by having acted as law clerks to the Constitutional Court and with an interest in continuing to share multidisciplinary debates. Susana was unable to attend the seminar on legality in November 2014, to both her and our own great sadness, as we know how much she would have enjoyed it and how much she would have enriched the other participants with the lucidity of her appreciations and the passion and the vivacity with which she expressed them. Susana was an exceptional penalist, a reference in the areas that she investigated and, among those, in the principle of legality, to which she dedicated a large number of works. During the autumn and the subsequent winter of 2014, Susana continued working on the task she had accepted, but was unable to finish it. As we were unable to imagine this book without her presence, we decided to request permission from the *Revista Jurídica de Cataluña* to reproduce her work on the Del Río Prada judgement here. We are grateful to the journal and especially to its director, Eugenio Gay, for the extensive cooperation extended to us, which has enabled us to include her work alongside our own.

Susana often stated that "the Constitutional Court never passes through the life of a penalist without leaving its mark", expressing the evolution that her conception of criminal law and her priorities as a researcher had experienced since her first stage as a law clerk to the Constitutional Court. All of us who with Susana shared in the work at the Constitutional Court know that she was right, although she also modestly limited her remark to penalists: whatever your area of legal expertise, the Court never passes through your professional life without leaving its mark. This book is, without a doubt, evidence of that and a thankful testimony of another even more important mark: the indelible one that Susana Huerta has left among her friends and fellow colleagues.

Madrid, Spain — Mercedes Pérez Manzano
Madrid, Spain — Juan Antonio Lascuraín Sánchez

Contents

Abbreviations

AAN	Auto de la Audiencia Nacional (Decision of the *Audiencia Nacional*)
ACHR	American Convention on Human Rights
ATC	Auto del Tribunal Constitucional (Decision of the Spanish Constitutional Court)
AG	Attorney General
CFD	Council Framework Decision
CFREU	Charter of Fundamental Rights of the European Union
CISA	Convention Implementing the Schengen Agreement
EAW	European Arrest Warrant
ECHR	European Convention on Human Rights
ECJ	European Court of Justice
ECtHR	European Court of Human Rights
FD	Fundamento de Derecho (legal ground)
FJ	Fundamento jurídico (Point of Law, Legal Ground)
IACtHR	Inter-American Court of Human Rights
LEC	Law on Civil Procedure
LECrim	Law on Criminal Procedure
par.	Paragraph
PC	Penal Code (in force, 1995)
PC73	Penal Code of 1973
p./pp.	Page/pages
SC	Spanish Constitution
SCC	Spanish Constitutional Court
SSC	Spanish Supreme Court
STC	Sentencia del Tribunal Constitucional (Judgement of the Spanish Constitutional Court)

STS	Sentencia del Tribunal Supremo (Judgement of the Spanish Supreme Court)
TEU	Treaty on European Union
TFEU	Treaty on the Functioning of the European Union
UK	United Kingdom
VAT	Value-added tax

Part I
Multilevel Protection of Fundamental Rights

Material Limits on the Criminal Legislator: Their Interpretation by the Spanish Constitutional Court and the European Court of Human Rights

Enric Fossas Espadaler

1 Introduction

The aim of this contribution is to study the material limits on the criminal legislator set forth in the Spanish Constitution and in the European Convention of Human Rights, as interpreted by the Spanish Constitutional Court (SCC) and by the European Court of Human Rights (ECtHR).

Constitutionalism places an onus on all the powers, even the legislative branch, to subject themselves to limits and material obligations.[1] Therefore, the penal and procedural guarantees that define the model of minimal criminal Law are also considered constitutional safeguards that are binding even for the legislator.[2] These principles, as is well known, have their grounding in enlightened criminal philosophy, which not only proposes a formal limit on Criminal Law (*how to* punish) but also a substantive one (*what* and *how much* to punish), as it understands that Criminal Law should be used for sanctioning only those conducts that effectively harm relevant legal assets, as is proclaimed in Art. 8 of the Declaration of the Rights of Man and of the Citizen of 1789.[3]

The norms that place material limits on the criminal legislator take effect today within the framework of constitutional pluralism; in other words, in a situation in

Former Law Clerk at the Spanish Constitutional Court (1999–2003; 2005–2008), Professor of Constitutional Law at Universitat Autònoma de Barcelona.

[1]Ferrajoli (2007), p. 567.

[2]Prieto Sanchís (2011), p. 31.

[3]The article stated: "The law should establish only penalties that are strictly and evidently necessary. (. . .)".

E. Fossas Espadaler (✉)
Universitat Autònoma de Barcelona, Campus UAB, 08193 Bellaterra (Cerdanyola del Vallès), Barcelona, Spain
e-mail: enric.fossas@uab.cat

M. Pérez Manzano et al. (eds.), *Multilevel Protection of the Principle of Legality in Criminal Law*, DOI 10.1007/978-3-319-63865-2_1

which there is a plurality of normative institutional orders, each with a constitution, at least in the sense of a corpus of hierarchical norms that establish and condition the exercise of political power and in which each one mutually recognizes the legitimacy of others, but without affirming the supremacy of one over another.[4] It happens to be so in Spain, where the Spanish Constitution of 1978 (SC), the European Convention on Human Rights, signed in Rome, in 1950 (ECHR), and the Treaty of Lisbon of 2007 prevail. The last two, of a different nature, affect the freedom of the Spanish criminal legislator, although European Law does so in the form of obligatory criminal protection of the legal interests of the European Union, which follow a harmonizing logic that is completely different from constitutional and convention-related limits, tied to fundamental rights. Hence, the limits imposed by European Law will not be discussed.

This contribution will, therefore, analyse the limits that the SCC and the ECtHR have respectively found in the SC and in the ECHR. We adopt a broad concept of limits, which includes the norms that establish prohibitions on the legislator in the form of rules, those which proclaim values, principles and rights, and even the norms that contain mandates of punishment, which can be seen as limits to decriminalization. And this concept centres on limits directed at a specific manifestation of punitive power: the promulgation of criminal norms through the selection of criminal conduct and the determination of the corresponding sanctions. Moreover, only the material limits are approached and not the formal or procedural limits to the punitive power of the State, exercised through the law that defines offences and fixes penalties. The formal limits are often designated as "constitutional guarantees" related with Criminal Law, among which the principle of legality is prominent. The main purpose of this principle is to set an external limit to the monopolistic exercise of *ius puniendi* by the State, arising as an impediment so that the executive and judicial authorities may freely define crimes and penalties.[5] The principle of criminal legality is therefore not understood as a material limit, but as a formal limit of *ius puniendi* in a State under the Rule of Law,[6] and for that reason will not be discussed.

An attempt is made through this work to contribute to the debate over the so-called "minimum Criminal Law", of which the maximum exponent is has Ferrajoli,[7] and its comparison with the so-called "expansiveness" of Criminal Law, understood as a dominant tendency in the legislation towards the introduction of new criminal categories, as well as an aggravation of those already in existence.[8] This tendency implies flexibility of categories and the relativization of principles, in view of which it is proposed to develop the norms of international Criminal Law that are protective of human rights.[9] All of these issues lead us to ask ourselves how

---

[4]This definition, in line with McCormick's, is from Bustos Gisbert (2012), p. 21.

[5]Huerta Tocildo (2000), p. 513; Ruiz Robledo (2003), pp. 61 and ff.

[6]Mir Puig (2011), p. 71.

[7]Ferrajoli (1993).

[8]Silva Sánchez (1999), Rodríguez Montañés (2009).

[9]Mir Puig (2011), p. 13.

the criminal legislator is limited in the frame of constitutional pluralism, and to compare the responses that the highest judicial interpreters have given to that question. The comparison of the pronouncements of the SCC with those of the ECtHR will allow us to advance some considerations on the relation between criminal guaranteeism and constitutional pluralism.

In pursuit of these aims, the first section will be dedicated to explaining the position that the SCC and the ECtHR maintain with respect to the criminal legislator (2); while in the second, the case-law of both the SCC and the ECtHR on the material limits to criminal law will be studied (3); drawing to a close with some conclusions (4).

2 The Position of the SCC and of the ECtHR with Regard to the Criminal Legislator

The identification of the material limits to criminal law by the SCC and the ECtHR cannot be delinked from the position in which these Courts are placed with regard to the legislator. In as many words: the understanding of the two courts as to the character and the scope of the control that they should exercise over criminal law conditions in large part their interpretation of the material limits contained in the SC and the ECHR.

2.1 The Position of the SCC with Regard to Criminal Law

An overall vision of constitutional case-law in criminal matters clearly shows that the SCC has intervened in greater depth on the definition of procedural criminal Law than in substantive criminal Law, following the pattern of other courts.[10] On the latter point, there is coincidence in pointing to the cautious, deferential and respectful attitude that the Constitutional Court has maintained towards the criminal legislator. For some authors, this attitude may be resumed in a single phrase: "little ponderation and very deferential".[11] Others underline the "cautious attitude" that the Court itself proposed towards the use of the principle of proportionality in its control over criminal laws.[12] Some have also argued that the SCC has been rather more exacting in the setting of the constitutional framework and rather more

[10]Tiedemann (1991), p. 157.

[11]Prieto Sanchís (2009), p. 288.

[12]Lopera Mesa (2006), p. 562; Díez-Ripollés (2005), p. 84; Rodríguez Mourullo (2002), p. 76; González Beilfus (2003), p. 65; Ferreres Comella (2012), p. 115; Rodríguez Montañés (2012), p. 59.

deferential in the final judgement over the inclusion of the norms that are challenged in that setting; the deference towards the criminal legislator being "manifest".[13]

The STC 55/1996 of 28 March 1996 is usually cited as the decision that contains the doctrine of the Court on its position in relation to controls over the constitutionality of criminal law. That Judgement includes *"a reflection that already anticipates the limits that the jurisdiction of this Court has on this matter with regard to the legislator"* (FJ 6). Such a reflection begins with the first declarations of the Court on its own jurisdiction, from which it derives the position of the criminal legislator: *"In the exercise of his competence to select the legal assets that emanate from a particular model of social coexistence and from the threatening behaviours against them, as well as the determination of the necessary criminal sanctions for the preservation of the aforementioned model, the legislator enjoys, within the limits established in the Constitution, a wide margin of freedom that arises from his constitutional position and, in the last instance, his specific democratic legitimacy. Not only may it be affirmed, therefore, as could not be otherwise in a social and democratic State, that under the rule of Law, the design of criminal policy corresponds exclusively to the legislator, but also, with the exception of the aforementioned elemental guidelines that are taken from the Constitution, that he has full freedom to do so"*. This freedom is translated into *"the exclusive power of the legislator to organize the criminally protected assets, the criminally reprehensible behaviours, the type and the amount of criminal sanctions, and the proportion between the conducts that he seeks to avoid and the penalties with which he seeks to achieve them"*.

As this position of the criminal legislator is that control over constitutionality should be far less intense: *"Far, therefore, from proceeding to the evaluation of its convenience, of its effects, of its quality or perfectibility, or of its relation with other possible alternatives, we have to refer solely, when asked to do so, to its constitutional framework"*, which does not mean that it *"is possible to renounce all material control over the punishment as the area of criminal legislation is not a constitutionally exempt area"*.

This doctrine based on STC 55/1996 has been reiterated by the Constitutional Court in subsequent decisions (SSTC 161/1997 of 2 October 1997, FJ 9; 59/2008 of 14 May 2008, FJ 6; 45/2009 of 19 February 2009, FJ 3; 127/2009 of 26 May 2009, FJ 3; 41/2010 of 22 July 2010, FJ 5), in which the scope of constitutional control over criminal law has been achieved: *"The judgement that takes place in this court, in protection of fundamental rights, should therefore be very cautious. It is limited to verifying that the criminal norm will not produce 'a patent useless waste of coercion that converts the norm into an arbitrary matter and that undermines the principal elements of justice inherent to the dignity of the person and to the Rule of Law'"* (STC 55/1996, FJ 8).

---

[13] This is the conclusion of the excellent study of constitutional case-law in criminal matters from Lascuraín Sánchez (2012), p. 23.

The position of the Court towards the criminal legislator can be statistically demonstrated, through an examination of the twenty-four headline judgements delivered in constitutional control processes over the past thirty years. Only nine were favourable to the appellants and declared the unconstitutionality of some legal precepts, grounded essentially in a violation of "constitutional guarantees", and in one case (STC 136/1999 of 20 July 1999) of those nine judgements was the unconstitutionality concluded on the basis of the principle of proportionality.[14] In the controversial Judgement *Herri Batasuna*,[15] no change was apparently introduced in the general doctrine in relation to control over the punitive power of the State, but only a different application of that doctrine to a case that was also different.[16]

This self-restrictive attitude of the Court against criminal law was also prominent in the interpretation of constitutional mandates directed at the criminal legislator, such as the one contained in Art. 25.2 SC, according to which custodial sentences will be oriented towards re-education and social rehabilitation and may not consist of forced labour. The Court has declared that the aforesaid norm contains no fundamental right but a constitutional mandate to the legislator (ATC 15/1984 of 11 January 1984). And it has maintained that it can *"serve as a parameter of the constitutionality of [criminal and prison] law"* (STC 75/1988 of 25 April 1988, FJ 29), but that neither rehabilitation nor re-education *"may be considered in each case as a condition of legitimacy of the punishment"* (STC 35/1994 of 31 January 1994, FJ 2). Hence, it has been affirmed that in reality neither rehabilitation nor re-socialization would be conditions for the constitutional legitimacy of the punishment; in such a way that it would be practically impossible, when designing a penalty, to invalidate a legal norm of this type for non-compliance with constitutional objectives.[17]

2.2 *The Position of the ECtHR with Regard to State Criminal Law*

Although the ECtHR is not a Constitutional Court, it assumes a role close to that of a constitutional judge in so far as it supervises the actions of state powers to verify their compatibility with the rights that it interprets. That proximity is reinforced by the supervision that it can initiate, in order to control the compliance of State laws with the Convention.[18] The Court could in this way issue a "judgement of conventionality", declaring that the existence of certain legislation can produce a violation

[14]Lascuraín Sánchez (2012), pp. 22–23.
[15]Bilbao Ubillos (2000), pp. 277–342.
[16]Prieto Sanchís (2009), p. 293.
[17]Urías Martínez (2001), p. 65.
[18]Saiz Arnáiz (1999), p. 145.

of a right, but also, considering that the right is violated by the punitive passivity of the state legislator.[19]

However, that proximity in no way implies a comparison with the control of constitutionality. Essentially, because the ECHR establishes a minimum European standard of fundamental rights arising from the legal and the political heterogeneity of the States. And that reasoning explains the harmonizing rather than the uniformizing function of the European systems that the ECtHR performs. Hence, important consequences ensue for the parameter of ECtHR judgements; which is not one of identity-conformity with the European standard, but one of proximity-compatibility, understood in terms of the principle of non-contradiction.[20]

A different question is that of the interpretative value that the ECHR has in the Spanish legal order, arising from the clause contained in art. 10.2 SC, according to which all Spanish public powers are obliged to interpret the norms relating to fundamental rights and liberties recognizes in the Constitution in accordance with international treaties and agreements on the same matters ratified by Spain. One of the functions of art. 10.2 SC is its operation as a rule of "conforming interpretation", a constitutional expression that denotes a process of comparison between two interpretations and the incorporation or the reception of the European *acquis* in matters of human rights.[21] It could, for example, lead to a comparison of the interpretation of art. 15 of the SC by the SCC, and that of art. 3 ECHR by the ECtHR when specifying how the prohibition of "inhuman and degrading punishments" limits the criminal legislator.

Due to its position with respect to the sovereign state legislators, the ECtHR in principle clearly manifests a position that is even more respectful towards them than the SCC. The ECtHR has defined its deferential position not only in relation to the criminal legislator, but in relation to the regime of criminal justice, when affirming that the latter is in principle outside of the control exercised by the Court, provided that the system does not ignore the principles of the Convention (ECtHR Judgement of 29 March 2006, c. Achour v. France; ECtHR Judgement of 12 February 2008, c. Kafkaris v. Cyprus), and in consequence, it should give the States a margin of appreciation to determine an acceptable duration of the term of imprisonment corresponding to the different offences (ECtHR Judgement of 9 July 2013, c. Vinter and others v. the United Kingdom).

The position of the ECtHR would likewise be conditioned by the interpretative criterion of "autonomous concepts", according to which the meaning of the terms of the Convention will not necessarily correspond with the meaning that those same terms are found to have in their internal legal orders.[22] Criminal Law has been one of the areas in which the autonomous concepts have been used more than any other,

[19]Ruiz Miguel (1997), p. 41.

[20]Queralt Jiménez (2008), p. 104.

[21]Arzoz Santisteban (2014), p. 180.

[22]Casadevall (2012), p.140.

where both their notions and the "criminal matter", which condition the application of art. 6 ECHR, are interpreted in an autonomous manner by the Court.[23]

3 Case-Law of the SCC and the ECtHR on the Material Limits on the Criminal Law

Having seen the position adopted by the CC and the ECtHR towards the criminal legislator, the material limits that each one of them has identified in their respective interpretations of the SC and the ECHR will be set out in this section.

3.1 The Case-Law of the Spanish Constitutional Court

Constitutional case-law could be summarized in one idea: identification of few material limits and, essentially, through the principle of proportionality. The SC contains more limits than those identified in constitutional case-law. Thus, some explicit material limits in the SC have been underlined in the doctrine,[24] and other limits linked to the specific functions of the social and democratic State (art. 1 SC) have been "discovered".[25] However, the SCC has identified the material limits on the criminal legislator, basically through a none-too-intense application of the principle of proportionality.[26]

3.1.1 The Principle of Proportionality as the Limit of Limits

It is worth asking why and how the SCC has applied the principle of proportionality as a substantive limit and what results it has achieved. The response to the first

[23] Burgorgue-Larsen (2005), p. 324.

[24] For example, the prohibition of inhuman and degrading punishments (Art. 15 CE). See Cuerda Riezu (2011) on life imprisonment. The topic has sprung into the news following the last reform of the Spanish Criminal Code in 2015, which has introduced the so-called "reviewable life sentence" for a series of very serious crimes (art. 92), which have been considered unconstitutional by numerous criminologists. See Arroyo Zapatero et al. (2016).

[25] Carbonell Mateu (1996) maintained the validity, among others, of the "principle of excessive prohibition (or proportionality)" as a limit to legislative power (pp. 82–192). Mir Puig (2011) presented the principle of proportionality, the principle of culpability, the principle of humanity and the principle of rehabilitation as constitutional limits of *ius puniendi* in the social and democratic State subject to the rule of Law (p. 94).

[26] The majority of authors who have dealt with the question coincide with this appraisal: Prieto Sanchís (2009), p. 285; Mir Puig, p. 96; Lopera Mesa (2006), p. 561; González Beilfus (2003), p. 49; Díez-Ripollés (2005), p. 83; Rodríguez Montañés (2012), p. 57; Rodríguez Mourullo (2002), p.73; Lascuraín Sánchez (2012), p. 15.

question is that the SC contains no definitive catalogue of legal criminal assets, and given that criminal laws restrict the exercise of fundamental rights, the parameter of its control should be the principle of proportionality in a broad sense. The SCC states that disproportion between the end that is pursued and the means that are employed to achieve it, "can give rise to a control from the constitutional perspective when that lack of proportion implies excessive or unnecessary sacrifice of the rights that the Constitution guarantees" (STC 55/1996, FJ 3).

But that control has to consider the special relation that exists between the law and the Constitution, since *"the legislator does not limit himself to enforcing or applying the Constitution, but he freely adopts the political options that at each time he considers most advisable within the framework that the Constitution outlines. In fact, unlike what happens with respect to other institutions that are entrusted with the task of interpreting and applying the law, the legislator, when establishing the sanctions, obviously lacks the guidance of a precise table that unequivocally relates the means to the ends, and has not only to pay attention to the essential and direct objective of protection that the norm upholds, but also to other legitimate ends that it may pursue with the sanction and to the various ways in which it operates"* (STC 55/1996, FJ 6).

How has the SCC used the principle of proportionality in its control over the criminal legislator? Well, unlike other courts, it has acted so cautiously that the principle has not operated as a material limit derived from the Constitution, in other words, as a limit of limits. The SCC states that the principle of proportionality in no way constitutes *"an autonomous canon of constitutionality"* but rather *"a principle that may be inferred from certain constitutional precepts and, as such, it essentially operates as a criterion for interpretation that permits an appraisal of the possible violations of specific constitutional norms"*. In that way *"if the existence of disproportion is adduced, it should first be asserted and then judged to what extent this disproportion affects the content of the constitutional norms that are invoked"*.

This perspective of the SCC has in general been accepted into the doctrine, on the basis of different arguments: the affirmation that the Constitution contains no "criminal programme", and the difficulties of the Court when performing complex criminological and evaluative judgements that would disempower the role of the legislator.[27] It has been said that to control the law through the principle of proportionality implies a high degree of discretionality, and if the control is excessive, it entails risks that justify a rigorous attitude of deference towards the legislator.[28]

The case-law of the SCC raises two questions. The first is if such a broad freedom of the criminal legislator, at a time of the expansion of criminal Law, can seriously compromise the guaranteeist political programme of

[27]See Lopera Mesa (2006), pp. 569–570; Lascuraín Sánchez (2012), p. 16.

[28]Lascuraín Sánchez (2014), p. 320. A difference stance was taken by Huerta Tocildo (2000), for whom *"the necessary attitude of caution when delivering a judgement of proportionality on criminal norms is practically converted into the concession of a 'open cheque' to the criminal legislator to design criminal policy..."*, p. 63.

decriminalization. The times we live in are not only marked by the "pulverization" of legislative law, and the increasingly marked "contractualization" of the contents of the law,[29] but also by the resurgence of a "legislation of struggle"[30] against new criminal behaviour to which a response is sought, pressured by social demand for punishment. It could be paradoxical that when exercising the most terrible of powers, the power of punishment, the legislator is subjected to so few and to such weak material limits derived from the Constitution. It suggests that perhaps the guardian of the Constitution makes no assurance that the criminal order is reserved for the most intolerable abuses of fundamental assets, as enlightened philosophy always maintained.

The second question that this case-law raises is whether the Constitutional Court, when renouncing the exercise of strict control over criminal laws, prevents a real and profound debate over the decisions of the majorities, which affect fundamental rights. If the Constitutional Court is so unexacting in its appraisals, the legislator will see no need to deliberate and to try to justify his decisions on the controversial questions in society.[31] In any case, it will not be done through a deliberative process that is developed through constitutional case-law. Instead, by using the mechanisms of a democratic State: the submission of the majorities and their decisions to the scrutiny of the electorate, and to the judgement of public opinion. That being so, it may be asked up to what point the Constitution operates as a material limit to the criminal legislator and what its efficacy is to ensure the guaranteeist program of minimum Criminal Law.

3.1.2 Other Material Limits on the Criminal Legislator

As has been seen, fundamental rights have operated as a limit to the limiting capability of rights that the criminal legislator has, whose control has been exercised through the deferential application of the principle of proportionality. But the rights, for the SCC, have also been recognized as a limit, because their "essential content" is raised as an "impassable limit for the criminal legislator". This much was affirmed in the judgement of the constitutionality of art. 607.2 Penal Code, which defined as an offense the diffusion of ideas or doctrines through any medium that deny or justify crimes of genocide. The majority of the Court justified the mere inclusion of "denial" in the criminal definition as unconstitutional because it violated art. 20.1 SC. Its reasoning was that the freedom of definition of the criminal legislator finds its limit in the essential content of the right to freedom of expression, in such a way that the constitutional order does not permit the definition of the mere communication of ideas as a crime (STC 235/2007 of 7 November 2007, FJ 6).

---

[29]Zagrebelsky (2005), p. 37.

[30]An expression from German terminology, employed by Rodríguez Montañés (2009), p. 1657.

[31]Lopera Mesa (2006), p. 571.

A third channel for the use of rights as conditioners of the freedom of the criminal legislator could, as the ECtHR has done, be in the form of mandates of punishment. However, the Constitutional Court has declared that *"the Constitution does not guarantee, as a content of fundamental rights, the criminal repression of their violations"* (ATC 261/1993 of 20 July 1993, FJ 3), which does not imply that the legislator decides, as he has done, to define some conducts as offences that violate fundamental rights.

Another limit for the legislator, rather than in terms of criminalization, may be the decriminalization of certain conducts. In these circumstances, the Court carries out a "positive control" in the sense that the legislator is obliged to suppress a gap in criminal protection through the definition of criminal offences, as has been stressed in the German doctrine.[32] I think that the SCC pronounced on this matter in the historic STC 53/1985 of 11 April 1985, where it judged the alleged unconstitutionality of the decriminalization of consensual abortion in certain circumstances or situations. The Court understood that the protection offered to the *nasciturus* by the SC placed an obligation on the State to establish *"a legal system for the defence of life that implies its effective protection and that, given the fundamental nature of life, also includes, as a final safeguard, the criminal norms"* (FJ 7). The question was whether the legislator can exclude in certain circumstances the life of the *nasciturus* from criminal protection. However, the Judgement declared that *"the legislator (...) can also forego the criminal sanction of a conduct that could objectively represent an unbearable burden, notwithstanding that, if applicable, the duty of protection from the State still exists with regard to the legal asset in other areas"* (FJ 9). I believe that it may be inferred from this Judgement, and from that of STC 215/1994 of 14 July 1994, on the decriminalisation of sterilization authorized by the judge of incapacitated persons who suffer serious psychotic disabilities, that the Court has also considered the criminal protection of certain constitutional assets as a limit on the legislator.

Finally, the Court has pronounced on the mandate of rehabilitation in art. 25.2 SC, and has accepted that the constitutional precept can serve as a parameter of the constitutionality of criminal and prison laws. But once again, its application has highlighted the weakness of the mandate as a parameter of control. So, in STC 120/2000 of 10 May 2000, the constitutionality of art. 586 bis Penal Code was questioned, among other reasons, for establishing a penalty deemed unfit to achieve the ends of rehabilitation, as it had to be served at home and without judicial supervision. The Court rejected such reasoning, declaring that the mandate that established art. 25.2 SC operates as a parameter for pondering *"the complete system of the enforcement of sentences and the institutions that they integrate"*. So, a single prison sentence cannot be evaluated, but must be considered within the framework of a system in which there are institutions such as the sentence and conditional release, alternatives to imprisonment, and, finally, the different regimes for serving the prison sentence (FJ 4).

[32]Tiedemann (1991), p. 165.

3.2 *The Case-Law of the European Court of Human Rights*

The case-law of the European Court in criminal matters has essentially focused on the interpretation of procedural guarantees contained in the Convention and the Protocols (arts. 6, 7 ECHR; arts. 2 and 4 of Protocol 7); and on the "proceduralization" of certain substantive rights (arts. 2 and 3 ECHR).[33] All those aspects are related to procedural guarantees[34] but are not aimed at placing substantive limits on the criminal legislator with the objective of establishing a minimum criminal Law.

But the Court, whether directly or indirectly, has also faced substantive limits over three types of decisions: those that have interpreted the explicit limits contained in the Convention itself; those that have established limits on the restrictions of rights imposed by criminal laws; and those that have declared the obligation of the criminal legislator to protect some rights.

3.2.1 Interpretation of the Substantive Limits of the Convention

The European Convention contains some clear material limits, for instance, the right to life (art. 2 ECHR), the prohibition of torture or inhuman or degrading treatment or punishment (art. 3 ECHR), and the total abolition of the death penalty (art. 1 of Protocol num. 13). The ECtHR has pronounced on some of these matters in several judgements. It is worth highlighting the one relating to the death penalty (ECtHR Judgement of 12 March 2003, c. *Öcalan v. Turkey*), delivered before the entry into force of Protocol num. 13 (1 July 2003), which declared the abolition of the death penalty "under all circumstances". In that decision, the Court noted an evolution towards the almost total abolition of the death penalty in Europe in times of peace (art. 2 of Protocol num. 6 still allowed it *"for acts committed in wartime or imminent danger of war"*), which would demonstrate *"an agreement of the States to abrogate, or at least to make substantial modifications to the exception to the death penalty covered in art. 2 ECHR"*. It went on to conclude that the death penalty in peacetime has been considered as an unacceptable form of sanction, in other words as an inhuman one, which is not authorized by art. 2 of the Convention.[35] In this way, the Spanish legislator could constitutionally reinstate the death penalty through "military criminal law in times of war" (art. 15 SC), but that would be contrary to art. 2 ECHR as interpreted by the Court of Strasbourg.[36]

---

[33]Burgorgue-Larsen (2005), p. 373.

[34]Burgorgue-Larsen (2007).

[35]Earlier, the Court had qualified the death penalty as "inhuman and degrading treatment" in ECtHR Judgement of 7 July 1989, c. *Soering v. the United Kingdom*.

[36]According to Rey Martínez (2009), p. 75, art. 15 SC would not prevent Spain from ratifying the Convention, because it contains no obligation to foresee the death penalty in this circumstance, but only a permissible possibility that would be validly renounced in case of ratification of the Protocol, as Spain indeed did on 27 November 2009.

Other decisions may be included in this group, relating to the prohibition of "inhuman or degrading treatment or punishment" (art. 3 ECHR), which have been the object of numerous sentences of life imprisonment.[37] ECtHR Judgement of 12 February 2008, c. Kafkaris v. Cyprus, par. 98, stands out, in which the Court pronounced on the compatibility of life imprisonment for a crime of murder with art. 3 ECHR. The Court held that such a punishment for an adult is neither prohibited by Art. 3 nor by any other provision of the Convention. This provision grants no right to re-examine the punishment by the national authorities, with a view to its remission or definitive interruption, although this possibility is a factor to take into account to appreciate the compatibility of life imprisonment with Art. 3 ECHR. And having noted that there is no clear tendency among the States on life imprisonment and the possibilities for review, it concluded that the appellant, given the possibilities of release or remission by the president of the Cypriot Republic, had neither been deprived of all perspectives of release, nor that his continuance in prison constituted "inhuman or degrading treatment".

In the subsequent ECtHR (GC) Judgement of 9 July 2013, c. Vinter and others v. the United Kingdom, the Grand Chamber faced the compatibility of the regulation of life imprisonment (in force at the time in the United Kingdom) with the Convention, following the *Criminal Justice Act* of 2003. The application of that law to the appellants involved their conviction to an obligatory 'whole life order' (life imprisonment in perpetuity) for murder. This punishment is exclusively foreseen in cases of exceptional severity and may only be reviewed at the discretion of the Home Secretary for humanitarian reasons, mortal illness or invalidity, therefore with no possibility of conditional freedom. The Court declared that the punishment raised a question in connection with Art. 3, if it could be demonstrated that no legitimate reason of a penological order could justify the continued imprisonment of the inmate, or that the punishment was irreducible both *de facto* and *de iure*. But at the same time, it pointed out that the States should enjoy a margin for appreciation. Life imprisonment should offer a possibility for release and a possibility for review, to be compatible with art. 3 ECHR, as the imperative of rehabilitation also applies to those sentenced to life imprisonment (sec. 119). The national authorities should therefore permit a review of life imprisonment, in order to note whether in the course of serving the sentence, the convicted person has progressed along the road of rehabilitation, the States exercising a margin of appreciation on the administrative or jurisdictional procedures of any such review. The Court concluded that

[37]The majority made no pronouncement on the law that contemplates that penalty but on the form and the circumstances of its application: ECtHR Judgement of 25 October 1990, c. of Thynne, Wilson and Grunnel v. United Kingdom (by violation of art. 5.4 ECHR); ECtHR Judgement of 21 February 1996, c. Singh v United Kingdom, (art. 5.4 ECHR); ECthHR Judgement of 28 May 2002, c. Stafford v. the United Kingdom, (art. 5.1 ECHR); ECtHR Judgement of 16 December 1999, c. V. v. the United Kingdom (violation of art. 3 ECHR due to various factors, among others, the young age of criminal liability).

the requirements of art. 3 ECHR were not fulfilled in that case, given that the legislation of the United Kingdom was not clear on the exceptional possibilities for the release of prisoners, and it contained no special mechanism allowing the review of whole life orders.

However, in ECtHR Judgement of 3 February 2015, c. Hutchinson v. the United Kingdom, par. 23, in which the appellant was also a British inmate serving a discretional whole life order, the Court held that there had been no violation of Art. 3 ECHR. And that decision was because the British Court of Appeal had incorporated the criteria of *Vinter and others v. the United Kingdom* in a judgement of 2014 (*Regina v. Newell; Regina v. McLoughlin*), declaring that the power of discretional review of the sentence by the Home Secretary should be done in accordance with the requirements of art. 3 ECHR. In particular, that the decision of the governmental authority should consider all of the exceptional circumstances that might justify a release of the convicted person, which should be reasoned and subject to judicial review.

3.2.2 Limits to the Restrictions on Rights Imposed by Criminal Laws

There are other types of decisions in which the ECtHR has declared a certain criminal legislation contrary to the Convention, because it disproportionally restricts a substantive right. Here, the Court makes complex judgements in which it balances the protection of legal assets and the rights that are affected.

One of the most interesting is ECtHR Judgement of 6 October 2005, c. Hirst v. the United Kingdom, where the Court was confronted with a British law (the *Representation of the People Act* 1983) that deprived convicted and imprisoned persons of their right to vote in local and parliamentary elections. The applicant claimed that it violated Art. 3 of Protocol num. 1. The Grand Chamber confirmed ECtHR (GC) Judgement of 30 March 2004, c. Hirst v. the United Kingdom, par. 82, rejecting—and this is a notable aspect—the objection of the British Government that criticized the Court for having in abstract appreciated the compatibility of the statutory law with the Convention. With regard to the merits of the case, the Court accepted that the purpose of the restriction (preventing the crime and reinforcing a sense of civic duty and respect for the Rule of Law) were acceptable, but confirmed that it was disproportionate when considering that the *"general, automatic and indifferential [restriction] of a right enshrined in the Convention, and one that is of crucial importance, surpasses the margin of appreciation, as wide as it might be, and is incompatible with art. 3 of Protocol num. 1"*. The subsequent ECtHR Judgement of 4 July 2013, c. Anchugov and Gladkov v. Russia, once again declared the violation of art. 3 of Protocol num. 1. In this case, two Russian citizens sentenced to fifteen years imprisonment had been deprived of the right to vote, in application not of an Act of Parliament, but of art. 32.3 of the Russian Constitution, which establishes the total prohibition of the right to active and passive suffrage of citizens sentenced to a term of imprisonment by a court.

On the other hand, in ECtHR Judgement of 4 December 2007, c. Dickson v. the United Kingdom, the Grand Chamber declared that the rejection by the Home Secretary of the petition from a prisoner and his wife to use artificial insemination was in violation of art. 8 ECHR, which enshrines the right to respect for private and family life. Once again, the Court turned to the judgement of proportionality and to the margin of appreciation, but on this occasion, the violation was not attributed to criminal law, but to a decision of the Home Secretary, which in application of the *Prison Act 1952* followed a particular policy in relation to the petition for artificial insemination from prisoners.

In this group of decisions, we find the judgements relating to homophobic criminal legislation, which the Court deemed contrary to the right to a private life enshrined in art. 8.1 ECHR. For instance, in ECtHR Judgement of 22 October 1981, c. Dudgeon v. United Kingdom, par. 61, concerning Northern Irish legislation dating back to the 19th c., the Court considered that from the point of view of proportionality, the harmful consequences that the very existence of those legislative provisions might cause for the life of a homosexual person prevailed over the arguments of the Government. "Decriminalization", it stated, is not the same as approval, and the fear of drawing erroneous conclusions following a reform of the legislation does not constitute a reason for it to remain in force. The Judgement concluded that the restriction imposed by Northern Irish law on the right to a private life (art. 8 ECHR) constituted a violation of that right.

The reasoning in this Judgement would subsequently be applied in ECtHR Judgement of 26 October 1988, c. Norris v. Ireland, where the Court upheld the request of a teacher from Dublin, who criticized the effects of Irish legislation on his right to respect for private and family life (art. 8.1 ECHR), declaring that it had been contravened by the contested "legislation". And in ECtHR Judgement of 27 September 1999, c. Smith and Grady v. the United Kingdom, where the appellants were dismissed from the British Royal Air Force because of their declared homosexuality. Following those precedents, the Court considered, in ECtHR Judgement of 22 April 1993, c. Modinos v. Cyprus, that the Cypriot Penal Code, by punishing homosexual relations, involved a violation of that right.

Finally, the Judgements on criminal legislation that are considered contrary to the Convention, because they violate freedom of expression (art. 10 ECHR), should be mentioned. In this ECtHR Judgement of 25 June 2002, c. Colombani and others v. France, the Court examined the conviction of the director of the newspaper *Le Monde* for an offence of insulting a foreign Head of State contemplated in the Law of the Press of 1881. The Court held that the offense was in violation of freedom of expression and that it did not respond to any "pressing social need" likely to justify that restriction. Likewise, it affirmed that despite the margin of appreciation of the national authorities, no reasonable relation of proportionality existed between the restrictions on freedom of expression of the appellants and the legitimate purposes that were pursued. In this case, the Court not only controlled the decision of the French criminal judge, but it dared to judge the content of the criminal law, which would demonstrate that the control exercised by the ECtHR can lead to a declaration of the non-conventionality of a Law.[38]

The *Colombani* doctrine has subsequently been reiterated in other decisions, in which the violation of art. 10 ECHR was not attributed to criminal legislation, but to its application by the courts that had delivered the unfavourable sentence. Similarly, in ECtHR Judgement of 26 June 2007, c. Artun and Güvener v. Turkey; ECtHR Judgement of 15 March 2011, c.Otegi Mondragón v. Spain; and in ECtHR Judgement of 14 March 2013, c. Eon v. France.

3.2.3 Obligations of the Criminal Legislator to Protect the Rights of the Convention

Following the path of the Inter-American Court of Human Rights, the ECtHR has contemplated a duty to protect rights through criminal law. As has been pointed out,[39] the Court has understood that such a duty could be violated in different ways: (a) a gap in the punishability of a conduct (ECtHR Judgement of 26 March 1985, c. X and Y v. the Netherlands; (b) the absence of a criminal offense to criminalize the violation of a fundamental right in an effective way (ECtHR Judgement of 4 December 2005, c. Siliadin v. France); (c) the existence of overly extensive causes for justification (ECtHR Judgement of 23 September 1988, c. A. C. v. the United Kingdom); (d) amnesty laws that prevent criminal action against crimes in violation of fundamental rights (ECtHR Judgement of 2 November 2004, c. Abdülsamet Yaman v. Turkey); (e) the provision of very weak penalties (ECtHR Judgement of 5 February 2010, c. Paduret v. Moldavia). In addition to those mentioned above, the case may be added in which the definition of an offense is considered contrary to the Convention, because it requires a conduct of the victim. In particular, when raped is only defined in criminal law as a crime if the victim has shown physical resistance, there is a risk that certain sorts of rape may go unprosecuted (ECtHR Judgement of 4 December 2003, c. M.C. v. Bulgaria).

The interpretation advanced in this case-law on the obligations for criminal protection of rights raises some doubts over changes in the role of rights: from establishing limits on the power of punishment, to becoming the object of punishment, and therefore a factor in the expansion of criminal Law. But it also raises doubts over the absence of democratic legitimization of the international courts to impose obligations on the exercise of State *ius puniendi*, which would question the principle of *nullum crimen sine lege*.[40]

---

[38]Burgorgue-Larsen (2005), p. 369.

[39]On this point, I follow the work of Viganò (2012), p. 316.

[40]Viganò (2012), p. 327.

4 Conclusions

The SCC has been very deferential towards the criminal legislator when sustaining that it has a broad margin of freedom for the design of criminal policy, which is derived from its constitutional position and its democratic legitimacy. Hence, it has up until today identified few material limits in the Constitution, and essentially through the principle of proportionality, which has been used with great caution, up to such a point that it has almost no longer operated as a limit of limits. This jurisprudence has in general been accepted by the doctrine, based on two arguments: that the Constitution contains no "criminal programme", and that control over constitutionality through the principle of proportionality implies a high degree of discretionality, the exercise of which would disempower the democratic legislator of his function. The SCC has indeed expressly identified an impassable limit to the freedom of the criminal legislator to draft legislation: the essential content of fundamental rights.

In turn, the ECtHR has also shown itself to be deferential towards the criminal legislator, affirming that the regime of criminal justice in principle evades European control, provided that the principles of the ECtHR are not ignored. The Court of Strasbourg has also turned to the principle of proportionality, as well as the margin of appreciation, to examine the compatibility of criminal laws with the European standard of the protection of rights. But it has not been as cautious as the SCC in its use, by considering as disproportionate various restrictions imposed by the criminal legislator on the right to private life and freedom of expression. Moreover, the ECtHR has interpreted the material limits expressly formulated in the Convention, especially the prohibition on inhuman or degrading treatment, as well as the prohibition on the death penalty. And it has identified obligations in the Convention for the legislator to grant criminal protection to certain rights, which would range from placing limits on the power of punishment to becoming the object of punishment.

The earlier conclusions raise some questions. The first is that the fact of giving the criminal legislator such broad freedom to draft legislation at a time of the expansion of criminal Law will not seriously compromise the decriminalizing guaranteeist political programme. It suggests that perhaps the guardian of the Constitution in no way assures that the criminal order has to be used only for the most intolerable attacks against fundamental values. The second question refers to the role of the Court that, when abandoning the exercise of strict control over criminal laws, prevents a real and profound debate on the decisions of the majorities that affect fundamental rights. If the Court is so loose in its control, the legislator should justify its decisions before the electorate and public opinion, but not before the constitutional judge. It is worth asking, therefore, up to what point the Constitution operates as a material limit on the criminal legislator and whether it is really effective to ensure the guarantist programme. Finally, the third question that is proposed is whether the State criminal legislator is subjected to more material limits when he operates in a framework of constitutional pluralism.

References

Arroyo Zapatero L, Lascuraín Sánchez JA, Pérez Manzano M (eds) (2016) Contra la cadena perpetua. Ed. Universidad de Castilla-La Mancha, Cuenca
Arzoz Santisteban X (2014) La concretización y actualización de los derechos fundamentales. CEPC, Madrid
Bilbao Ubillos JM (2000) La excarcelación tenía un precio. El Tribunal enmienda la plana al legislador (Comentario a la STC 136/1999, en el caso Mesa Nacional de HB). Revista Española de Derecho Constitucional 58:277–342
Burgorgue-Larsen L (2005) La Corte Europea de los Derechos Humanos y el Derecho penal. Anuario de Derecho internacional 21:317–378
Burgorgue-Larsen L (2007) Aspectos recientes de la jurisprudencia de la Corte Europea de los Derechos Humanos en asuntos penales. In: García Ramírez S, Islas de González Mariscal O (eds) Panorama internacional sobre justicia penal: proceso penal y justicia penal internacional. Universidad Nacional Autónoma de México, México, pp 351–369
Bustos Gisbert R (2012) XV proposiciones generales para una teoría de los diálogos judiciales. Revista Española de Derecho Constitucional 95:13–63
Carbonell Mateu JC (1996) Derecho penal: concepto y principios constitucionales. Tirant lo Blanch, Valencia
Casadevall J (2012) El Convenio europeo de Derechos Humanos, el Tribunal de Estrasburgo y su jurisprudencia. Tirant lo Blanch, Valencia
Cuerda Riezu A (2011) La cadena perpetua y las penas muy largas de prisión (Por qué son inconstitucionales en España). Atelier, Barcelona
Díez-Ripollés JL (2005) El control de constitucionalidad de las leyes penales. Revista Española de Derecho Constitucional 75:59–106
Ferrajoli L (1993) Derecho y razón. Teoría del garantismo penal. Trotta, Madrid
Ferrajoli L (2007) Principia iuris. Teoria del diritto e della democracia. Laterza, Roma
Ferreres Comella V (2012) El control de las leyes penales por parte de los jueces ordinarios In: Mir Puig S, Corcoy Bidasolo M (eds) Constitución y sistema penal. Marcial Pons, Madrid, pp 109–122
González Beilfus M (2003) El principio de proporcionalidad en la jurisprudencia del Tribunal Constitucional. Aranzadi, Madrid
Huerta Tocildo S (2000) Principio de legalidad y normas sancionadoras In: El principio de legalidad. Actas de las V Jornadas de la Asociación de Letrados del Tribunal Constitucional. CEPC, Madrid
Lascuraín Sánchez JA (2012) ¿Restrictivo o deferente? El control de la ley penal por parte del Tribunal Constitucional. InDret 3/2012
Lascuraín Sánchez JA (2014) Cuándo penar, cuánto penar. In: Lascuraín Sánchez JA, Rusconi M (eds) El principio de proporcionalidad penal. AdHoc, Buenos Aires
Lopera Mesa GP (2006) Principio de proporcionalidad y ley penal. CEPC, Madrid
Mir Puig S (2011) Bases constitucionales del Derecho Penal. Iustel, Madrid
Prieto Sanchís L (2009) Justicia y Derechos Constitucionales. Trotta, Madrid
Prieto Sanchís L (2011) Garantismo y Derecho Penal. Iustel, Madrid
Queralt Jiménez A (2008) La interpretación de los derechos: del Tribunal de Estrasburgo al Tribunal Constitucional. CEPC, Madrid
Rey Martínez F (2009) La protección jurídica de la vida ante el Tribunal de Estrasburgo: un derecho en transformación y expansión. In: García Roca J, Santolaya P (coords), La Europa de los Derechos. CEPC, Madrid, pp 73–105
Rodríguez Montañés T (2009) Expansión del Derecho Penal y límites constitucionales, In: Carbonell Mateu JC, González Cussac JL, Orts Berenger E (dirs) Constitución, derechos fundamentales y sistema penal (Semblanzas y estudios con motivo del setenta aniversario del profesor Tomás Salvador Vives Antón), vol 2. Tirant lo Blanch, Valencia

Rodríguez Montañés T (2012) Libertad de expresión, discurso extremo y delito (Una aproximación desde la Constitución a las fronteras del derecho penal). Tirant lo Blanch, Valencia

Rodríguez Mourullo G (2002) Delito y pena en la jurisprudencia constitucional. Civitas, Madrid

Ruiz Miguel C (1997) La ejecución de las Sentencias del Tribunal Europeo de Derechos Humanos. Tecnos, Madrid

Ruiz Robledo A (2003) El derecho fundamental a la legalidad punitiva. Tirant lo Blanch, Valencia

Saiz Arnáiz A (1999) La apertura constitucional al derecho internacional y europeo de los derechos humanos. El artículo 10.2 de la Constitución española. CGPJ, Madrid

Silva Sánchez JM (1999) La expansión del Derecho Penal. Aspectos de la política criminal en las sociedades postindustriales. Civitas, Madrid

Tiedemann K (1991) Constitución y Derecho Penal. Revista Española de Derecho Constitucional 33:145–171

Urías Martínez J (2001) El valor constitucional del mandato de resocialización. Revista Española de Derecho Constitucional 63:43–78

Viganò F (2012) Sobre las obligaciones de tutela penal de los derechos fundamentales en la jurisprudencia del TEDH. In: Mir Puig S, Corcoy Bidasolo (eds) Garantías constitucionales y Derecho penal europeo. Marcial Pons, Madrid, pp 311–328

Zagrebelsky G (2005) El derecho dúctil. Ley, derechos, justicia, 6th edn. Trotta, Madrid

The Conformation of Fundamental Rights by the Court of Justice of the European Union

Cristina Izquierdo Sans

1 Introduction

The Treaty of Lisbon grants a binding character to Charter of Nice, in its version of 12 December 2007,[1] establishing in section 1 of article 6 of the Treaty on European Union (TEU) that *"The Union recognises the rights, freedoms and principles set out in the Charter of Fundamental Rights of the European Union of 7 December 2000, as adapted at Strasbourg, on 12 December 2007, which shall have the same legal value as the Treaties"*. It is important to add that the Charter is not only binding for the Union since, as in accordance with art. 51 of the Charter, its provisions are also applicable to the Member States, although solely when they apply the Law of the Union.[2]

Art. 6 TEU addresses two further questions. On the one hand, it affirms that *"The provisions of the Charter shall not extend in any way the competences of the Union as defined in the Treaties"* anticipating what art. 51 of the Charter[3] clarifies: it is

Former Law Clerk at the Spanish Constitutional Court (2006–2014), Professor of Public International Law at Universidad Autónoma de Madrid.

[1]The Treaty of Lisbon included the incorporation by reference. In relation to the technique of incorporation by reference, Vid. Andrés Sáenz de Santamaría (1985), p. 37.

[2]Article 51 of the Charter: "*Scope. 1. The provisions of this Charter are addressed to the institutions and bodies of the Union with due regard for the principle of subsidiarity and to the Member States only when they are implementing Union law. They shall therefore respect the rights, observe the principles and promote the application thereof in accordance with their respective powers*".

[3]Article 51 of the Charter: "*Scope. 1 (. . .) 2. This Charter does not establish any new power or task for the Community or the Union, or modify powers and tasks defined by the Treaties*".

C.I. Sans (✉)
Universidad Autónoma de Madrid, 28049 Madrid, Spain
e-mail: cristina.izquierdo@uam.es

M. Pérez Manzano et al. (eds.), *Multilevel Protection of the Principle of Legality in Criminal Law*, DOI 10.1007/978-3-319-63865-2_2

only a commitment to respect fundamental rights in the exercise of the normative competences attributed to the Union in other areas, but there is no transference of competences in this matter. On the other hand, taking into account this lack of competences, in its last paragraph, art. 6 refers to arts. 52 and 53 of the Charter to determine the criteria for the interpretation and the application of the Charter.[4]

Hence the importance of arts. 52 and 53 that include—as well as the Charter—the work of the European Court of Justice (ECJ) over the years. Article 53 affirms, in relation to the level of protection granted to fundamental rights, that "*Nothing in this Charter shall be interpreted as restricting or adversely affecting human rights and fundamental freedoms as recognised, in their respective fields of application, by Union law and international law and by international agreements to which the Union, the Community or all the Member States are party, including the European Convention for the Protection of Human Rights and Fundamental Freedoms, and by the Member States' constitutions*". Likewise, article 52 was also intended to send out a reassuring message: the European Union declares that in its normative process it will affect fundamental rights, but it will not limit their substantive contents, unless it is essential for the general interest, and in these cases limitations will be established by law.[5] In section 2, article 52 lists the interpretative criteria that it will apply to give content to the fundamental rights. The mentions produce no surprises at all. As it should be, the criteria are: the ECHR, the constitutional traditions of the Member States and the explanations approved having drafted the Charter of Nice. Section 3 of art. 52 contains a warning that the meaning and the scope of the fundamental rights of the Charter may be superior to those conferred by the European Convention of Human Rights. Besides, the Treaty of Lisbon incorporates a new art. 4 from the TEU that asserts the respect of the Union for the fundamental political and constitutional structures of the Member States[6] and, as we all known, it incorporates a commitment of accession to the ECHR under art. 6.[7] Neither element

[4]Art. 6.1 TEU, 3rd paragraph: "*The rights, freedoms and principles in the Charter shall be interpreted in accordance with the general provisions in Title VII of the Charter governing its interpretation and application and with due regard to the explanations referred to in the Charter, that set out the sources of those provisions*".

[5]Take into account the new denomination of normative acts in the EU, introduced by the Treaty of Lisbon.

[6]"*The Union shall respect the equality of Member States with respect to the Treaties as well as their national identities, inherent in their fundamental, political and constitutional, structures inclusive of regional and local self-government. It shall respect their essential State functions, including ensuring the territorial integrity of the State, maintaining law and order and safeguarding national security. In particular, national security remains the sole responsibility of each Member State*".

[7]Art. 6.2 TEU: "*The Union shall accede to the European Convention for the Protection of Human Rights and Fundamental Freedoms. Such accession shall not affect the Union's competences as defined in the Treaties*". Art. 6.3 TEU: "*Fundamental rights, as guaranteed by the European Convention for the Protection of Human Rights and Fundamental Freedoms and as they result from the constitutional traditions common to the Member States, shall constitute general principles of the Union's law*". Vid. Pastor Ridruejo (2008), p. 151.

is surprising, but together they both highlight a major commitment and a strong involvement of the Union with the pillars of the Members States in matters of fundamental rights: their own Constitutions, the ECHR and the ECtHR.[8]

Among the above-mentioned set of provisions that regulate fundamental rights in the EU, it is worth reflecting on whether the absence of the normative competences of the EU in fundamental rights, declared in articles 6 of the TEU and 51.2 of the Charter, is real.[9] The following study, together with a concrete case, seeks to highlight the work of the ECJ in matters of fundamental rights and, along those lines, it cannot be dismissed that the conformation of fundamental rights by the ECJ is, in practice, of greater scope.

2 The *Melloni* Case

In the *Melloni* case, the Spanish Constitutional Court (SCC) submitted the first request for a preliminary ruling to the ECJ in its history, through a Court Order of 9 June 2011. The controversy revolved around the incompatibility of the case-law of the SCC in the context of procedural guarantees and the European directive in regulation of the European Arrest Warrant (EAW). For the SCC, the enforcement of an EAW to comply with a sentence delivered in abstentia must always be subject to the condition that the convicted person has the right to a new trial in the issuing Member State. Otherwise, the surrender of the requested person would violate article 24 of the Spanish Constitution (SC). This matter is explained through the doctrine of the absolute content of fundamental rights, the major exponent of which is STC 91/2000 of 30 March, which basically declares that access to extradition for the enforcement of a conviction for a serious offence delivered in the absence of the accused, indirectly violates the right to a fair trial and due process, except if the surrender is subject to some guarantees sufficient in themselves to remedy the initial shortcoming. The indirect violation arises from the –unconditional– recognition of a foreign judicial decision handed down in "direct" violation of a fundamental right.[10] Up until the *Melloni* case, the SCC considered that there was nothing, at that time, in the Law of the Union, which would prevent the application of the doctrine of the absolute content of fundamental rights to the EAW. But at the time of the Melloni case, the legal framework of the EAW had changed with the approval of

[8]The agreement relating to the accession of the Union to the ECHR stipulates the specific modalities of the possible participation of the Union in the supervisory bodies of the European Convention and b) the necessary mechanisms to guarantee that the appeals submitted by third-party States and individual appeals are correctly submitted against the Member States, against the Union or against both, where applicable. Protocol on the adhesion of the EU to the ECHR. On this matter, Stoffel Valloton (2008), p. 179.

[9]Cámara Villar (2004), pp. 9–42.

[10]STC 30/2006 of 30 January 2006, STC 177/2006 of 5 June 2005, STC 199/2009 of 28 September 2009.

Council Framework Decision (CFD) 2009/299/JHA, of 26 February 2009. This norm, with the purpose of limiting the discretionality of the executing authority to refuse the enforcement of an EAW expressly excluded the possibility of refusing surrender when made aware that the accused knew of the cause or might have instructed legal counsel who would have acted in his defenced, even though the accused may have been absent at the trial. The impossibility of an interpretation of Spanish constitutional case-law in accordance with art. 4 bis CFD 2009/299 was clear. While the latter expressly excluded the possibility of refusing surrender when aware that the accused knew of the cause or had given instructions to Counsel to act in his defence, the presence of the accused was, in constitutional case-law, an essential guarantee of the proceedings that, if not respected, violated the absolute content of the right to a fair trial. Taking it a step further, SCC Judgement 91/2000 had declared that the surrender of a convicted person who, in another State, had been judged in abstentia, indirectly violated the same fundamental right.

In this context, the SCC requested the preliminary ruling and questioned the validity of article 4 bis of the CFD. It called on the ECJ to define—for the first time—the scope of article 53 of the Charter of Fundamental Rights of the European Union (CFREU), that states that *"nothing in this Charter shall be interpreted as restricting or adversely affecting human rights and fundamental freedoms as recognised, in their respective fields of application, by (...) the Member State's constitutions"*. The Spanish Constitutional Court assembled various reasons to initiate the dialogue with Luxembourg.[11] On the one hand, it was aware that with the case-law of the ECtHR to hand, there is no violation of the right of defence, if the absence of the convicted person at a trial is voluntary and that person has been defended in an effective way in the proceedings by a lawyer.[12] On that point, the Constitutional Court felt isolated in its interpretation of the procedural guarantees. Additionaly, an internal division had emerged within the Court over maintaining the doctrine of indirect violations in a united and integrated Europe.[13] On the other hand, this was a question –the non-appearance of the accused at a criminal trial–, in which there were as many situations as nuances to be derived from each one of them[14]; and as it was the first time that the conflict had clearly emerged between the Constitutional Court and the ECJ, in relation to the level of protection of a

[11]Arroyo Jiménez precisely justifies the preliminary request for a ruling from the Constitutional Court and explains how the Court refused the negative reply from the Office of the Public Prosecutor for the submission of a question, because it understood the non-application of *ratione temporis* of the CFD 2009/299 to the appeal for relief that originated it. Vid. Arroyo Jiménez (2011).

[12]In relation with the case-law of the ECtHR relating to the non-appearance of the accused, Pérez Manzano has called attention to the fact that neither was CFD 2002/584 really in harmony with the case-law of Strasbourg. The author clearly observed that the standard of protection of the ECtHR is more protective than that of the EU. Vid. Pérez Manzano (2012), p. 311.

[13]Vid. the dissenting opinion of the magistrate Pablo Pérez Tremps in Constitutional Court judgment STC 199/2009 of 28 September 2009.

[14]Vid. Pérez Manzano, p. 324.

fundamental right, the Constitutional Court decided to present a preliminary request for a ruling to the Court at Luxembourg. The Constitutional Court drafted a Court Order—ATC 86/2011—a well-structured and carefully composed text, with abundant citations of both classic and more recent case-law of the ECtHR and the ECJ,[15] so it therefore turned out to be a good starting point.

3 The Conclusions of the Advocate General

On 2 October 2012, the advocate General (AG), M. Yves Bot, made public his conclusions in the *Melloni* case. They were, in general terms, well received. On the first question, relating to whether article 4 bis, section 1 (a) of the Council Framework Decision permitted the national executing authority to make the EAW conditional upon whether the affected person had the right to a new trial in the issuing Member State, the AG strongly disagreed with the viewpoint of the SCC by which article 4 bis prevented enforcement of the EAW, but would not necessarily prevent submitting its enforcement to conditions. The AG rejected the idea that letters (a) and (b) of article 4 bis, paragraph 1 contemplated circumstances in which the interested party could have the right to a new trial.

The AG made all of his reasoning for the interpretation of article 4 bis, section 1 (a) revolve around the objective pursued by the normative regulation of the Union; in a word, to eliminate the faculty of the judicial authority of the Member States to refuse enforcement of the EAW and to determine the circumstances in which surrender was obligatory and unconditional. Making it conditional upon a new trial would, in many cases, be equivalent to a refusal to execute. It may, it appears, be assumed that, in the opinion of the AG, it is the objective that justifies the scope and/or intensity of the action.

In relation to the second question, which directly questioned the validity of article 4 bis, paragraph 1 (a) because of its possible violation of the right of defence as a guarantee of the proceedings, the AG justified its validity reasoning in a twofold manner: (1) the standard of the EU is the same as that of the ECtHR; and, (2) there are no constitutional traditions in the Member States—in plural—that can be seen as a *leitmotiv* for reflection directed at changing such a standard.

With regard to the coincidence between the standard of protection of the EU and of the ECtHR, the AG referred to article 52 of the Charter to affirm that the Court at Strasbourg establishes a level of protection that is identifiable with the level that is provided in CFD 2002/584, in so far as it understands that there is no violation of the right to a defence if the accused tried in *absentia* has been defended by legal counsel, as in those cases there is a voluntary refusal to appear. In fact, the AG came to the conclusion that, under those conditions, article 4 bis, section 1 (a) of the CFD not only respects the requirements stated by the ECtHR but that it also codifies them

[15] Vid. Andrés Sáenz de Santamaría (1985), p. 193.

in a very accurate manner. Furthermore, with respect to the constitutional traditions of the Member States, the AG made an important contribution. He declared that there was no reason to go beyond the balanced position adopted by the ECtHR. The ECJ could not support the constitutional traditions common to Member States to apply a broader level of protection, because the CFD 2009/299 had sprung from the initiative of seven Member States and had been adopted by all Member States. It may therefore be assumed, with sufficient certainty, that the large majority of Member states do not share the same understanding of the guarantees of the proceedings that the Constitutional Court upholds in its case-law in Spain. In my view, it is important to highlight in this second question that, for the AG, the reference in art. 53 of the Charter to the constitutional traditions of the Member States cannot be identified with the level of protection of a fundamental right in a Member State, but this is a referral to the opinion of all Member States, as a whole.

Finally, the AG reflected on the core of the request for a preliminary ruling raised by the Constitutional Court in Spain: the legal content and scope that should be attributed to article 53 of the Charter. It concludes that the precept will not allow the executing judicial authority to subordinate the execution of an EAW to the condition that the requested person will have the right to a new trial in the issuing Member State, in application of its national constitutional law. The foundations of this affirmation are as follows: (1) the terms *"in their respective fields of application"* that are found in article 53 of the Charter were chosen by those drafting it so as not to harm the principle of primacy; (2) the interpretation of the rights protected by the Charter should tend towards a higher level of protection, as may be deduced from article 52.3, but it should be a matter of a level of protection adapted to the Law of the Union; (3) in the concrete case of CFD 2009/299, the level of protection of the right of defence is not established in the abstract, but even before with the adaption to the requirements inherent in the construction of the area of freedom, security and justice (par. 113). So, it all comes back once again to the objectives of the normative action of the Union as determinants of the level of protection of a fundamental right.

Although, with these arguments, the AG would have granted a satisfactory response to the third question raised by the Constitutional Court, far from stopping there, he continues to examine the question further and sets out, on the one hand, what the margin of action is of the Member States to establish the level of protection of fundamental rights that they wish to guarantee in the context of the application of Union Law and, on the other hand, establishes what role art. 53 of the Charter really fulfils. With regard to the first question, the AG is very clear: setting a common definition of a fundamental right within the scope of the Union is marked by the objectives of Union actions and will be reflection of a balance—achieved by the Union legislator—between the efficacy of European action and the protection of fundamental rights; in these cases, the European norm will reflect a consensus between the Member States and, it is precisely that consensus that will leave no room for the application of divergent standards of national protection. In a contrary sense, the AG affirmed that when the level of protection of a fundamental right has not been the object of a common definition in Europe, the Member States have a certain degree of manoeuvre to guarantee levels of protection in the national legal order, even in the scope of the application of Union Law, provided that they are compatible with due application of the Law of the Union and that they harm no other fundamental rights.

With regard to the role that article 53 of the Charter plays, the AG defended both its political value and its close relation and necessary interpretation with articles 51 and 52, of which it constitutes a prolongation. Article 53 has the purpose of guaranteeing that the adoption of the Charter should not serve as a pretext for a Member State to reduce the protection of fundamental rights in the field of application of national law, but not beyond that field.

4 The *Melloni* Judgement, of 26 February 2013

On 26 February 2013, the ECtHR delivered its judgement in the Melloni case (C-399/11), seeking to respond to the request from the SCC to the ECJ for a preliminary ruling.

In the Melloni judgement, the ECJ declared that article 4 bis, section 1 (a) of FD 2002/584 should be interpreted in the sense that it does not permit the judicial authority that executes an EAW, for the enforcement of a punishment, to make its enforcement conditional upon a new trial (par. 35). The ECJ has lent support to the objective of the action: the EAW has the purpose of substituting the system of multilateral extradition between Member States for a system of surrender of convicted persons between legal authorities that is essentially based on the principle of mutual recognition. For the ECJ, the CFD has sought to establish a new simplified and efficient system of surrender of convicted persons or those suspected of having violated criminal law, basing themselves on the high degree of confidence that should exist between the Member States and it is through that lens that article 4 bis, par. 1, of the CFD should be interpreted. In that sense, the national court can only make the execution of an EAW subject to the requirements established in article 5 of the CFD.[16]

Its reply and reasoning was more limited in relation to the validity of article 4 bis of CFD 2002/584, as the ECJ declared that the interpretation is in accordance with the content of the right of defence established in the Charter, in particular articles 47 and 48, section 529. As a reason to sustain its validity, it only made clear that it was the same interpretation that the ECtHR had given to the rights guaranteed under article 6, sections 1 and 3 of the ECHR, as well as the harmonization of the conditions for the enforcement of the EAW contained in CFD 2009/299 that tend –as highlighted in its article 1–, to reinforce the procedural rights of the accused in a criminal proceeding (par. 50–53).

---

[16]The requirements established in article 5 of Framework Decision 2002/584 were analysed by the ECJ in its Judgment of 29 January 2013, Radu (C-396/2011) par. 33.

Finally, the ECJ pronounced itself in favour of the compatibility of art. 4 bis understood alongside article 53 of the Charter and declared that article 53 of the Charter did not permit a Member State to subject the surrender of a person convicted in *absentia* to the condition that the conviction may be reviewed in the issuing Member State, on the grounds of preventing a violation of its Constitution (par. 64). The problem with this pronouncement is not its content—despite that interpretation implying a reduction in the level of protection of the procedural guarantees established for the Constitutional Court–, but the short road that the ECJ took to reach it. The ECJ limited itself to affirming that the principle of the primacy of the Law of the Union is an essential characteristic of the European legal order and, that principle, implies that the Member State cannot invoke the provisions of national law even though they are at a constitutional level, to affect the efficacy of the Law of the Union in the territory of that State (par. 59). Then, the ECJ declared that *"It is true that Article 53 of the Charter confirms that, where an EU legal act calls for national implementing measures, national authorities and courts remain free to apply national standards of protection of fundamental rights, provided that the level of protection provided for by the Charter, as interpreted by the Court, and the primacy, unity and effectiveness of EU law are not thereby compromised"* (par. 60); it went on to recall that, in the present case, article 4 bis of the CFD claimed no national measures of enforcement and, therefore, did not attribute the faculty of refusing execution to the Member States in application of national standards of protection of fundamental rights (par. 61). Although known by everybody, it is worth noting that article 53 of the Charter only says that *"Nothing in this Charter shall be interpreted as restricting or adversely affecting human rights and fundamental freedoms as recognised, in their respective fields of application, by (...) the Member States' constitutions"*. It is more than likely that what is stated in par. 60 of the *Melloni* judgement may be and should be extracted from this provision, but that was not the way to put it; simply because that is not what may be directly understood from article 53.

5 Complements to the Melloni Judgement and Its Assessment

The ECJ caused surprise when handing down its scantily argued judicial decision, –in great measure—lacking useful signposts for future conflicts. The position that was adopted is not relevant. Nobody in the Constitutional Court expected any other response. It was clear that the value at stake was a nuanced matter, as well as its position that was supported by the constitutional traditions of other Member states, previously reflected in the case-law from Strasbourg. But the *leitmotiv* of the request for a preliminary ruling was the search for the terms of the relation between the Constitutional Courts and the ECtHR in matters of fundamental rights. And in its response, the ECJ did not wish to outline all sides of that relation.

It is true that it had magnificent examples with which to enrich its own case-law—especially in relation to articles 51–53 of the Charter–, both in SSC court order ATC 86/2011, on the submission of the preliminary question, and in the conclusions of the Attorney General, M. Yves Bot. But above all, as J. Díez Hochleitner[17] made clear, the ECJ had already adopted an approximation to the position in its earlier case-law, as in 1989, in the *Hoesht* case, the ECJ argued that, when uniform solutions are not necessary in the Union, the Union is obliged to respect the levels of protection laid down in national law[18] in the field of fundamental rights. The author deduced an interesting competency-related perspective from this case-law, affirming that it corresponded to the ECJ to determine whether an acceptable level of protection was offered by the act, whose validity was in question, taking into account the objectives pursued by the action of the Union. It all implies considering the harmonizing competences that the EU is exercising, that are very few in the case of harmonization in matters of fundamental laws and, normally, only permit minimum norms to be adopted. The author thereby linked the determination of the level of protection of a fundamental right in the European Union to the exercise of competences of the Union and affirmed that the ECJ has on multiple occasions been aware of the collision between the Union Law and fundamental rights enshrined in the national Constitutions, when instituting controls over national norms and establishing their conformity with the Union Law and, in particular, with the basic freedoms of the internal market. In that case-law, the ECJ has accepted that the Member State defines the level of protection of the fundamental right and restricts the community freedom, provided that the restriction responds to a legitimate end, but above all in so far as the ECJ considers that there is no need for a measure that establishes a conception shared by the Member States with regard to the modalities of the level of protection of the fundamental right under consideration.[19] Things being so, beginning with the non-necessity of a shared conception of the level of protection of a fundamental right in the set of Member States, the ECJ accepts that the Member State has a margin for manoeuvre when laying down a restrictive measure that affects community freedoms, if its purpose is the protection of the fundamental right and the measure is proportional to the end that is pursued, which might implicate its conformity with Union Law. Along these lines, the author analyzed judgements in the *Omega* case, the *Schmidberger* case, and the *Winner Wetten* case[20]; in all of which the ECJ ponders a weighting between two values that are at play: on the one hand, a community freedom and on the other, the level of protection of the fundamental right as determined by national law that enforces the Law of the Union. It is interesting to

[17] Díez-Hochleitner Rodríguez (2013).

[18] ECJ Judgment of 21 September 1989, Hoescht (C-46/87 and C-227/88).

[19] ECJ Judgment of 14 February of 2008, Dynamic Medien (C-244/06), par 36.

[20] ECJ Judgment of 14 October of 2004, Omega (C-36/02), par. 37; ECJ Judgment of 12 June 2003, Schmidberger (C-112/00) par. 65 and ECJ Judgment of 8 September of 2010; Winner Wetten (C-409/06) par. 60.

add the judgement in the *Mangold* case, as the ECJ, even accepting the margin for manoeuvre of the Member State, understood that the national legislator had violated the principle of non-discrimination, when using the age of the worker as the sole criteria for the application of a works contract of a particular duration, without having demonstrated that the setting of an age limit as such was objectively necessary to achieve the objective of the professional insertion of unemployed workers of an advanced age. It exceeded what was appropriate and necessary to achieve the objective that was pursued, was not proportional and as it did not conciliate the principle of equal treatment with the requirements of the objective that was pursued, it violated the principle of non-discrimination by reason of age. The following is a good example of the arguments of the ECJ in the *Melloni* case: *"where an EU legal act calls for national implementing measures, national authorities and courts remain free to apply national standards of protection of fundamental rights, provided that the level of protection provided for by the Charter, as interpreted by the Court, and the primacy, unity and effectiveness of EU law are not thereby compromised"* (par. 60).

The ECJ confirmed this line of case-law in *Åkerberg Frasson*, of 26 February 2013, adopted on the same day as the *Melloni* Judgement and relating to a national measure of enforcement of the order of the Union in Sweden. In the *Åkerberg Frasson* case, the ECJ questioned whether the principle of *non bis in idem* established in article 50 of the Charter was opposed to the national order of a Member State instituting a criminal action for a tax offence against a person upon whom a tax surcharge had already been applied for the same facts of submitting false returns. Against the decision in the *Melloni* case, the ECJ declared that article 50 of the Charter allowed the Member State to impose, for the same facts of non-compliance with the obligations of making VAT-related declarations, a combination of tax surcharges and criminal sanctions. It was a question of measures for the ECJ to guarantee the collection of all VAT-related income, thereby protecting the financial interests of the Union. In this context, the ECJ affirmed that the Member States enjoy freedom of choice over the applicable sanctions and that those sanctions may be administrative sanctions, criminal sanctions or a combination of both. For the ECJ, only when the income-tax sanction is of a criminal nature, and cannot be the object of an appeal may it be considered that article 50 of the Charter is opposed to a criminal action for the same facts against the same person. As may be seen in the present case, the ECJ understands that the States are the ones that have to chose the means for the applicable sanctions with a view to the protection of the financial interests of the Union and that, in that selection of means, they are not limited by the principle of *non bis in idem*, enshrined in article 50 of the Charter, except where the tax sanction is of a criminal nature and cannot be appealed against. A clear example, therefore, of a scarcely intense harmonization in which the Member States will be the ones that determine the standard of protection of the principle of *non bis in idem* in the national orders within the scope of application of Directive 2006/112, on VAT and article 325 TFEU. Notwithstanding which, it may be affirmed that this second judgement of the ECJ of

26 February 2013, incurred in the same—even more intense—shortcoming, than the *Melloni* judgement, in other words, a clear lack of reasoning, of legal construction and of explanation of the shortcoming.

The difference with the question that is the object of the *Melloni* judgement is that in the area of freedom, security and justice and, in this particular question of the European Arrest Warrant, the Union legislator has considered it necessary to adopt the enforcement measure by himself, as the requirements of the objective pursued by the Union have made it clear in that way and, in consequence, it is competent to determine the level of protection of the fundamental right affected by the measure that is adopted, provided that the competence has been exercised in accordance with the principle of proportionality of the legal framework of the Union.

The truth is that it is easy to share this interpretation of article 53 of the Charter of Fundamental rights of the Union, although the sparseness of its arguments cannot be shared. It makes sense, is sensible and fits in perfectly with the needs of the process of European construction. The terms *"in their respective fields of application"* that article 53 of the Charter contains were chosen by those who drafted it, so as not to harm the principle of primacy, but also so that the Member States would have the security that the Charter was not intended to replace their national Constitutions with regard to the level of protection that it guarantees within the scope of application of national law. In this sense, linking the scope of application of one order or another to the attributed competence is inevitable and, from a competency-related perspective, we may know where we are. Nevertheless, taking into account the complex competency-related system of the Union—competence of functional attribution and, on the majority of occasions, shared with the Member States–, it may only be determined on a case-by-case basis whether we are at one level or another, as the Union legislator in accordance with the principle of proportionality, has to define the intensity of the action of the Union that is necessary to reach the pre-set objectives. Nevertheless, in general terms it may be affirmed that when an act of the Union Law requires national measures for its execution, the authorities and national courts continue to be empowered to apply national standards of protection of fundamental rights, even though that application can neither affect the level of protection foreseen in the Charter, nor the primacy, the unity, and the effectiveness of the law of the Union (*Melloni*, par. 60).

References

Andrés Sáenz de Santamaría P (1985) La incorporación por referencia en el Derecho de los Tratados. Revista Española de Derecho Internacional 37:7–40

Arroyo Jiménez L (2011) Sobre la primera cuestión prejudicial planteada por el Tribunal Constitucional, bases, contenido y consecuencias. InDret 4/2011

Cámara Villar G (2004) Los derechos fundamentales en el proceso histórico de construcción de la Unión y su valor en el Tratado Constitucional. Revista de Derecho Constitucional Europeo 1:9–42

Díez-Hochleitner Rodríguez J (2013) El derecho a la última palabra: ¿Tribunales Constitucionales o Tribunal de Justicia de la Unión? In: Aa.Vv., Tribunal Constitucional y diálogo entre tribunales: XVIII Jornadas de la Asociación de Letrados del Tribunal Constitucional, pp 57–130

Pastor Ridruejo A (2008) La adhesión de la Unión Europea a la Convención Europea sobre Derechos Humanos y libertades Fundamentales. In: Martín Pérez de Nanclares J (ed) El Tratado de Lisboa. La salida de la crisis constitucional. Iustel, Madrid, pp 151–178

Pérez Manzano M (2012) El Tribunal Constitucional español ante la tutela multinivel de derechos fundamentales en Europa. Sobre el ATC 86/2011, de 9 de junio. Revista Española de Derecho Constitucional 95:311–345

Stoffel Valloton N (2008) La adhesión de la Unión Europea a la Convención Europea sobre Derechos Humanos y libertades Fundamentales: evolución de la cuestión, previsiones y posibles consecuencias. In: Martín Pérez de Nanclares J (ed) El Tratado de Lisboa. La salida de la crisis constitucional. Iustel, Madrid, pp 179–191

Part II
Multilevel Protection of the Principle of Legality in Criminal Law

A Dialogue Between Courts. The Case-Law of the European Court of Human Rights and the Spanish Constitutional Court on the Principle of Legal Certainty

Ignacio Villaverde Menéndez

1 Preliminary Considerations

Art. 7 ECHR and art. 25 of the Spanish Constitution (SC) guarantee the principle of the rule of law in relation to punishments; a similar wording may be found in art. 49 CFREU. All these norms have been interpreted in the sense of prohibiting the punishment of any offense, or the application of any punishment, in the absence of a prior, written, strict, and precise legal norm. But the fact is that neither art. 7 ECHR nor art. 25 SC refer to norms that are "written" Acts of Parliament—under the "democratic-representative principle" *or* within the *legal reservation*—"strict"—i.e. describing elements of a specific criminal behaviour (*legal crime definition*)—nor "precise"—in reference to legal certainty. The requirement for a prior written, strict and precise legal norm is essentially the product of a jurisprudential and doctrinal interrelation of those provisions. These imply an interpretation that leads one to uphold that the basic principles of a democratic society imply a "legal reservation"—or democratic-representative principle, because only the citizens, through their political representatives, are entitled to decide on the *ius puniendi*; and that the principle of legal certainty and the prohibition of retroactivity of laws demand that all statutes be non-retroactive, legally defined, and subject to legal certainty. It is from these affirmations that the prohibitions arise on analogical or extensive interpretation *in malam partem*, the abusive use of indeterminate legal terms, and "*carte blanche*" criminal statutes. Nothing of this is stated literally in the

Former Law Clerk at the Spanish Constitutional Court (1998–2001), Professor of Constitutional Law at Universidad de Oviedo.

I.V. Menéndez (✉)
Universidad de Oviedo, 33001 Oviedo, Spain
e-mail: nacho@uniovi.es

M. Pérez Manzano et al. (eds.), *Multilevel Protection of the Principle of Legality in Criminal Law*, DOI 10.1007/978-3-319-63865-2_3

aforementioned conventional and constitutional provisions, but it is in accordance with their spirit.[1]

Despite the existence of established and undisputed case law regarding the principle of legality in criminal law, the ECtHR (GC) Judgement of 21 October 2013 c. Del Río Prada *v*. Spain has profoundly altered the way in which art. 25.1 SC has been applied in Spanish case-law.

What is interesting to emphasize here, regarding this judgement of the ECtHR, is the Court's manner of construing the principle of "legal certainty" that diverges from the one used by the Spanish Constitutional Court (SCC). For the ECtHR, the requirement of legal certainty of the punishing norm is met when the relevant law has "*been formulated with sufficient precision to enable the applicant to discern to a reasonable degree the scope of the penalty imposed and the manner of its execution*". For the SCC, at least until this judgement of the ECtHR, the condition was deemed to be satisfied when the criminal or administrative sanctioning law, or the judicial application of the criminalizing criminal provision, is so reasonable that the consequence of its actions are foreseeable to those it addresses. The SCC considers that this foreseeability exists when the sentencing judge does not stray from the literal tenor of the provision and desists from applying extravagant interpretative and value-laden parameters to the existing constitutional body of laws. Nonetheless, for the SCC *"not every construal or application of a criminalizing criminal definition that is incorrect, inopportune or inadequate entails a violation of the principle of legality or of fundamental law that are the contents of art. 25.1 SC"* (STC 137/1997 Of 21 July 1997, FJ 7 and 185/2014 of 6 November 2014, FJ 8).

It is here that the divergence between the ECtHR and the SCC is found, when testing compliance with the principle of legality. For the SCC, it is a matter of knowing whether the consequences of criminal or administrative sanctions applied to particular conducts are reasonably predictable, in view of the literal tenor of the criminal or administrative provision that sanctions. What is important for the ECtHR is that these consequences should be foreseeable for the individual, in view of the circumstances of the case (ECtHR).[2] Obviously, the competencies and parameters of control used by the two jurisdictions are different, which doubtless conditions their criteria of judgement. The ECtHR lacks competency to carry out an abstract control of the "conventionality" of the provision for the criminal or administrative sanction, hence, perhaps, its tendency to judge the pronouncements of judges and courts from a subjective perspective.[3] But the SCC does exercise competency for control over the constitutionality of the criminal-sanctioning norm; hence to a considerable degree the canon that it employs—in the case of the principle of legal certainty that concerns us here—to assess (the constitutionality) of the norm conditions the canon that it uses to do so in its judicial and administrative spheres.

---

[1]See STC 137/1997 of 26 August 1999 FFJJ 6–7. Lamarca Pérez (1987), p. 102 ff. Kuhlen (2012), *passim;* Lagodny (1996), pp. 15, 78.

[2]This doctrine is summed up to perfection by Huerta Tocildo (2008), pp. 733–734.

[3]Matscher (1993), pp. 322 ff.

Thus, the present article sets out to examine this divergence. For this purpose, I shall, in the first place, restrict the content of the principle of legality to the case-law of the ECtHR and the SCC. The following pages examine their respective formal and material guarantees with special attention to the principle of legal certainty. Finally, I shall indicate the divergences that separate both jurisdictions regarding the mandate of legal certainty, and the role that may be played in the future by the ECJ.

2 The ECtHR's Doctrine on Art. 7 ECHR

The ECtHR (GC) Judgement of 21 October 2013 c. Del Río Prada v. Spain sums up the Court's doctrine in the following terms (par. 78)[4]:

> Article 7 of the Convention is not confined to prohibiting the retrospective application of the criminal law to an accused's disadvantage (concerning the retrospective application of a penalty, see Welch v. the United Kingdom, 9 February 1995, par. 36, Series A no. 307-A; Jamil v. France, 8 June 1995, par. 35, Series A no. 317-B; Ecer and Zeyrek v. Turkey, nos. 29295/95 and 29363/95, par. 36, ECHR 2001-II; and Mihai Toma v. Romania, no. 1051/06, par. 26-31, 24 January 2012). It also embodies, more generally, the principle that only the law can define a crime and prescribe a penalty (nullum crimen, nulla poena sine lege – see Kokkinakis v. Greece, 25 May 1993, par. 52, Series A no. 260-A). While it prohibits in particular extending the scope of existing offences to acts which previously were not criminal offences, it also lays down the principle that the criminal law must not be extensively construed to an accused's detriment, for instance by analogy (see Coëme and Others v. Belgium, nos. 32492/96, 32547/96, 32548/96, 33209/96 and 33210/96, par. 145, ECHR 2000-VII; for an example of the application of a penalty by analogy, see Başkaya and Okçuoğlu v. Turkey [GC], nos. 23536/94 and 24408/94, par. 42-43, ECHR 1999-IV).

Up to this point, there is no difference as regards the doctrine of the SCC. We might say that this is the European and Spanish standard of the principle of legality in criminal law. But thereafter the divergences begin (par. 79):

> It follows that offences and the relevant penalties must be clearly defined by law. This requirement is satisfied where the individual can know from the wording of the relevant provision, if need be with the assistance of the courts' interpretation of it and after taking appropriate legal advice, what acts and omissions will make him criminally liable and what penalty he faces on that account (see Cantoni v. France, 15 November 1996, par. 29, Reports of Judgments and Decisions 1996-V, and Kafkaris, cited above, par. 140).

This insistence on the subjective perception of the person concerned is reiterated in the Judgement with expressions such as the following: "*...when the latter [the convicted person] could not have imagined such a development at the time when the offence was committed or the sentence was imposed*" (par. 89). The ECtHR's reasoning culminates in reaffirming the capital importance of the interpretation in criminal and sanctioning case law. This is what will be required by the inevitable abstraction and generality of the normative provision in art. 7 ECHR, and that is

[4]A painstaking analysis of the ECtHR's jurisprudence can be found in Murphy (2010), *passim*.

what constitutes the ultimate bulwark of individual certainty regarding the foreseeability of the juridical consequences of an individual's behaviour. The ECtHR says (par. 92):

> It is a logical consequence of the principle that laws must be of general application that the wording of statutes is not always precise. One of the standard techniques of regulation by rules is to use general categorisations as opposed to exhaustive lists. Accordingly, many laws are inevitably couched in terms which, to a greater or lesser extent, are vague and whose interpretation and application are questions of practice (see Kokkinakis, cited above, par. 40, and Cantoni, cited above, par. 31). However clearly drafted a legal provision may be, in any system of law, including criminal law, there is an inevitable element of judicial interpretation. There will always be a need for elucidation of doubtful points and for adaptation to changing circumstances. Again, whilst certainty is highly desirable, it may bring in its train excessive rigidity and the law must be able to keep pace with changing circumstances (see Kafkaris, cited above, par. 141).

The ECtHR goes on to demand of case-law the same precision and certainty that, in principle, art. 7 ECHR (like Art. 25 SC) imposes upon the criminal or administrative sanction code (par. 93):

> The role of adjudication vested in the courts is precisely to dissipate such interpretational doubts as remain (ibid.). The progressive development of criminal law through judicial law-making is a well-entrenched and necessary part of legal tradition in the Convention States (see Kruslin v. France, 24 April 1990, par. 29, Series A no. 176-A). Article 7 of the Convention cannot be read as outlawing the gradual clarification of the rules of criminal liability through judicial interpretation from case to case, provided that the resultant development is consistent with the essence of the offence and could reasonably be foreseen (see S.W. v. the United Kingdom, cited above, par. 36; C.R. v. the United Kingdom, cited above, par. 34; Streletz, Kessler and Krenz, cited above, par. 50; K.-H.W. v. Germany [GC], no. 37201/97, par. 85, 22 March 2001; Korbely v. Hungary [GC], no. 9174/02, par. 71, ECHR 2008; and Kononov v. Latvia [GC], no. 36376/04, par. 185, ECHR 2010). The lack of an accessible and reasonably foreseeable judicial interpretation can even lead to a finding of a violation of the accused's Article 7 rights (see, concerning the constituent elements of the offence, Pessino v. France, no. 40403/02, par. 35-36, 10 October 2006, and Dragotoniu and Militaru-Pidhorni v. Romania, nos. 77193/01 and 77196/01, par. 43-44, 24 May 2007; as regards the penalty, see Alimuçaj v. Albania, no. 20134/05, par. 154-62, 7 February 2012). Were that not the case, the object and the purpose of this provision – namely that no one should be subjected to arbitrary prosecution, conviction or punishment – would be defeated.

The problem with this slant is that it alters the standard of protection of the right to criminal or administrative sanctioning legality, because it converts the mandate of certainty and precision that is directed at the legislator into a duty of foreseeability directed at the judges and the courts.

3 The Formal Guarantee: The Criminal or Administrative Sanctioning Norm

3.1 *Absolute "Legal Reservation" in the Case of Art. 25.1 SC*

It is an undisputed principle—and from the beginning, the SCC has regarded it as such—that the state's *ius puniendi* can only be regulated by law[5] (hence art. 25.1 SC would contain an implicit "Legal reservation"; SSTC 8/1981 of 30 March 1981, FJ 3; 15/1986 31 January 1986, FJ 2; 42/1986 of 10 April 1986, FJ 3 and 4; 52/2003 of 17 March 2003, FJ 7; 283/2006 9 October 2006, FJ 5). Consequently—and for what concerns us now—the first guarantee of the principle of legality is the normative predetermination of violations, of punishable or sanctionable offenses. The second consists in the identification of the constitutionally established legal procedure for determining infractions. Here we find the first divergence with the ECtHR. The Court at Strasbourg has recourse to the material concept of "Law" so that what it requires of national codes on this point is to dispose of an accessible and foreseeable norm which is what must establish the categories of each criminal or administrative sanction. The SCC, however, identifies the criminal or administrative sanctioning norm with the formal law (not necessarily the parliamentary statute, as it happens) and excludes any other legal form that does not possess that status and force. On that point, I disagree with Huerta Tocildo, who fears the possibility that the European standard in relation with the proper norm for fixing criminal-sanctioning categories might weaken the strict requirement for formal law in the case of the Spanish standard.[6] I do not agree that this interpretation of the ECtHR necessarily leads to a flexibilization of the requirement for absolute *Legal reservation* that the SCC has inferred from art. 25 SC.[7]

From the literal tenor of art. 25.1 SC one cannot deduce the existence of an absolute and formal "reserve of law" in the criminal-sanctioning area. But at an early date the SCC affirmed that the aforesaid article establishes a formal guarantee of the principle of legality in criminal law, consisting in an absolute *Legal reservation* (from STC 15/1981 of 7 May 1981, FJ 7). Art. 25.1 SC regulates the conditions of production of criminal or administrative sanctioning norms in the Spanish legal code. But the constitutional provision in no way identifies this norm with any of the legal forms of our system of sources. If the constitutional conditions under which one may be sentenced or sanctioned constitute the object of the principle of legality, it is obvious that such conditions are not identifiable with the definition of categories defined in criminal or administrative law. Likewise, those categories do not constitute limits to law, because they do not contemplate

[5]"Law" must be understood in all this text as "Parliamentary or legislative Act".

[6]Huerta Tocildo (2014), pp. 402 ff.

[7]Others who have voiced concern are Ruiz Robledo (2003), pp. 132ff; and Burgorgue-Larsen (2007), pp. 337 ff.

exceptions or restrictions on the constitutional mandate of normative predetermination of prohibited and punishable conducts. Nor do the norms of a criminal or administrative sanction establish conditions as regards time, mode and place of exercise of this fundamental right. Rather, what they do is precisely to establish the conditions of production of those norms (which is not the object of the fundamental right, since the latter does not guarantee the power to create criminal-sanctioning norms). Neither does the criminal or administrative sanctioning norm develop the content of the right to legal punishment certainly, because the *reaction* of the individual sentenced or sanctioned in violation of the constitutional conditions, is not regulated in criminal or administrative sanctioning norms. Any such regulation takes place in the procedural rules. Hence, there appears to be no constitutional reason that in all cases demands ordinary regulatory law (art. 53.1 SC) or an organic law to guide its development (art. 81.1 SC), except for those norms that contemplate infractions sanctioned by a punishment involving privation of liberty (as such a sanction constitutes a limit to the fundamental right to freedom of art. 17 SC), or that constitute limits to fundamental rights or punish conducts harmful to fundamental rights, or establish the general conditions of punishability. Beyond those cases, the sanctioning norms are not an expression of the content (in the broad sense) of the right, but are what is addressed by the mandate contained in art. 25.1 SC.

The SCC seems to view the matter in this light (SSTC 8/1981 of 30 March 1981, 25/1984 of 23 February 1984 and 32/1984 of 8 March 1984). In fact, the SCC affirms that the state's *ius puniendi* can only be formalized in a norm with the status of law, because this is what is required by the principle of legality and the democratic principle of Arts. 1.1 and 9.1 and 3 SC (SSTC 8/1981 of 30 March 1981, FJ 3; 133/1987 of 21 July 1987, FJ 4; 3/1988 of 21 January 1988, FJ 6; 101/1988 of 8 June 1988, FJ 3; 142/1999 of 22 July 1999, FJ 3; 77/2006 of 13 March 2006; 144/2011 of 26 September 2011, FJ 4). The principle of legality requires the predetermination by law of the norm that establishes in which cases the state may make use of force, thus prohibiting its arbitrary use. The democratic principle incorporates in the "Legal reservation" contained in art. 25.1 SC the duty of the legislator as the representative of the public to regulate the criminal category and its sanction in material terms. And it is this last-mentioned obligation, that it is the legislator, and only the legislator who, as a representative of the general public, materially regulates the criminal category and its sanctioning that gives rise to the requirements of criminal definitions and legal certainty (STC 34/1996 of 11 March 1996, FJ 5).

3.2 The ECtHR's Jurisprudence: The Criminal or Administrative Sanctioning Norm in Art. 7 ECHR

It is not possible to extract the same consequences regarding the status and form of the criminal or administrative sanction norm from art. 7 ECHR as can be drawn from art. 25 SC. The ECHR contains no system of sources subject to particular structural principles such as legality or the democratic principle. Art. 7 ECHR does, however, contain a formal guarantee of the principle of legality in criminal law, but expressed in a different way from the way it would be done in a national constitution.

The ECtHR has construed art. 7 ECHR as an expression of the "Rule of Law", of the principle of legality in the punishing and sanctioning sphere, that seeks to proscribe the arbitrary behaviour of the state in criminal sentencing or its application of administrative sanctions. On this point, the Court regards art. 7 ECHR as a manifestation of the Democratic State under the Rule of Law.[8] The Court has expressed this much in ECtHR (GC) Judgement of 21 October 2013 c. Del Río Prada v. Spain, summing up its reiterated doctrine, as follows (par. 77):

> The guarantee enshrined in Article 7, which is an essential element of the rule of law, occupies a prominent place in the Convention system of protection, as is underlined by the fact that no derogation from it is permissible under Article 15 even in time of war or other public emergency threatening the life of the nation. It should be construed and applied, as follows from its object and purpose, in such a way as to provide effective safeguards against arbitrary prosecution, conviction and punishment (see S.W. v. the United Kingdom, 22 November 1995, par. 34, Series A no. 335-B; C.R. v. the United Kingdom, 22 November 1995, par. 32, Series A no. 335-C; and Kafkaris, cited above, par. 137).

The ECtHR has taken particular care to point out that the norm to which any criminal sentence or administrative sanction must be subject is a synonym of "Law". A term repeated on numerous occasions in the ECHR, especially in arts. 9, 10 and 11. The ECtHR has defined that concept in ECtHR Judgement of 26 April 1979, c. The Sunday Times *v.* United Kingdom (par. 47) and Judgement of 24 February 1994, c. Casado Coca *v.* Spain (par. 43). It is, for the ECtHR, a material and not a formal concept, in which—with the aim of reconciling the continental tradition with the Anglo-Saxon, and with the tacit referral to what each system of national sources (or international legislation) ordains—what is required of the criminal or administrative sanctioning norm is not that it be construed in accordance with a particular procedure (the legislative one) or by a particular subject (the legislator), but that it be an accessible and foreseeable norm. This much has been set forth by the ECtHR in connection with the following Judgements of 22 November, 1995, c. S.W. *v.* United Kingdom, and 22 November 1995, c. C.R. *v.* United Kingdom, par.34–36 and par.32–34 respectively; 15 November 1996, c. Cantoni *v.* France, par.29; 12 February 2008, c. Kafkaris *v.* Cyprus, par. 139 and 140; 18 October, 2000, c. Cöeme et al. *v.* Belgium, par. 145; 22 March 2001, c. Streletz, Kessler and Krenz *v.* Germany, par. 50; 7 February 2002, c. EK *v.* Turkey, par. 51; 17 November 2009 c. Scoppola *v.* Italy (no. II), par. 99–102; 10 May 2010, c. M. *v.* Germany, par. 117; 18 March 2014, c. Öcalan *v.* Turkey (no. II), par. 171–174. I am unware of any judgement by the ECtHR that questions the status or form of a criminal or administrative sanctioning norm, as long as the

---

[8]Murphy (2010), pp. 194 ff.

system of sources of the state appealed against is not seen to be extravagant.[9] But it has not hesitated to demand of the norm those conditions that it regards as unwaivable; that it should be accessible and its consequences foreseeable.

The ECtHR has required that criminal or administrative sanction laws be sufficiently accessible. It has considered that a law is accessible if the citizen can have sufficient information at hand regarding its existence and contents in application to a particular situation (viz. Judgement of 26 April 1979, c. The Sunday Times v. Unit Kingdom, par. 49; Judgement of 28 March 1990, c. Groppera Radio AG et al. *v*. Switzerland, par. 67 ff.).[10] In Burgorgue-Larsen's words, the ECtHR has demanded, in the framework of the requirement of accessibility to such norms, "*a clear definition of the law and a reasonable interpretation of the criminal judge*".[11] For the former case, the ECtHR judged that the norm must be sufficiently clear for a member of the public to understand it, with the help of "clarifying advice" if necessary, admitting that absolute precision in laws is unattainable and that the "*level of precision required of the domestic legislation can vary in accordance with the text under consideration, the matter that it covers and the function of whoever it addresses*".[12] Both the clarity of the norm and its jurisprudential interpretation must be of such reasonableness, that the ECtHR has described the latter as a "*complement of written law*".[13] The ECtHR has considered on numerous occasions (in particular in its Judgements of 22 November 1995, c. S.W. *v*. United Kingdom, and of 11 November 1996, c. Cantoni *v*. France,) that case-law contributes to clarifying the sense of the criminal or administrative sanctioning norm and must be taken into account, in order to establish whether the effect was accessible and foreseeable. The ECtHR has, nonetheless, required of jurisprudence a strict and restrictive interpretation of criminal or administrative sanctioning laws, prohibiting analogy or broad interpretations *in malam partem*. The Court has declared admissible a margin of judicial appreciation in the application of the criminal or administrative sanctioning norm as long as the result "*is consistent with the essence of the offense and can reasonably be foreseen*" (Judgement of 22 November 1995, c. S.W. *v*. United Kingdom, par. 36).[14]

---

[9]Tomuschat (2013), *passim;* Murphy (2010), pp. 200 ff.; Bartole et al. (2001), pp. 249 ff.; Cadoppi (2002), *passim*; Dijk and Hoof (1990), p. 365 ff.; Frowein and Peukert (1996), pp. 325 ff.; Harris et al. (1995), pp. 274 ff.; Renucci (2007), *passim*; and Loucaides (2007), *passim*.

[10]Bartole et al. (2001), pp. 260–261; Murphy (2010), p. 200.

[11]Burgorgue-Larsen (2007), pp. 339 ff.; Bartole et al. (2001), *ibid*.

[12]Burgorgue-Larsen (2007), p. 340; ECtHR Judgement of 25 August 1993, c. Chorherr *v*. Austria, par.25.

[13]Burgorgue-Larsen (2007), p. 341; Huerta Tocildo (2014), pp. 415 ff.

[14]The ECtHR accepted the "evolutive" and "finalist" interpretation of the British courts of the crime of rape, according to which a husband could commit the offense of rape against his wife; despite the fact that at the time the acts took place English criminal law did not contemplate that possibility and actually regarded it as excluded. The same could be said regarding the cases of Judgement of 22 March 2001, c. Streletz, Kessler, and Krenz *v*. Germany and Judgement of 22 March 2017, c. K.H.W *v*. Germany, in which, in application of punishing norms of the reunified

The second requirement refers to the condition of foreseeability. The ECtHR has broken this requirement down into two conditions. The first requires that the criminal or administrative sanctioning norm must be formulated clearly and precisely by the competent agents. For the effects of art. 7 ECHR, the ECtHR considers that a norm can only be regarded as "Law", if it is formulated with sufficient precision for a member of the public to regulate his own conduct—if need be with appropriate legal counsel—so as to be able to foresee, to a degree that is reasonable in the circumstances, the consequences that a given action may entail. The ECtHR has admitted a certain degree of generality and has not demanded absolute precision in the norm, and has taken into account the sort of individual addressed in the norm and his circumstances, as well as those of its own jurisprudential or administrative interpretation. The second refers to the reasonableness of the criminal or administrative sanction norm and its interpretation, conceived as the interpretation of the norm, especially the case-law interpretation, that enables its sphere of application to be predicted. This condition is fulfilled when for the individual it is possible to identify which acts or omissions are punished or sanctioned (Judgements of 26 April 1979, c. The Sunday Times v. Unit Kingdom., *ibid.*; of 15 November 1996, c. Cantoni *v*. France, par. 30; or Judgements of 25 May 1993, c. Kokkinakis *v*. Greece, par. 40; of 8 July 1999, c. Baskaya and Okçuoglu *v*. Turkey, par. 36; of 25 September 2009, c. Liivik *v*. Estonia, par. 101–104).[15]

It seems reasonable that the ECtHR should examine the punitive context of each case, in order to know, in the absence of a formal, certain and precise norm, whether it was subjectively foreseeable to the defendant that his conduct was prohibited. In the absence of a formal law, the only option available is to examine whether the passive subject of the state's *ius puniendi* could, with a reasonable degree of security, be aware of the consequences of his acts.[16]

Germany and international criminal law, three border guards of the extinct Democratic Republic of Germany were convicted of wilful murder, concerning the deaths of various individuals who were attempting to escape to the Federal Republic. As Burgorgue-Larsen (2007), p. 343, wisely pondered when commenting on both cases: "*One must not forget that there are close links between such interpretations and the principle of non-retroactivity(...). Every judicial interpretation, every change introduced through case law has necessarily a retroactive aspect. How can one reconcile this with the prohibition of retroactivity of the punishing law enshrined in Article 7?*" Murphy (2010), p. 206.

[15]Bartole et al. (2001), p. 263.

[16]To a certain extent this is the conclusion at which Huerta Tocildo also arrives on considering that the ECtHR replaces the mandate of legal certainty by the criterion of foreseeability in cases where it is not possible to appeal, in the national system of reference, to an absolute legal reservation (Huerta Tocildo (2014), pp. 414–415).

3.3 Two Standards for the Same Guarantee. A Proposal of Interpretation that Avoids Weakening the Guarantee of Art. 25.1 SC

In view of what has already been said, the formal standard of protection of art. 7 ECHR as defined by the ECtHR in no way entails a relaxation of national standards—in this case that of Spain, according to which the criminal or administrative santioning norm must have the status of law—that might serve to justify a criminal sentence or an administrative sanction in application of a customary norm or doctrine arising out of case law (*mutatis mutandis* ECtHR Judgement of 14 April 2015, c. Contrada *v.* Italy (N° 3), *passim*).[17] To a certain extent, the demand for prior exhaustion of the national judicial recourses, before appealing to the ECtHR constitutes a guarantee that the system of sources generative of criminal or administrative sanctioning norms has been respected in the respective national body of law. If in that system of sources, customary law or the judicial precedents are acceptable for the definition of criminal categories, it is not within the ECtHR's competence to correct the conditions of that system of sources or to alter them.

It therefore seems clear that the requirements of accessibility and foreseeability of the ECtHR in application of art. 7 ECHR are none other than those of the existence of a statutory conceptual definition and its legal certainty, in terms of art. 25 SC. But neither of these conditions affect or alter in the slightest the criminal or administrative sanction, or the identification in each national juridical codification of the norm with the capacity for defining—criminally or administratively—a conduct as anti-juridical. Let it not be forgotten that, as Loucaides points out, for the ECtHR the principle of "Rule of Law"—by its very essence as a founding principle of democratic society—presupposes a democratic regime (ECtHR Judgements of 23 November 1993, c. Poitrimol *v.* France; of 30 March 2004, c. Hirst *v.* United Kingdom; of 15 July 2005, c. Colacai *v.* Italy; of 13 July 2001, c. Refah Partisi *v.* Turkey). A corollary of this reasoning is that the "Law" must possess certain material qualities: in particular, to have been drafted by authorities and institutions of state competent to do so; in other words, the ECtHR will limit itself to trying whether in each case the system of criminal and sanctioning sources of that national codification has been respected. The use of the expression "Law" in the ECHR, particularly in its art. 7.1, does not constitute a material reference to a concrete juridical form, but a referral to the system of sources of the national codifications. These are what specify in each case the juridical form suitable for establishing

[17]The SCC has not hesitated to deny mere custom the condition of a sanctioning or punishing norm, STC 26/1994 of 27 January 1994, FJ 5. Huerta Tocildo (2014), pp. 402 ff.; Burgorgue-Larsen (2007), pp. 337, and criticizes recognition of such established practices as weakening the formal guarantee of the domain of legality, and thus widening to an alarming extent each state's "margin of appreciation". Thus the ECtHR has come to regard a wide variety of juridical forms as source of punishment norms, such as military proclamations (ECtHR Judgement of 19 December 1994, c. Vereinigung Demotratischer Soldaten Ósterreichs and Gubi *v.* Austria,), or mere public statements before the House of Commons (Report of the Commission on Human Rights on Rai, Allmond and Negotiate Now *v.* United Kingdom of 6 April, 1995).

criminal or administrative infractions and their respective penalty.[18] The ECtHR only requires of that norm that it be "accessible and foreseeable" and drafted by the authority that is competent to do so.

To sum up, although art. 7 ECHR does not incorporate into the European principle of legality a general requirement of parliamentary law, and permits the sources of the criminal or administrative sanctioning norm to be any other, including customary law or judicial precedent, by doing so it does not weaken the formal guarantee of the Legal reservation (*Legal reservation*) enshrined in art. 25.1 SC.

4 The Material Guarantee. The Principle of Legal Certainty

4.1 The Standard of Art. 25.1 SC and ECtHR Case Law in Reference to Art. 7 ECHR

Another well-settled point in Spanish case law concerns the principle of determination, or legal certainty, as one of the contents of the principle of legality enshrined in art. 25.1 SC.[19] This principle imposes on the legislator of the criminal or administrative sanction the duty to draw up clear and precise criminal or administrative sanction norms regarding the definition of criminal categories and their respective penalties or sanctions. There is no space for doubt that this mandate derives from the absolute Legal reservation contained in art. 25.1 SC and is connected with the principles of the legal guarantees enshrined in art. 9.3 SC (STC 62/1982 of 15 October 1982 and STC 137/1997 of 21 July 1997). If it is only the law that can formalize the state's exercise of *ius puniendi* by defining those cases in which it is to be employed, then reasonably clear and precise terms must be employed in the statutes of criminal and sanctioning law (STC 69/1989 of 20 April 1989, FJ 1 and STC 137/1997 of 21 July 1997, FJ 7), thus avoiding situations in which judges and Administration supplant the legislator, invading or infringing the absolute Legal reservation of criminal or administrative sanctioning law via the construal of offences that the legislator has not defined (STC 105/1988 of 8 June 1988, FJ 2).

There is no doubt that the mandate of legal certainty operates in the sphere of legislation (clarity and precision are required of criminal or administrative sanction law), while the mandate of criminal definitions regulates the judicial and administrative interpretation and application of criminal or administrative sanctioning law.[20] The requirement of such statutory descriptions of each offence implies that

---

[18] Murphy (2010), p. 207.

[19] Ferreres Comella (2002), *passim*; Navarro Frías (2010), *passim;* Huerta Tocildo (2000), pp. 39 ff.; (2014), pp. 413 ff.; Lascuraín Sánchez (2009), par. 35, III; Navarro López and Manrique (2005), *passim*.

[20] Lascuraín Sánchez (2009), par. 34, III.

no other criminal categories exist apart from those defined by law.[21] The requirement of legal certainty establishes that the law must define the offence with precision and clarity. The joint operation of both mandates, addressed first and foremost to the legislator and not the judge, prohibits whoever might apply the criminal or administrative sanctioning law from any construal or application of the criminal law that might sanction what is not legally defined as an offence, by using interpretations of an extravagant and unreasonable nature, or that unduly extend the scope of a norm beyond its obvious literal meaning. Not to do so would raise judges or the administration to the status of creators of new criminal norms or penalties *praeter legem* or even *contra legem*. This possibility violates the absolute Legal reservation established in art. 25.1 SC and the legal security of art. 9.3 SC.

The principle of legal certainty on the other hand requires the clear and precise predetermination of the sanctioning categories; only thus can a member of the public reasonably foresee the consequences of his conduct (STC 199/2014 of 15 December 2014, FJ 3). But, as the Constitutional Court admits, the literal sense of the criminal or administrative sanctioning norm will always leave space for judicial interpretation, so that the mandate of determination is also binding upon judges and courts in the construal and application of the norm that regulates the criminal or administrative sanction (STC 185/2014 of 6 November 2014, FJ 5).

In the words of Huerta Tocildo: "*hence the demand addressed to criminal legislators in the sense of seeking to use clear and comprehensible language when describing prohibited conducts, avoiding as far as possible the use of equivocal legal concepts that might give rise to the appearance of undesirable divergences of interpretation [. . .]. Only thus can one avoid situations in which the criminal judge who has to interpret the norm finds himself transformed into a legislator, contravening the idea of the division of powers, so intimately connected with the principle of legality, and with the consequent risks of 'decisionism' and arbitrariness that this entails; and only thus can a sufficient degree of foreseeability be attained to satisfy the demand for legal certainty*". The citizen has the right to know what to expect in accordance with the letter of the criminal or administrative sanction norm, and not on the basis of unpredictable interpretations or judicial applications of the law. For this reason criminal or administrative sanction statutes must be clear and precise, because such clarity and precision produce legal certainty (STC 118/1992 of 16 September 1992, FJ 2; STC 53/1994 of 24 February 1994, FJ 4; 137/1997 of 21 July 1997, FJ 7; 38/2003 of 27 February 2003, FJ 8; 218/2005 of 12 September 2005, FJ 6; 283/2006 of 9 October 2006, FJ 5).[22]

Since STC 62/1982 of 15 October 1982 (FJ 7c), the SCC has considered that the requirement of legal certainty is, in reality, a mandate to optimize the clarity and precision of the criminal or administrative sanction norm, indicating, however, an

[21]Lascuraín Sánchez (2009), par. 39, IV.

[22]Huerta Tocildo (1993), p. 109; Navarro López and Manrique (2005), pp. 810, 819 ("*Las leyes precisas sirven para generar certeza jurídica*").

insurmountable limit: the impossibility of a criminal or administrative sanction norm that is unquestionably precise and clear.[23] Hence the existence of *carte blanche* laws or the use of referrals or indeterminate legal terms is not in itself contrary to art. 25.1 SC, as long as such practices are not just a way of covering for the evident lack of precision or clarity of the law on the criminal or administrative sanction (STC 127/1990 of 5 July 1990, FJ 3b). The SCC has always required in those cases "*that the normative referral be express and justified in terms of the legal good protected by the criminal norm*"; "*that the law, besides stating the penalty, should contain the essential nucleus of the prohibition*"; and that "*the requirement of certainty be satisfied*". The latter requirement is deemed to be met when "*the conduct qualified as an offence is defined with sufficient precision by means of the indispensable complement of the norm referred to in the criminal statute…, with the possibility of knowledge of the criminally proscribed behaviour*" (STC 127/1990 of 5 July 1990, FJ 3; STC101/2012 of 8 May 2012, FJ 3).

However, when the SCC assesses the constitutionality of criminal or administrative sanction laws that are "relatively" imprecise or insufficiently clear—statutes that need, in order to clarify their sense, referral to other statutes—it also specifies that, "together with the aforementioned formal guarantee, the principle of legality of art. 25.1 SC also comprises another of material character, that reflects the overriding importance of the mandate of legal certainty in this sphere limitative of individual freedom and which, in relation with the legislator—and this is what concerns us most here—means in practice the absolute requirement of the normative predetermination of illicit conducts and their corresponding sanctions by means of a classification as precise and exacting as can be attained in the incorporated description, so that citizens may be aware in advance of the sphere of prohibition and thus foresee the consequences of their actions" (STC 283/2006 of 8 October 2006, FJ 5).

However, the foreseeability to which the SCC alludes in no way implies that in each case the courts must weigh up, as the ECtHR does, whether the sentenced or sanctioned member of the public really could know the consequences of his actions or omissions in advance of his sentencing or sanctioning. For the SCC, that requirement of foreseeability is a demand upon the legislator aimed at avoiding judicial activism in the matter of criminal law and the application of sanctions. The punishing norm must be precise and clear, and hence foreseeable, and the judges and courts may not be a substitute for the legislator when the norm is obscure or imprecise (STC 26/2005 of 14 February 2005, FJ 3).[24]

The ECtHR, on the other hand, seems to be less demanding as regards the mandates of typicality and the certainty of criminal or administrative sanctioning norms.[25] Indeed, the Court does not use these terms. In its judgements it is very

[23] Lascuraín Sánchez (2009), par. 39, IV; Moreso (2001), p. 11; Navarro López and Manrique (2005), p. 822.

[24] Huerta Tocildo (2008), p. 733; Lascuraín Sánchez (2012), p. 18.

[25] Huerta Tocildo (1993), p. 96; Murphy (2010), *passim*.

permissive with the role played by case-law, in complementing the criminal or administrative sanctioning norm. In those cases, what the ECtHR examines is whether case-law (as legitimate in a democratic society as its parliament), in supplying the absence or imprecision of a criminal or administrative sanctioning norm, has done so in such a way that the sentenced or sanctioned person could have foreseen the consequences of his acts or omissions. It is true that the SCC uses a very similar standard to that used by the ECtHR; except that for the SCC the sentence or sanction is foreseeable to the extent that the norm prescribing the criminal or administrative sanction is not manifestly imprecise or obscure in its literal sense or that its interpretation by judges and courts is not manifestly unreasonable or extravagant. For the ECtHR, in contrast, the sentence or sanction is foreseeable if, in view of the circumstances of the case, the sentenced or sanctioned individual is in a situation to be aware of, understand, and foresee the criminal or administrative sanction consequences of his acts or omissions.

The ECtHR Judgement of 11 November 1996, c. Cantoni *v*. France, is a clear example of this subjective foreseeability. In this case, a person was sanctioned for selling medicines in a supermarket. The appellant argued, among other pleas, that the punishing statute applied to his case did not define what ought to be considered "medicines". In its judgement, the ECtHR held that it was not necessary to enumerate exhaustively what ought to be regarded as medicine in order for the law in question to be considered precise; and that, besides, the appellant—given his profession—could be expected to be aware of that information; hence it was not admissible to conclude that in this particular case the appellant could not have foreseen his conviction (par. 35).[26] The ECtHR emitted a similar judgement on the ECtHR Judgement of 6 October 2011, c. Soros *v*. France, relating to a sentence for the commission of an offense regarding the use of privileged information, in which—given the appellant's profession and experience—it considered that he was in a position to understand and foresee the consequences. In the ECtHR (GC) Judgement of 21 October 2013, c. Del Río Prada v. Spain, however, the ECtHR considered that, in view of a change in jurisprudence of the Spanish courts, it was impossible for the appellant to foresee the modification of the conditions for serving his criminal sentence.

[26]Perhaps, in the light of its case law, the SCC might have emitted a different sentence. Not, however, because of the unforeseeability of the conviction for the appellant, but because the referral of the punishing law did nothing to clarify for any citizen what, for punishing effects, should be considered "medicine". In fact, the Commission in its report on the matter of April 12, 1995, expressed quite the contrary opinion to the judgement handed down subsequently by the ECtHR, stating that the definition of "medicine" lacked "a reasonable degree of foreseeability" (par. 63).

4.2 Two Divergent Standards Regarding the Principle of Legality

There is no doubt that an important discrepancy exists here between the standard of art. 7 ECHR and that of art. 25.1 SC. Spanish legal culture has always tended to see a rule on the adherence of the institutions of the state to Law (principles of legality and legal certainty) in the right to criminal or administrative sanctioning legality. The ECtHR, on the other hand, has seen art. 7 ECHR as a guarantee of the certainty of members of the public regarding the consequences of their actions or omissions. What concerns the ECtHR is possible formal observance of the principle of legality that is used as a pretext for convictions or sanctions that, unforeseeable for the public, leave people in a state of "defencelessness" (breach of defence rights) before decisions of state regarding what, when and how to punish or sanction a particular conduct, since the citizen is unable to foresee such decisions.[27]

Perhaps the origin of the discrepancy is found in the reasons that underlie each standard. In the case of art. 25.1 SC, the principle of legality guarantees the prohibition of conviction or sanctioning in the absence of a prior written, clear and precise law. It is from the mandate upon the legislator contained in the constitutional precept and the democratic principle that the principles of elements of the criminal definition and the legal certainty of the norm prescribing the criminal or administrative sanction are deduced. The principle of legality is violated when legislators fail to comply with those principles: when their definition of what is to be punished or sanctioned is not clear and precise, or when courts on construing and applying the criminal or administrative sanction law do so in an extravagant or unreasonable way, punishing or sanctioning conducts that are not defined in the law (violating elements of the criminal definition), or doing so in a way that makes it impossible or very difficult for the public within reason to predict the consequences of their acts or omissions (violating legal certainty).[28]

The standard of protection of art. 25.1 SC turns on the existence of a formal law; it is what the law says that constitutes the measure of control of its constitutionality or of its interpretation and application. But in the case of art. 7 ECHR, where there is no Legal reservation, the measure of control of compliance with the standard of protection can no longer be what the law or the sanctioning or punishing norm says, but how it is interpreted and applied by courts and judges. It can be said that, for the standard of protection of art. 25.1 SC, what is important is the guarantee of "juridical" certainty; what matters for the standard of protection of art. 7 ECHR is the safeguard of "*de facto*" certainty. In the first case, in relation with the mandate of legal certainty, the important thing is to know whether the criminal or administrative sanctioning norm enables one reasonably to foresee the consequences of an act or its omission. In the second, what matters is to prove that it would have been

[27]Navarro Frías (2010), pp. 20, 27.

[28]Ferreres Comella and Mieres (1999), p. 293.

possible for the member of the public to foresee his sentence or sanction with regard to the circumstances of the concrete case.[29] The ECtHR has construed art. 7 ECHR as a subjective right to the foreseeability of a sentence or a sanction. For the SCC, art. 25.1 SC guarantees a subjective right to legality.

If the inexistence of a formal guarantee of the absolute "requirement of law" in art. 7 ECHR leads to transforming the principle of legal certainty into the principle of foreseeability, the consequence is that the whole of the ECtHR's doctrine on this precept revolves around the requirement to define all elements of the crime and the limits that this mandate imposes on interpretation and application by courts of the norm on the criminal or administrative sanction. In the Spanish constitutional system, given the existence of an absolute Legal reservation in the criminal and sanctioning sphere, the principle of legal certainty consists in the mandate of clarity and precision of wording of the norm. The SCC will assess whether in effect the criminal or administrative sanction is reasonably clear in law and precise in its terms, and whether qualifies as those laws as reasonably clear and precise that enable the member of the public to judge the consequences of his acts or omissions in advance. In the Spanish case, the principle of legal certainty also extends to the judicial interpretation or application of the criminal or administrative sanction norm, confusing itself here with elements of the criminal definition, requiring that the interpretation or application of the criminal or administrative sanction norm by judges and courts will not frustrate the reasonable clarity and precision of the criminal or administrative sanctioning norm, by means of unreasonable or extravagant interpretations or applications that make it impossible or seriously difficult for an average individual to know in advance whether his acts or omissions are punishable). The norm must be predictable in its interpretation and application (hence the norm must be clear and precise in its literal sense, reducing the margins of ambiguity subject to the will of the interpreter), and this predictability is a consequence of the reasonable clarity and precision of its terms.

In the case of art. 7 ECHR, in the absence of absolute Legal reservation, the mandate of determinacy is fulfilled if the norm on the criminal or administrative sanction is accessible and foreseeable (which is not the same as being clear and precise). Accessibility and foreseeability of the norm is examined by assessing the objective conditions of accessibility to the norm and the subjective conditions of the foreseeability of its consequences. For the ECtHR what is decisive is to know whether in a concrete case the sentenced or sanctioned individual could foresee and know that his conducts were punishable.[30]

The SCC deliberates upon a possible violation of art. 25.1 SC by employing an objective standard of foreseeability of the judicial interpretation. The analysis of legal certainty is carried out in two successive phases: first assessing whether the criminal or administrative has a clear and precise norm, so that it is possible for any

[29]Huerta Tocildo (2014), pp. 414–415.

[30]Frowein and Peukert (1996), p. 325; Harris et al. (1995), p. 274; Jacobs and White (1996), p. 162; Murphy (2010), p. 203.

citizen to foresee the legal consequences of his behaviour; and then, besides, that the jurisprudential application of the norm is likewise foreseeable in the sense that it is adjusted to the letter of the law. After all, legal certainty is an objective judgement on the letter of the law and on its judicial application; it is not a judgement on whether in a particular case the subject was in a position to know whether his behaviour was punishable or not.

4.3 The Irruption of the Court of Justice of the European Union in Defence of Art. 49 CFREU

Following the Melloni case—ECJ (GC) Judgement of 26 February of 2013, Melloni (C-399/11), and its application in STC 26/2014 of 13 February 2014—a new perspective has been opened in relation to the principle of legality in criminal law, in so far as it has recognized art. 49 CFREU as a fundamental European right. Despite its formal lack of competence in punishing matters,[31] the guarantee of the right in the cited provision—and in particular following the Opinion 2/13 of ECJ (full Court) of 18 December, 2014 (Opinion pursuant to Article 218(11) TFEU), in relation to the accession of the Union to the ECHR—leads one to anticipate the possibility of a categorical pronouncement in the near future by the Court of Justice on the scope of the binding nature of what is enshrined therein upon the member States of the Union, and likewise on the necessary homogenization of their national standards of protection of the principle of legality with future decisions by the ECJEU. The warning in the Melloni case has been very clear: the national standard must conform to that of the European Union, even though the national standard might offer a higher degree of guarantee, if such an "excess" of guarantee is utilized by national courts as a pretext for not observing, or for violating, the Laws of the Union. In view of the contents of the above-mentioned Judgement, we must add to this doctrine that the ECJ may lend specific content of its own to art. 49 CFREU that differs from the standard interpretation of art. 7 CEDH and of art. 25 SC.

It is neither the time nor the place to venture ideas about this possible scenario, which would require a detailed examination that would exceed both the reasonable extension and the purpose of these lines. But it is not a scenario for the distant future, given that the ECJ has already applied art. 49 CFREU and the specific principle of legality on several occasions (ECJ Judgements of 13 December 2001, Ingemar Nilsson (C-131/00); of 7 January 2004, Commission *v*. Spain (C-58/02). The SCC (STC 145/2012 of 2 July 2012) has even taken into account the consequences of a declaration of *inconventionality* for violation of EU law by Spanish sanctioning norms, considering them inapplicable, because of their infringement of

[31] See Bernardi (2002), pp. 773 ff.

art. 25.1 SC, because they were not in force at the time of the facts sanctioned as a consequence of that *inconventionality* (if I may be forgiven the expression).[32]

The doctrine seems to point to an interpretation of art. 49 CFREU that would take into account the "constitutional traditions of the member states", to use an expression of the CJEU, in order to extract from this norm the precise rules of a European law on criminal and sanctioning legality that contains the same formal and material guarantees that are summed up in the principle "*nullum crimen sine prævia lege, scripta et certa*", enshrined in the European constitutional systems.[33]

References

Bartole S, Conforti B, Raimondi G (2001) Commentario alla Convenzione Europea per la Tutela dei Diritti Dell'Uomo e delle Libertà Fondamentali. CEDAM, Padova

Bernardi A (2002) Il Principio di Legalità dei reati e delle pene nella Carta Europea dei Diritti: Problemi e prospettive. In: AA.VV, I diritti fondamentali in Europa (Atti del XV Colloquio biennale dell'Associazione Italiana di Diritto Comparato). Giuffrè, Milano, pp 729–725

Burgorgue-larsen L (2007) Aspectos recientes de la jurisprudencia de la Corte Europea de los Derechos Humanos en asuntos penales. In: García Ramírez, Islas de González Mariscal (coords.), Panorama internacional sobre justicia penal. Proceso penal y justicia penal internacional. Culturas y sistemas jurídicos comparados. Ed. Universidad Nacional Autónoma de México, México, pp 351–369

Cadoppi A (2002) Principio di legalità, Carta europea, e law in action In AA.VV., I diritti fondamentali in Europa (Atti del XV Colloquio biennale dell'Associazione Italiana di Diritto Comparato). Giuffrè, Milano, pp 775–778

Ferreres Comella V (2002) El principio de taxatividad en materia penal y el valor normativo de la jurisprudencia (una perspectiva constitucional). Civitas, Madrid

Ferreres Comella V, Mieres J (1999) Algunas consideraciones acerca del principio de legalidad penal (A propósito de las sentencias 111/1993 y 150/1997 del Tribunal Constitucional). Revista Española de Derecho Constitucional 55:287–321

Frowein J, Peukert W (1996) Europäische MenschenrechtsKonvention. EMRK-Kommentar. 2nd edn. Engel, Kehl

Grandi G (2010) "Nullum crimen sine lege" parlamentaria y Derecho Penal europeo. In: Díez-Picazo LM, Nieto Martín A (eds) Los derechos fundamentales en el Derecho penal europeo. Civitas/Thomson, Madrid, pp 183–250

Harris DJ, O'Boyle M, Warbrick C (1995) Law of the European convention on human rights. Butterworths, London

Huerta Tocildo S (1993) El derecho fundamental a la legalidad penal. Revista Española de Derecho Constitucional 39:81–114

Huerta Tocildo S (2000) Principio de legalidad y normas sancionadoras. In: AA.VV Actas de las V Jornadas de la Asociación de Letrados del Tribunal Constitucional. Centro de Estudios Políticos y Constitucionales, Madrid, pp 11–76

Huerta Tocildo S (2008) Artículo 25.1. El derecho a la legalidad penal. In: Casas Baamonde, Rodríguez-Piñero y Bravo-Ferrer (eds) Comentarios a la Constitución Española. XXX Aniversario. Kluwer, Madrid, pp 727–747

[32]Scoletta (2010), pp. 270 ff.; Grandi (2010), *passim*; Cadoppi (2002), *passim*.

[33]Scoletta (2010), *passim*.

Huerta Tocildo S (2014) El contenido debilitado del principio europeo de legalidad penal. In: García Roca J, Santolaya Machetti P (coords) La Europa de los derechos, 3rd edn. Centro de Estudios Políticos y Constitucionales, Madrid, pp 399–427

Jacobs FG, White RCA (1996) The European convention on human rights. Clarendon Press, Oxford

Kuhlen L (2012) Sobre la relación entre el mandato de certeza y la prohibición de analogía. In: Montiel JP (ed) La crisis del principio de legalidad en el nuevo Derecho Penal: ¿decadencia o evolución? Marcial Pons, Madrid, pp 151–172

Lagodny O (1996) Strafrecht vor den Schranken der Grundrechte. JCB Mohr, Tübingen

Lamarca Pérez C (1987) Legalidad penal y reserva de ley en la Constitución española. Revista Española de Derecho Constitucional 20:99–138

Lascuraín Sánchez JA (2009) Sólo penas legales, precisas y previas: el derecho a la legalidad penal en la jurisprudencia constitucional. Aranzadi, Cizur Menor

Lascuraín Sánchez JA (2012) ¿Restrictivo o deferente? El control de la ley penal por parte del Tribunal Constitucional. InDret 3:1–33

Loucaides LG (2007) The European convention on human rights. Collected essays. Martinus Nijhoff, Leiden-Boston

Matscher F (1993) Methods of interpretation of the convention. In: Macdonald J, Matscher H, Petzold F (eds) The European system for the protection of human rights. Martinus Nijhoff, Dordrecht, pp 63–81

Moreso JJ (2001) Principio de legalidad y causas de justificación. Doxa 24:525–546

Murphy CC (2010) The principle of legality in criminal law under the ECHR. Eur Hum Law Rev 2:192–207

Navarro Frías I (2010) Mandato de determinación y tipicidad penal. Granada, Comares

Navarro López P, Manrique L (2005) El desafío de la taxatividad. Anuario de Derecho penal y Política criminal 58:807–836

Renucci JF (2007) Traité de Droit Europeén des Droits de l'Homme. LGDJ, Paris

Ruiz Robledo A (2003) El derecho fundamental a la legalidad punitiva. Tirant lo Blanch, Valencia

Scoletta M (2010) El principio de legalidad penal europeo. In: Díez-Picazo LM, Nieto Martín A (dirs) Los derechos fundamentales en el derecho penal europeo. Civitas-Thomson, Madrid, pp. 251–304

Tomuschat C (2013) Democracy and the rule of law. In: Shelton D (dir) The Oxford handbook of international human rights law. Oxford University Press, Oxford, pp 469–496

van Dijk P, van Hoof GJH (1990) Theory and practice of the European convention on human rights, 2nd edn. Kluwer, Deventer

How Judges Are Bound by the Legal Definition of the Crime

Juan Antonio Lascuraín Sánchez

1 Introduction

In the late 1990s, Spanish constitutional case-law developed a carefully constructed doctrine establishing that, as part of the legality principle, judges are bound by the legal definition of the crime. The classic dilemma concerning the boundary between legitimate and necessary judicial interpretation, on the one hand, and the proscribed judicial creation of offences and penalties, on the other (Sect. 2). That constitutional canon was welcomed greatly by the doctrine, but raised some partial controversy and left other points for development (3). The aim in this work is to shed light on both aspects—to explain that controversy and to advance in the canon—and it will to do so in two jurisdictions of human rights: that of the European Court, which is binding upon us (4), and that of the Inter-American Court, whose enlightenment will be compared and will move us to emulation (5).

2 The Canon of the Spanish Constitutional Court

The canon of the linkage between the judge and legal definitions of the crimes was outlined for the first time in a judgement from the Spanish Constitutional Court (STC 137/1997 of 21 July 1997), in the circumstances of a conviction for unlawful duress in a labour conflict in which the interpretation of the concept of violence was under discussion. It has an immediate extension to administrative sanctions—for

Former Law Clerk at the Spanish Constitutional Court (1994–1998; 2004–2009), Professor of Criminal Law at Universidad Autónoma de Madrid.

J.A. Lascuraín Sánchez (✉)
Universidad Autónoma de Madrid, Campus UAM, 28049 Madrid, Spain
e-mail: juanant.lascurain@uam.es

M. Pérez Manzano et al. (eds.), *Multilevel Protection of the Principle of Legality in Criminal Law*, DOI 10.1007/978-3-319-63865-2_4

the subjection of the Administration to the law—in STC 151/1997 of 29 September 1997, in the curious case of the captain given a dishonourable discharge for bringing military honour and dignity into disrepute *"for permitting the adultery of his wife with a lieutenant"*.

These judgements attempted to sketch out the boundaries of the constitutional response to the none-too infrequent complaints that judges were not interpreting a previous regulation, but were in reality creating a new one. A norm that would therefore be established subsequent to the conduct to which it was applied and that would be pronounced by a judge and not by a parliament.

The starting point for the new case-law doctrine was one of values that are considered harmed in these reproaches and that are constitutive of the principle of legality: the legal certainty of the citizen and parliamentary authorship over the definition of offences and penalties. Such certainty and respect shown by the judge towards the decision of the legislator requires above all that the judge takes as a starting point the *"wording of the letter of the law, that in all cases marks out an unquestionable area of exclusion of behaviours"*, as *"the regulatory message is expressed in words and with words is made known to its addressees"* (STC 137/1997, FJ 7). It so happens that the meaning of words is potentially very wide. Due respect from the reader will not guarantee a foreseeable interpretation of the norm; an application that is not the result of the creation, but of the *"judicial administration of popular sovereignty"*.[1] An application of a norm of that type (foreseeable and respectful towards the legislator) needs to be backed up by new reasons of value and method. Judicial measures will have to be reasonable *"from the axiological patterns that guide our Constitutional Text and from models of reasoning accepted by the legal community itself"*. Conversely, *"it not only violates the principle of the legality of sanctioning decisions that are sustained in a subsumption of the facts external to the possible meaning of the terms of the norm that is applied. Other applications may also be rejected on constitutional grounds if, because of their methodological –illogical or undeniably extravagant reasoning– or axiological support –a valuative basis external to the criteria that uphold our constitutional order–, they lead to solutions that are essentially opposed to the material orientation of the norm and that are, therefore, unforeseeable for those it addresses"* (STC 137/1997, FJ 7; 151/1997, FJ 4).

The canon of analysis of complaints arising from violations of the right to legality in criminal law is completed by requesting a new condition from the enforcer of the norm: that he reasons his decision. An absence of reasoning is not only a generic problem of a lack of judicial protection. It is not only a problem of

---

[1]As reflected in the same STC 137/1997, "*[t]his respect does not always guarantee a sanctioning decision in accordance with the essential guarantees of legal certainty or the interdiction of arbitrariness, as, among other factors, the language is relatively vague and versatile, the regulations are necessarily abstract and refer implicitly to a standardized underlying reality, and within certain limits (among others, STC 111/1993), the legislator himself can strengthen that malleability to facilitate the tuning of the norm to reality (as in judgement STC 62/1982; and more recently, STC 53/1994)*" (FJ 7).

lack of explanations. It may also be a problem of the principle of legality. The break with sanctioning legality could arise not from improper subsumption, but from a doubtful and unexplained subsumption. Regarding this rule, it should be taken into account that the less precisely defined the sanctionable offence, the greater the requirement for reasoning. What the legislator does not specify, the judge should specify. As STC 151/1997 clearly affirms, *"the deficit of the law is only compatible with the requirements of the principle of legality if the Judge makes up for it"* (FJ 3).

It is not superfluous to recall that from the constitutional point of view of respect for fundamental rights, the problem neither is nor can it be that of the best interpretation of sanctioning norms from the point of view of constitutional values. The problem lies in whether it may be foreseen that the penalized conduct was defined and, if so, whether it may be affirmed that such a definition came originally from the legislator and not from the judge. The question is whether we may reasonably interpret the legal definition that is applied as inclusive of the conduct that is sanctioned. And so the fundamental right to sanctioning legality (following its vector of judicial subjection to legal definitions of the crimes) is breached, not because the judge adopts a possible interpretation of the normative wording that is less favourable for the accused than any other available interpretation, but that the judge adopts an impossible interpretation. And in this context "impossible" means unforeseeable, and unforeseeable means unreasonable. Unreasonable in accordance with the words of the law, with the interpretative criteria accepted by the legal community and with constitutional values. It was so recalled in STC 129/2008 of 27 October 2008: *"Determination of the final interpretation, or more properly, of a criminal sentence is not therefore the task of this Court, not even on the basis of the parameters that define the constitutional values and principles. And neither is its task the demarcation of the possible interpretations of that sentence. In a much more restricted way, and from the external perspective that corresponds to it as a Court outside the criminal process, our task is restricted to assessing the constitutional sustainability of the specific interpretation carried out by the courts. Such sustainability refers [. . .] to respect for values of legal certainty and parliamentary authorship of the definition of the offences and the penalties, and is translated into the semantic, methodological and axiological reasoning of the legal interpretation of the norm and the legal subsumption of the facts within it"* (FJ 3).

It is a worthy summary of Spanish constitutional case-law: the principle of legality guarantees to the citizen the foreseeability of his conviction and from that point of view, in so far as the judicial application of the law is concerned, what is foreseeable is that the judge adjusts his interpretation to the meaning of the legal provision and to constitutional values and accepted methods of interpretation. What is foreseeable is that the judge will be reasonable: both axiologically and methodologically reasonable.

3 Open Questions

I think that this scheme of analysis appears to be easily shared. And in fact it has been well received in the doctrine. But, as we know, in Law, the devil is in the detail. It has its details at each (semantic, axiological, and methodological) level of analysis of the subjection of normative interpretation to the requirements of the principle of legality: open questions arise in response to which this work directs its gaze at the case-law of both the European Court of Human Rights and the Inter-American Court of Human Rights.

3.1 Semantic Reasonability

In relation with the semantic reasonability of the interpretation, the first doubt that arises in the reader of the judgements of the Spanish Constitutional Court (STC) is whether we face either a limit or a principle. The doubt is whether, as it appears, reasonableness always exists in the broad framework of the possible literal meaning of the words used by the legislator. Or, whether it is a matter of approaching a particular meaning of the words as much as possible,[2] the most accessible for the majority of those addressed in the norm, and, as happens with the other principles as mandates of optimization, to situate unconstitutionality at a certain distance from the optimal point. That intolerable distance could situate itself precisely in the over-excessively literal tenor or at a point closer to the ideal, which would mean that unconstitutional meaning might fit in the possible literal tenor.

3.2 Axiological Reasonability

It is enough for the reader to interpret one from among various semantically possible understandings of the legal sentence, which is in valuative terms in accordance with the Constitution, for the axiological criteria of control over the interpretation to be respected. Only an interpretation of that sort may be expected; only that sort of interpretation appears to respond to a legislator who had to keep constitutional principles in mind.

As that axiological doubt adds a further constitutional perspective (in addition to the perspective of legality in criminal law), pertaining to the value or the principle that is perhaps ignored, it is worth asking how the two analyses of constitutionality are related: if both are necessary or if we should select one, either because both have the same content, or because one of them displaces the other.

---

[2]On the inconveniences of this criteria, Ortiz de Urbina Gimeno (2012), p. 202.

In relation with the axiological control of criminal interpretations, the doctrine of the chilling effect that inhibits the exercise of fundamental rights is of great interest, as it not only means that interpretations that incriminate the exercise of fundamental rights are proscribed, but also those interpretations that generate their inhibition. This doctrine, which arises from reflections on freedom of expression and information means that the constitutional coverage of these freedoms extends to *"communication of diligently confirmed, although potentially false information"*, and it radically proscribes *"the inhibition of [...] upright informative activity"* (STC 190/1996 of 25 November 1996, FJ 3).[3] Such inhibitions will occur whether excess in the legitimate exercise of the freedom is harshly (criminally) sanctioned and whether in addition it is diffuse, and it usually is so, on the frontier between such legitimate and illegitimate forms of exercise.[4]

It is hardly necessary to underline the importance of this doctrine for the delimitation of legal descriptions of offences and punishments and their interpretation, which will have to be restrictive, if the conduct is originally framed in the exercise of a fundamental right, of which it implies an excess. Thus, if the apparently offensive conduct in no way constitutes the exercise of fundamental rights, which would obviously force its justification, but is an excess in itself *"which does not go so far as to denaturalize it or disfigure it"*, in such a way that *"the act is framed within its content and its finality and, therefore, in the raison-d'être of its constitutional enshrinement"*, it should be interpreted that the conduct falls outside of the legal description. Taking the constitutional axiology into account demands that it be so: the principle of proportionality in the treatment of the right that is at stake. To do otherwise would imply a disproportionate forbearance of the right, because of the chilling effect on its exercise that the punishment would imply.[5]

3.3 Methodological Reasonability

All in all, from the start, what was of most surprise in the construct of our Constitutional Court was the use of the adjective "extravagant" to define methodological unreasonableness. Through the use of this adjective, it was expressed that what the addressee of a norm legitimately expects is that the norm is interpreted with generalizable and not contradictory guidelines.

---

[3]Also, SSTC 110/2000 of 5 May 2000, FJ 5; 88/2003 of 19 May 2003, FJ 8.

[4]See, ECtHR Judgement of 15 March 2011, c. Otegi Mondragón v. Spain, par. 59.

[5]STC 104/2011 of 20 June 2011, FJ 6, in relation to the right to strike. See also STC 136/1999 of 20 July 1999, FJ 29 c, in relation to the disproportionate nature of the punishment of the crime of collaboration with a terrorist organization for a political party that had issued a video of that organization.

Quite rightly, objections were raised that many interpretations of legal statements that are in principal radically heterodox (and in that sense "extravagant") end up imposing themselves as the fairest. Justice in this area is not necessarily a matter of majority adhesions, but of respect for certain rules of thought. Hence, it should it appears be stressed that the proscribed "extravagance" is not the result of the interpretation, but of the method that is used. Hence, it should likewise be reconsidered whether the term "extravagance" is the most appropriate to express what in the last place is nothing other than the break in legal logic, as the method (and not only the result) can be as novel as it is valuable. In fact, Spanish constitutional case-law has more recently tended to flee from the rather unfortunate concept of extravagance and to define its analysis as the appraisal of *"whether the exegesis and subsumption of the norm will not incur logical breaks and is in accordance with models of reasoning accepted by the legal community itself"* (SSTC 91/2009 of 20 April 2009, FJ 6; 153/2011 of 17 October 2011, FJ 8).

4 The Inter-American Court of Human Rights

I summarize on this point. At the end of the 1990s, the Spanish Constitutional Court prepared its doctrine relating to constitutional control over the boundaries of criminal law for the judge. In summary, such control involves the verification of a triple reasonability of both the interpretation and the application of the norm: semantic reasonability, axiological reasonability and methodological reasonability. This canon reveals its sense in the light of the values of legal certainty and democracy that uphold the principle of legality in criminal law, but still raises some questions. Is semantic reasonability only respect for the possible meaning of the words or does it require greater proximity to its usual or systematic significance? Is the analysis of legality excessive when what is discussed is that the interpretation is axiologically unreasonable, because it ignores another principle or constitutional law, which is the one that would demarcate the perspective of the analysis? In what does extravagance as methodological unreasonableness consist? Should whoever alleges it, prove it?

The over-arching question is now whether we may find some path to respond to these concerns in the case-law of the Inter-American Court of Human Rights. I already foresee a negative response. What the reading of its judgements reveals, is that beyond some resemblance with the Spanish constitutional jurisdiction, is the use of some instruments of conflict-resolution that are much less finely tuned than those of the Spanish Constitutional Court.

Its starting point is article 9 of the American Convention of Human Rights, which affirms that *"[n]o one shall be convicted of any act or omission that did not constitute a criminal offense, under the applicable law, at the time it was committed. A heavier penalty shall not be imposed than the one that was applicable at the time the criminal offense was committed. If subsequent to the commission of the offense the law provides for the imposition of a lighter punishment, the guilty person shall benefit therefrom"*. The first comparative impression with article 25.1 of the Spanish Constitution (SC) is that on the one hand its text has a wider content of principle, by including the mandate on favourable criminal retroactivity,[6] and on the other it directs its entire content to a more restricted area: the strictly criminal.[7] Unlike the Spanish text, which talks of sanctions[8] and expressly includes the administrative offences, the words of the Convention refer solely to the criminal offences and to the punishments. This wording has been no obstacle to the Court having judiciously understood that it is applicable to administrative violations and to administrative sanctions.[9] And that a mandate to the judge—to the sanctioning authority, in general—of links to criminal—sanctioning—law is inserted in article 9 of the Convention. It consists of the following paragraph reiterated in various judgements of the Court: *"In this regard, when applying criminal legislation, the judge of the criminal court is obliged to adhere strictly to its provisions and observe the greatest rigor to ensure that the behavior of the defendant corresponds to a specific category of crime, so that he does not punish acts that are not punishable by law"*.[10]

The Court has taken cognizance of some cases in which the lack of submission of the judge to criminal law was challenged. Against a relatively sophisticated Spanish canon of analysis (semantic, methodological and axiological reasonableness) what the reading of these sentences gives us is that, after a detailed presentation of the facts and some general points of law, the decision tends to be apodictic, hardly without reasoning in terms of its *ratio decidendi*.

Such is the case, for example, of the judgement in the case of *Vélez Loor v. Panama*, in which protection was afforded to a foreign citizen serving a sentence at an ordinary prison despite the express provision that the sentence—for returning to the country after deportation—should be served at a special prison, the Penal Colony of Coiba. He was protected because it was an "extensive" interpretation "of criminal law", substantively different from that envisaged in the law.[11] Of greater

---

[6]Neither expressed in the Spanish Constitution, nor implicit, by the way, in the prohibition of unfavourable retroactivity (see Lascuraín Sánchez 2000, p. 55 ff).

[7]For these and other reasons Guzmán Dalbora qualifies it as *"defective and uninspiring"* (Guzmán Dalbora 2010, p. 172).

[8]*"Nobody can be convicted or sanctioned..."*: as the sanction is also a conviction and the punishment is a sanction, it appears that it might have been better to refer only to a sentenced person.

[9]IACtHR Judgement of 2 February 2001, Case of Baena-Ricardo et al. v. Panama, par. 106; IACtHR Judgement of 31 August 2004, Case of Ricardo Canese v. Paraguay, par. 176.

[10]IACtHR Judgement of 18 November 2004, Case of De la Cruz-Flores v. Peru, par. 82; IACtHR Judgement of 25 November 2005, Case of García-Asto and Ramírez-Rojas v. Peru, par. 190; IACtHR Judgement of 6 May 2008, Case of Yvon Neptune v. Haiti, par. 125; IACtHR Judgement of 27 April 2012, Case of Pacheco Teruel v. Honduras, par. 105; IACtHR Judgement of 23 November 2012, Case of Mohamed v. Argentina, par. 132; IACtHR Judgement of 30 January 2014, Case of Liakat Ali Alibux v. Suriname, par. 61.

[11]However much the reason was the *"reconversion of the island of Coiba, from a Prison Centre into an ecological tourist site"* and even though the criminal norm had subsequently been repealed

transcendence than that case is the one of *De la Cruz Flores v. Peru*, in which a doctor was convicted of collaboration with a terrorist organization, because of providing medical attention to members of such an organization, despite the acts of which she was accused coming under other criminal categories (belonging to a terrorist organization and failing to report a crime) and despite there being no specification of which of the categorical modalities of collaboration with a terrorist organization were subsumed in the alleged conducts of the accused. The Court added that the violation of the principle of legality also occurred *"for penalizing a medical activity, which is not only an essential lawful act, but which it is also the physician's obligation to provide; and for imposing on physicians the obligation to report the possible criminal behavior of their patients, based on information obtained in the exercise of their profession"*.[12] The reason for which these two last reasons are reasons that relate to the principle of legality is not explained, although the clear undertone was that the conducts were included in permissive norms (grounds for justification) derived from the practice of medicine and the duty of confidentiality attached to it.[13]

In the case of *García Asto and Ramírez*, the Peruvian courts were reprimanded for a sentence that applied two *"exclusive criminal categories and mutually incompatible between each other"*: association with terrorists and collaboration with terrorists,[14] and additionally, as in the case of De la Cruz Flores, the lack of specification of the collaborative conduct[15] that was criminalized. The legal definitions of offences can be poorly interpreted not only because of how their words are read, but because what other concurrent definitions of offences say, which explicitly or implicitly delimit the former, is ignored. From such a perspective, it appeared clear, not perhaps that collaboration with a terrorist organization excludes membership per se, but that this membership, more severely punished, limited the scope of application of the collaboration, if understood not only as external, but also as internal collaboration. It is not so clear, in the end, that collaboration requires the externality of the actor, but it is clear that the same act is excluded due to its normative concurrence with membership and that the sanction for the two criminal categories, as always happens with ignorance of the concurrency of norms, implies a flagrant bis in idem.

The courts that convicted the appellants of collaboration with a terrorist organization are, both in the judgement of *De la Cruz Flores v. Peru* and in the judgement of *García Asto and Ramírez Rojas v. Peru*, reproached for not specifying in which

---

that foresaw deprivation of freedom for conducts such as those of the appellant (IACtHR Judgement of 23 November 2010, Case of Vélez Loor v. Panama, par. 186 and 18).

[12]IACtHR Judgement of 18 November 2004, Case of De la Cruz-Flores v. Peru, par. 88, 102.

[13]IACtHR Judgement of 18 November 2004, Case of De la Cruz-Flores v. Peru, par. 88, 95, 101.

[14]IACtHR Judgement of 25 November 2005, Case of García-Asto and Ramírez-Rojas v. Peru, par. 200. See, in a similar sense, STC 13/2003 of 28 January 2003.

[15]IACtHR Judgement of 25 November 2005, Case of García-Asto and Ramírez-Rojas v. Peru, par. 201.

of the categorical modalities of collaboration their behaviours were subsumed. This blemish of legality constitutes, according to the parameters of Spanish constitutional case-law, a peculiar infraction, consistent, neither in penalizing without a legal definition of the offence nor on the basis of an unreasonable interpretation of the definition, but in not explaining a subsumption of a definition that is not in itself explained.[16]

On the matter of reasoning the criminal subsumption, the interesting reflection in the judgement of Mohamed v. Argentina attracts our attention, coinciding with that of the Spanish Constitutional Court pertaining to judicial reasoning that should be painstaking wherever the legal definition of a crime is relatively diffuse. It requires greater justificatory effort from the judge in convictions for offenses involving negligence: *"The Court considers it necessary to add that, in dealing with an offense of negligence, whose unlawfulness is minor compared with that of intentional crimes and whose typical elements are defined in a generic manner, the judge or court is required to observe the principle of legality when ascertaining the effective existence of the defined conduct and determining criminal responsibility"*.[17]

The relation between the principle of legality and freedom of expression is established in different terms to those of Spanish constitutional case law, in which a particular dovetailing of both constitutional perspectives takes place on the basis of the parameter of axiological reasonability. The starting point in the judgements of *Kimel v. Argentina* and *Usón Ramírez v. Venezuela*[18] is the analysis of determination, of precision, of the regulation of the corresponding offences of expression, and they concluded with negative judgements in both cases. In the case of Argentina, for example, the words of the State itself are underlined: there is a lack of *"sufficient precisions in the framework of the criminal norms that sanction the slander and the defamations that prevent them from affecting freedom of expression"*.[19] I would call attention to the pertinence of this reflection, although I do not know whether the indetermination is as serious as to consider it as intolerable and to consider that the precept is unconstitutional. In any case, it hardly appears acceptable from the point of view of the principle of legality that the basic

[16]IACtHR Judgement of 18 November 2004, Case of De la Cruz-Flores v. Peru, par. 88; IACtHR Judgement of 25 November 2005, Case of García-Asto and Ramírez-Rojas v. Peru, par. 201.

[17]IACtHR Judgement of 23 November 2012, Case of Mohamed v. Argentina, par. 132.

[18]Not pleaded, but invoked by the Court itself "*in the light of the Inter-American Convention and based on the principle of* iura novit curia" (IACtHR Judgement of 2 May 2008, Case of Kimel v. Argentina, par. 61; IACtHR Judgement of 20 November 2009, Case of Usón Ramírez v. Venezuela, par. 53).

[19]IACtHR Judgement of 2 May 2008, Case of Kimel v. Argentina, par. 66. In the Case of Venezuela, "*Article 505 of the Organic Code of Military Justice does not strictly limit the elements of the criminal behavior, nor does it consider the existence of injury, resulting in a codification that is too vague and ambiguous in its formulation to comply with the legality requirements of Article 9 of the Convention*" (IACtHR Judgement of 20 November 2009, Case of Usón Ramírez v. Venezuela, par. 57).

parameters that define communicative liberties in their relation with honour and privacy, so consolidated in their basic guidelines, are not positivized and remain among the arcane collections of case-law.[20]

Having noted the reproach to the legislator and not to the judge with regard to legality, the judgements go on to analyze whether the criminal convictions imply a violation of the freedom of expression; a point affirmed in both cases on the basis of the canons of analysis of this freedom. There are no lack of commentaries that relate to the content of the chilling effect doctrine and that situate themselves in the analysis of the necessity and of the proportionality of the restriction of freedom of expression. Thus, *"[t]he Court does not deem any criminal sanction regarding the right to inform or give one's opinion to be contrary to the provisions of the Convention; however, this possibility should be carefully analyzed, pondering the extreme seriousness of the conduct of the individual who expressed the opinion, his actual malice, the characteristics of the unfair damage caused, and other information which shows the absolute necessity to resort to criminal proceedings as an exception"*.[21]

5 The European Court of Human Rights

In an article on the principle of legality in criminal law in the European Court of Human Rights, its author Cian C. Murphy concluded that, despite the almost absolute nature of the requirements of the principle of legality in the Convention—only comparable in that sense with the prohibition of torture and slavery[22]—, the Court has tempered it *"through a mixture of pragmatism in the definition and application of terms; selected deference to national criminal justice authorities; and the occasional use of a dubious balancing act"*. The result of this pragmatism *"is an under-developed and under-theorised nullum crimen principle"*.[23] This conclusion recalls the suggestion underlying the title of the article by Huerta

[20]On the matter, Lascuraín Sánchez (2002), p. 59.

[21]IACtHR Judgement of 2 May 2008, Case of Kimel v. Argentina, par. 78. Also, in similar terms IACtHR Judgement of 20 November 2009, Case of Usón Ramírez v. Venezuela, par. 67.

[22]Although it should be remembered that the same article 7 that firmly proclaimed the principle of legality relativizes its content. Under section 2, it affirms that *"This Article shall not prejudice the trial and punishment of any person for any act or omission which, at the time when it was committed, was criminal according to the general principles of law recognised by civilised nations"*. The Court itself has emphasized that we face an "essential element of the rule of law", that *"occupies a prominent place in the Convention system of protection, as is underlined by the fact that no derogation from it is permissible under Article 15 in time of war or other public emergency"* [ECtHR (GC) Judgement of 22 February 2013, c. Streletz, Kessler and Krenz v. Germany, par. 50].

[23]Murphy (2010), pp. 1, 15, 16. http://papers.ssrn.com/sol3/papers.cfm?abstract_id=1513623.

Tocildo "The weakened content of the European principle of legality in criminal law".[24]

I think that this diagnostic is quite accurate. But I also think that the task that the Court faces is no easy one, if it wishes to integrate the legal systems of common law into its jurisdiction, of such an opposing tradition to some of the basic precepts of the principle of legality in criminal law. So opposing in fact that its system of jurisdictional sources for the definition of crimes and punishments is losing its edge not only in the United States but even in the United Kingdom, where it is the object of critical doctrine[25] and where the judicial creation of crimes is no longer conceivable.[26] Nevertheless, on the one hand, classic offences from those same common-law sources—such as murder, imprudent manslaughter and public affray[27]—continue to exist, and, on the other hand, the case-law continues to hold a lot of weight; not only as in the Spanish system, to determine the indeterminate concepts of legal definitions of crimes, but also to establish the general criteria of criminal liability. On this point, certainly beyond abstract pronouncements, it is worth pausing to reflect on whether we are so very different. In the Spanish criminal order and, as far as my knowledge permits, a good part of the definition of such criteria in the other civil law orders is also case-law (jurisprudential)—What is the authorship? When is a result imputed to an action? When is it imputed to an omission? When does an attempted act begin?—, without losing sleep over it, which never ceases to be somewhat surprising. No surprise then that Lothar Kuhlen in a recent work pointed out that the time had come to require from judges not only the linkage to the legal definitions of the offences and the penalties, but also the determination (precision) of their reasoning[28]: a mandate of determination also for judges.

Some of the requirements of the principle of legality lack sense in a system of case-law-based criminal law, for the simple reason that this system as a starting point lacks one of the two great preoccupations at the root of the principle, which is Parliamentary authorship in the definition of crimes and punishments. Neither the

---

[24]Huerta Tocildo (2014), pp. 399–427.

[25]See, for example the manual of Simester et al. (2013): *"Today, English criminal law is no longer predominantly the result of judicial creativity, but is primarily enacted through parliamentary statutes and subordinate regulations. There are, it seems, over 10,000 different criminal offences on the statute books, by far the most important source of criminal law"* (p. 46). On the same page, the tendency to codification and some up until now, failed attempts to carry it out.

[26]LaFave points out that this practice was stopped in the mid-19th c. although he notes that in Rex v. Manley (1933) a crime was devised (termed *public mischief*) of false accusation. It points out that only rarely will an "offence" be created and that in no case would it be a serious crime or a felony. In the United States, the tendency to abolish common law crimes and to move towards codification is clearer. In any case, it is well founded that federal crimes cannot exist through such channels (LaFave 2009, pp. 74 ff.).

[27]See, Ormerod (2009), pp. 1, 7.

[28]Kuhlen (2012), pp. 163 ff.

requirement of the law nor the linkage of the judge to the law makes sense.[29] And yet the precepts that respond to the basic idea of legal certainty will indeed continue to make sense, cleansed when what is at stake is the deprivation of liberty: whether Parliament or the judges say so, what is not tolerable is that the pronouncement of what the offence is and how it is sanctioned is not clear or is subsequent to the conduct that is tried.

The European Court was forced into a degree of eclecticism. When it looks at the systems of common law, it begins with a wink at the definition of what the term law means in article 7 of the Convention, affirming that *"it encompasses the Law of origin both statute law and case-law"*.[30] If the problem comes from a criminal conviction of one of these legal systems, the basic judgement will be one of foreseeability and its anchorage will lack the formal point that the letter of a legal enunciation procures.

If the complaint arises from a legal system of full legality in criminal law, the Court will concern itself with the relation of the judicial decision with the text that is said to be applied, in such a way that the wording of the "legal provision" cannot be surpassed, not even by analogy. The starting point of its reflection is well known to us insofar as it is common to Spanish constitutional case-law[31]: that of the necessity of judicial interpretation, of the judicial contribution to the understanding of the legal wording. "*However clearly drafted a legal provision may be, in any system of law, including criminal law, there is an inevitable element of judicial interpretation. There will always be a need for elucidation of doubtful points and for adaptation to changing circumstances. [...] Article 7 of the Convention cannot be read as outlawing the gradual clarification of the rules of criminal liability through judicial interpretation from case to case, provided that the resultant development is consistent with the essence of the offence and could reasonably be foreseen*".[32] What such an article does set forth is *"that the criminal law must not be extensively construed to an accused's detriment, for instance by analogy"*.[33]

[29]See, on this Huerta Tocildo (2014), p. 218; Scoletta (2010), p. 259.

[30]ECtHR Judgement of 10 October 2006, c. Pessino v. France, par. 29.

[31]As *"due to the principle of the generality of laws, their texts cannot be of an absolute precision [...] Also, numerous laws make use of the force of more or less imprecise aspects of formulas, in order to avoid an excessive rigidity and to be able to adapt themselves to changes of situation"* (ECtHR Judgement of 24 May 2007, c. Dragotoniu and Militaru-Pidhorni v. Romania, par. 36; ECtHR Judgement of 6 October 2011, c. Soros v. France, par. 51). In this respect, Judgement STC 137/1997 of 21 July 1997, FJ 7).

[32]ECtHR Judgement of 22 November 1995, c. C. R. v. the United Kingdom, par. 34; ECtHR Judgement of 22 November 1995, c. S. W. v. the United Kingdom, par. 36; ECtHR Judgement of 10 October 2010, c. Pessino v. France, 10.10.06, par. 19; ECtHR Judgement of 24 May 2007, c. Dragotoniu and Militaru-Pidhorni v. Romania, par. 37; ECtHR Judgement of 25 June 2009, c. Liivik v. Estonia, par. 94.

[33]ECtHR Judgement of 25 June 1993, c. Kokkinakis v. Greece, par. 52; ECtHR Judgement of 22 November 1995, c. C. R. v. the United Kingdom, par. 33; ECtHR Judgement of 10 October 2010, c. Pessino v. France, 10.10.06, par. 28; ECtHR Judgement of 24 May 2007, c. Dragotoniu and Militaru-Pidhorni v. Romania, par. 33; ECtHR Judgement of 25 June 2009, c. Liivik v. Estonia, par. 92.

Here, we certainly come across the misunderstanding of the adjective "extensive" applied to the interpretation[34]: on the one hand, extensive is the interpretation that includes what is not there and makes the precept more extensive than the legislator wished, to which I believe the European Court refers; on the other, an extensive interpretation chooses a more extensive area of criminal categories from among the literally possible.[35]

The canon of analysis of judicial subjection to the principle of legality is therefore that of the reasonable foreseeability of condemnatory decisions. The questions that spring to mind are of what does that foreseeability consist, for whom should it be foreseeable, and by which criteria is the foreseeable defined.

Without the ordered construct of the Spanish Constitutional Court,[36] we can find some responses in the European Court,[37] some of which are revealing of the marked nature of minimums with which this jurisdiction works. It prompts us to recall that one thing is unconstitutionality and another contrariety with the Convention, and that surpassing this standard will not imply that the one demarcated in the Constitution is surpassed, which may be even higher.[38]

The first point on which we set our sights is the teleological criterion that accompanies foreseeability, which forms part of this concept and that is expressed in careful terms. It is not necessary that the judicial interpretation be justified by its functionality towards the end of protection from the crime, but a more modest relation will suffice: that the interpretation is *"consistent with the very essence of the offence"*.[39] Readings of criminal law that tend to adapt to changing social circumstances or that are the outcome of shared social valuations are in this sense foreseeable, as happened in the case of the punishment of rape within marriage or, supposedly, in the case of the conviction of the Berlin wall border guard, both cases to which reference will be made later on.

The Court in some cases mentions that the existence of favourable doctrinal interpretations or of previous case-law debate are discussed as evidence of foreseeability, in a tendency towards "extensive case-law".[40]

---

[34]See, in this respect Montiel (2009), p. 130.

[35]This is the meaning that Scoletta attributes to the use of the adjective in the European Court, from which he infers a restrictive requirement of interpretation of criminal law (Scoletta 2010, p. 270). The Spanish Constitutional Law also uses the expressions with ambiguity: *"application analogical or extensive* in malam partem" (STC 137/1997, FJ 7).

[36]Scoletta points out that European case-law does not insist on the principles-measure and it does on the final result of the cognoscibility of criminal law (Scoletta 2010, p. 259).

[37]Not many. As Huerta Tocildo affirms *"the same notion of foreseeability apparently destined to compensate the lack of a requirement of the absolute reserve of Law in criminal matters has not up until now been the object of excessive specifications"* (Huerta Tocildo 2014, pp. 404 and ff.).

[38]Thus, Huerta Tocildo (2014), p. 405.

[39]ECtHR Judgement of 22 November 1995, c. S. W. v. the United Kingdom, par. 43; ECtHR Judgement of 25 June 2009, c. Liivik v. Estonia, par. 94.

[40]ECtHR Judgement of 22 October 1996, c. Cantoni v. France, par. 30 and ff.; ECtHR Judgement of 6 October 2011, c. Soros v. France, par. 57. See, Scoletta (2010), p. 271.

The criterion of foreseeability is clouded at times in various senses: what is foreseeable is the risk of punishment, although only subjectively so and even though the prevision would have required legal assistance.

In effect, in the first place, the first enlargement of the concept begins with its objective, which is not necessarily the punishment, but the risk. What article 7 requires is that the law is sufficiently clear in the majority of cases, in such a way that those targeted can know that they run a real risk of incrimination.[41] It is what is known in the Anglo-Saxon world as "thin ice": attempts are made to advise the skaters that a sheet of ice on the lake might give way, not to point out the specific points where this is most likely to happen. In plain language: it is not necessary to be able to foresee that you are going to be punished, it is enough to be able to see that the possibility of punishment exists. The second point of flexibility refers to the subjective parameter of foreseeability, which arises in the case of professionals *"used to having to proceed with a high degree of caution when pursuing their occupation"* and those who are *"expected to take special care in assessing the risks that such activity entails"*.[42] More so, in third place: it is in general worth affirming foreseeability, even though the person involved would have had to turn to consultants to evaluate the legal consequences, to a reasonable degree in the circumstances of the case, that could result from a particular act.[43]

It is frequently the case that the canon of foreseeability in European case-law is added to that of accessibility,[44] without it being clear whether those are two forms of referring to the same thing—foreseeability as accessibility to the mind of the person addressed in the norm—or two different criteria for the analysis of the legality of a judicial decision, in so far as accessibility would refer to the formal quality of the law, to the precision or determination of its content.[45]

The judgement in *Fondi v. Italy* is very interesting, which appears to identify accessibility with subjective accessibility, opening an interesting door to the inclusion of some aspects of the principle of culpability in the Convention: *"article 7.1 of the Convention requires a link of a subjective nature (conscience and free will) that permits an element of responsibility to be detected in the material behavior of the perpetrator of the crime, in order to apply the punishment. If otherwise, the punishment would not be justified. It would in fact be incoherent, on the one hand, to demand an accessible and foreseeable legal base and, on the other, to allow a person to be held 'guilty' and to punish him for that when he was not able to know*

[41]ECtHR Judgement of 22 October 1996, c. Cantoni v. France, par. 32.

[42]ECtHR Judgement of 22 October 1996, c. Cantoni v. France, par. 33; ECtHR Judgement of 10 October 2010, c. Pessino v. France, 10.10.06, par. 33; ECtHR Judgement of 24 May 2007, c. Dragotoniu and Militaru-Pidhorni v. Romania, par. 35.

[43]ECtHR Judgement of 10 October 2010, c. Pessino v. France, 10.10.06, par. 33; ECtHR Judgement of 24 May 2007, c. Dragotoniu and Militaru-Pidhorni v. Romania, par. 35.

[44]ECtHR Judgement of 10 October 2010, c. Pessino v. France, 10.10.06, par. 29; ECtHR Judgement of 12 February 2008, c. Kafkaris v. Cyprus, par. 140.

[45]See Mururphy (2010), p. 9.

the criminal law because of an insurmountable error that can in no way be attributed to him".[46]

For a clearer understanding of the case-law doctrine of the European Court, it might be illustrative to present some of the applicable results to which it has led.

With regard to judgements upholding the claims of a breach of the right to legality in criminal law, the protection extended to a Lithuanian citizen is, in the first place, of interest. He had been convicted for abuse of his public-sector position "causing of significant damage" despite his conduct only having implied the danger of such damage, and with the affirmation that such a danger already implied a "moral" damage.[47] The judgement in the case of *Dragotoniu and Militaru-Pidhorni* was also favourable, in which two Romanian employees of a private bank had been sanctioned for passive corruption, only applicable to public-sector workers.[48] Finally, it is also worth underlining, the judgement of *Kasymakhunov and Saybatalov v. Russia*, in which the conviction of the second appellant by the Russian courts for membership of a terrorist organization (Hizb ut-Tahrir) is criticized, despite the legal declaration of this organization as a terrorist organization having been published after the acts that were on trial. Note that on the basis of a formal consideration of terrorist organization, what is complained of here is a retroactive application of the criminal norm, which like in all applications of this type meant that *"the second applicant could not reasonably have foreseen that his membership of Hizb ut-Tahrir amounted to criminal conduct"*, even though there may have been journalistic sources that at the time reported the decision of the Supreme Court qualifying the organization as a terrorist one.[49]

The best known judgements perhaps because of their controversy overturn the claim of violation of a criminal category. The first of them referred to two British nationals convicted of raping their wives. The appellants regretted that up until their conviction, it had been interpreted that rape within marriage was not within the category that encompassed "unlawful" sexual relations. In refusing its *amparo*, the Court used semantic arguments—as the English courts argued that it could be understood that the adjective "unlawful" was merely redundant—, axiological arguments—for "the essentially debasing character of rape"—and of a purely factual foreseeability, as the suppression of marital immunity had been discussed in Parliament and in the case-law, in which exceptions were beginning to appear.[50] Note that in any case, we were facing a problem of the interpretation of a written norm.

But perhaps the most important challenge which the European Court has faced is that of the claim of the "Berlin wall guard", who, as a border guard, while

[46]ECtHR Judgement of 20 January 2009, c. Fondi v. Italy, par. 116. The case originally judged was an urbanistic crime. See Grandi (2010), p. 218; Scoletta (2010), p. 278.

[47]ECtHR Judgement of 25 June 2009, c. Liivik v. Estonia, par. 99.

[48]ECtHR Judgement of 24 May 2007, c. Dragotoniu and Militaru-Pidhorni v. Romania, par. 43.

[49]ECtHR Judgement of 14 March, c. Kasymakhunov and Saybatalov v. Russia, par. 92, 94.

[50]ECtHR Judgement of 22 November 1995, c. S. W. v. the United Kingdom, par. 40, 41, 42.

completing his military service, was convicted of manslaughter after German reunification, for having shot and killed, a young man of 29 years old who was trying to emigrate from East-to-West Berlin, in 1972. The appellant argued that at the time, applying the Law of Popular Policing that referred to the use of arms, the border guards on the wall received orders and instructions in which it was said that they *"were therefore directly responsible for the situation which ensued at the border between the two German States"*; border guards were *ordered "not to permit border crossings, to arrest border violators [Grenzverletzer] or to annihilate them [vernichten] and to protect the State border at all costs"*. Having complied with his legal duty, he was then decorated for conduct that some 20 years later on led to his conviction and imprisonment for murder.[51]

The Court rejected the claim with two insufficiently convincing arguments from the value of legal certainty that underpins the principal of legality. That the punishable conduct was contrary to the laws of the Democratic Republic of Germany—which of course appears difficult to sustain from a conceptualization of minimally holistic and realist law[52]—and contrary to the most elemental human rights—which appears as obvious as it is beyond the essence of the discussion—, and what state practices such as border guards cannot be considered as "law",[53] which adds a material content to this concept that deprives the guarantee of judicial subjection to the law of its praiseworthily formal character[54]: it was not a matter of attempting to try the legal system that protected the horror, but of noting that such a system existed. As the dissenting vote to the judgement affirms, not only the convicted person, but nobody at that time, not even a lawyer, would have been able to foresee that his conduct could bring with it a sentence of murder.[55]

It is worth mentioning, finally, the Soros judgement, in which the conviction for the use of privileged information was not considered contrary to the principle of legality in criminal law: *"An 'institutional investor' familiarized with the world of business and accustomed to be contacted to participate in large-scale financial projects"*, a *"secondary initiate"*, who was considered a person who, *"by reason of the exercise of [his] profession and of [his] functions, had access to privileged information on the perspectives or the situation of an issuer"*.[56]

---

[51]ECtHR (GC) Judgement of 22 February 2013, c. Streletz, Kessler and Krenz v. Germany, par. 69, 78; ECtHR Judgement of 22 March 2001, c. K. H. W. v. Germany, par. 68, 71.

[52]Critically, Murphy (2010), p. 5: the criminal order of the Democratic Republic of Germany cannot be analyzed without taking into account the causes of exemption of responsibility.

[53]ECtHR Judgement of 22 March 2001, c. K. H. W. v. Germany, par. 90.

[54]Thus, Murphy (2010), p. 5. See also Scoletta (2010), p. 264.

[55]The judge Cabral Barreto.

[56]ECtHR Judgement of 6 October 2011, c. Soros v. France, par. 54 and ff. (non-official translation). Three of the eight judges dissented with the judgement, *"as neither the opinion of a jurist nor the Case-law analysis would have permitted the appellant to see clearly that the activities that were projected were prohibited upon the basis of the applicable legislation at the time"*.

6 Any Conclusion?

What have we learnt from our stroll through San José and Strasbourg? Not too much I think, probably due to the greater sophistication of the Spanish canons of the control of the judge over subjection to legal definitions of the offences and the penalties.

The concern in American case-law—that is common to Spanish case-law—captures our attention owing to the impact of the content of some norms on the delimitation of others: of how methodological reasonability has also to be in that sense a systematic reasonability.

Beyond the vector of the principle of legality with which this article has occupied itself, the criticism of the Court appears bold and pertinent in relation to the way that the indefinition of the scope of certain norms of permission affects the determination of the scope of those of prohibition, as also happens with the scope of freedom of expression in relation to the prohibition on slander and defamation.

The possibility of "conventionalizing" (integrating in the ECHR) some requirements of the principle of culpability through the principle of legality and its proscription of convictions on the basis of "inaccessible" norms attract our attention in European case-law. Likewise, the misty frontiers that exist between legal law and case-law.

If the cases of marital rape in the English order and the Berlin Wall border guard in the German order are seen as sufficiently reasonable alterations of previous case-law,[57] the reason why things are so different in comparison with an identical alteration but of legal origin have to be seriously thought through. As the example of the hypothetical consideration of cannabis as a hard drug (as a drug that "causes serious harm to health"—art. 368 of the Spanish Penal Code—) would show, perhaps certain case-law changes—but which and in accordance with which criteria—should only be prospective. In any case, a jurisdiction of human rights that seeks to encompass the weaknesses of legality in criminal law from common law orders and that therefore insists above all on the foreseeability of the final legal decision to do so, invites us to reflect on whether the law/case-law distinction is not too formal to appraise the foreseeability of a criminal decision. Indeed it is always unforeseeable if separated from a reasonable interpretation of the legal text. But is it always foreseeable if that is not so?

An innovative interpretative criterion would be to extend the principle of *in dubio pro reo* that is standard in the determination of the facts to the interpretation of the law. Such a step has not been taken by the jurisdictions under analysis,[58] probably due to its excessive guarantism and because the criminal norm never

---

[57] In the German example, Case-law rather than no Case law: the absence of criminal prosecution for acts such as those that were judged.

[58] Although it was affirmed in the judgement of Dragotoniu and Militaru-Pidhorni v. Romania that "*as a corollary of the principle of the legality of convictions, the provisions of criminal law are subjected to the principle of strict interpretation*" (ECtHR Judgement of 24 May 2007, par. 40).

ceases to be a particular balancing point between social interests and the interests of the accused whose best position is not always his possible proximity to these.[59] But this criterion has indeed been legalized by the Statute of Rome, perhaps as a reaction to some interpretive excesses of the ad hoc international criminal courts[60]: *"The definition of a crime shall be strictly construed and shall not be extended by analogy. In case of ambiguity, the definition shall be interpreted in favour of the person being investigated, prosecuted or convicted"* (art. 22.2).

It is not by chance that the introduction of this rule in the preparatory works of the Statute was accompanied by the exclusion of the *dolus eventualis* and the negligence of article 30.[61] And although the rule referred expressly to the definition of crimes, it appears extendable to punishments and to general rules of accusation. In the end, article 22.2 constrains the restrictive interpretation of crimes and is therefore not imposed on itself, with which the criteria of restrictive interpretation could be applied to other aspects of criminal responsibility.[62]

References

Alcácer Guirao R (2011) Fraude de ley y negocio simulado en el delito fiscal (SSTC 120/2005 y 129/2008): el derecho a la legalidad penal y los límites de intervención del Tribunal Constitucional. Revista Española de Derecho Constitucional 91:353–379

Grandi G (2010) Nullum crimen sine lege parlamentaria y Derecho Penal europeo. In: Díez-Picazo LM, Nieto A (eds) Los derechos fundamentales en el Derecho penal europeo. Civitas/Thomson, Madrid, pp 183–250

Guzmán Dalbora JL (2010) El principio de legalidad penal en la jurisprudencia de la Corte Interamericana de Derechos Humano. In: Steiner C, Ambos K, Malarino E (eds) Sistema interamericano de protección de los derechos humanos y Derecho Penal Internacional. Konrad-Adenauer, Montevideo, pp 171–192

Huerta Tocildo S (2014) El contenido debilitado del principio europeo de legalidad penal. In: García J, Santolaya P (eds) La Europa de los derechos, 3rd edn. Centro de Estudios Políticos y Constitucionales, Madrid, pp 399–427

Kuhlen L (2012) Sobre la relación entre el mandato de certeza y la prohibición de analogía. In: Montiel J (ed) La crisis del principio de legalidad en el nuevo Derecho Penal: ¿decadencia o evolución? Marcial Pons, Madrid, pp 151–172

LaFave WR (2009) Criminal law, 4th edn. Thomson, St. Paul

Lascuraín Sánchez JA (2000) Sobre la retroactividad penal favorable. Civitas, Madrid

Lascuraín Sánchez JA (2002) Protección penal y límites penales de las libertades comunicativas. In: Las libertades de información y de expresión. VII Jornadas de la Asociación de Letrados del

[59]In relation to constitutional control, Alcácer Guirao pointed out quite rightly that the extensive interpretation cannot form part of such control because it would lead the Constitutional Court to have to determine the correct interpretation of criminal law and because it is neither well coupled with the canon of foreseeability nor with the grounding of legal safety (Alcácer Guirao 2011, pp. 362 and ff.).

[60]On this point, Schabas (2010), p. 410.

[61]See. Schabas (2010), p. 410.

[62]On this point, Schabas (2010), p. 410.

Tribunal Constitucional. Centro de Estudios Políticos y Constitucionales, Tribunal Constitucional, Madrid, pp 45–83
Montiel JP (2009) Analogía favorable al reo. La Ley, Madrid
Murphy CC (2010) The principle of legality in criminal Law under the ECHR. Eur Human Law Rev 2:192–207
Ormerod D (2009) Smith and Hogan criminal law, 10th edn. Oxford University Press, Oxford
Ortiz de Urbina Gimeno I (2012) ¿Leyes taxativas interpretadas libérrimamente? Principio de legalidad e interpretación del Derecho penal. In: Montiel JP (ed) La crisis del principio de legalidad en el nuevo Derecho Penal: ¿decadencia o evolución? Marcial Pons, Madrid, pp 173–205
Schabas WA (2010) The International criminal court. Oxford University Press, New York
Scoletta M (2010) El principio de legalidad penal europeo. In: Díez-Picazo LM, Nieto A (eds) Los derechos fundamentales en el Derecho penal europeo. Civitas/Thomson, Madrid, pp 251–304
Simester AP, Spencer JR, Sullivan GR, Virgo GJ (2013) Criminal Law, 5th edn. Hart Publishing, Oxford

"*Ne bis in idem*" in Spain and in Europe. Internal Effects of an Inverse and Partial Convergence of Case-Law (from Luxembourg to Strasbourg)

Mercedes Pérez Manzano

1 Introduction: A Widely Recognized Right, with a Disparate Content

The prohibition of *bis in idem* contains a mandate addressed to the State of not reiterating the *Ius puniendi* concerning the same facts. It deals with a principle of punitive Law transformed into a fundamental right and has won wide recognition in the framework of international conventions for the protection of human rights and in state constitutions. It is included in the first versions of some international texts, such as Article 14(7) of the International Covenant on Civil and Political Rights (ICCPR) of 19 December 1966, while others have incorporated it through subsequent protocols, such as Article 4 of the Seventh Protocol to the European Convention on Human Rights (ECHR). And some states expressly recognize it in their constitutions, such as Germany in its Fundamental Law of Bonn—art. 103—and others through their constitutional case-law, such as Spain whose recognition was forthcoming in STC 2/1981 of 30 September 1981.

However, this broad national and international recognition will never hide, beyond the essential agreement entailed in such recognition, the remarkable discrepancies that are concealed in the different ways of defining the elements of the prohibition: the identity—*idem*—and the scope of the prohibition, in other words, the reiteration—*bis*—. These differences respond to disparate understandings built upon the foundation of this right and upon its pre-eminence over and above other

Former Law Clerk at the Spanish Constitutional Court (1998–2007), Professor of Criminal Law at Universidad Autónoma de Madrid.

M. Pérez Manzano (✉)
Universidad Autónoma de Madrid, Campus Cantoblanco, 28049 Madrid, Spain
e-mail: mercedesp.manzano@uam.es

M. Pérez Manzano et al. (eds.), *Multilevel Protection of the Principle of Legality in Criminal Law*, DOI 10.1007/978-3-319-63865-2_5

values at stake, and they are also due to the mixture of two different guarantees: the prohibition of both double punishment and double proceedings.[1]

Although this right raises many problems, I shall occupy myself in this paper with expounding and assessing the differences between the Spanish and the European standard of protection against the reiteration of sanctioning, only in so far as it concerns the concept of identity and the relevance of the "discounting" technique as a means of preventing the violation of the right. For that purpose, I will in the first place offer a brief presentation of internal and European case-law (Sects. 2, 3 and 4). Subsequently (Sect. 5), I will evaluate the consequences that the European standard entails.

2 The Standard in Spanish Constitutional Case-Law

2.1 *General Features*

The Spanish Constitutional Court recognized the constitutional dimension of the prohibition of *bis in idem* in STC 2/1981 of 30 September 1981. On the one hand, the judgement affirmed that, in principle, this right prohibits the accumulation of criminal and administrative penalties, provided that this accumulation was based on the same facts. The Court defined identity as the concurrency of three elements: identity of acts, of persons and of rationales. On the other hand, it declared that the recognition of the fundamental right takes effect in the framework of guarantees established in art. 25.1 of the Spanish Constitution (SC), due to the linkage of the prohibition on the accumulation of sanctions with the rights to legality and legal crime definition (*tipicidad*). Considering the connection of this right with the above-mentioned guarantees, the absence of any specific expression of the right in the Spanish Constitution was not considered relevant to prevent its recognition.

On the basis of this declaration, little by little the Constitutional Court began remodelling the scope of the prohibition and its foundation, by pointing out that the violation of the right will not always require the concurrence of two proceedings or punitive procedures and that this right is also linked to the principle of proportionality (STC 154/1990 of 15 October 1990, FJ 3). With this reasoning, the Court emphasized material *bis in idem*—dual punishment—affirming its independence with regard to procedural *bis in idem*—double prosecution or criminal trial—(also, SSTC 221/1997 of 4 December 1997; 77/2010 of 19 October 2010, FJ 4.c.).

Up until STC 2/2003 of 16 January 2003, in cases of the concurrency of two procedures, administrative and criminal, the punitive authority that had acted in the first place was considered irrelevant by the Spanish Constitutional Court, as it was held that the prohibited reiteration would always affect the second sanction. A paradigmatic case was decided in the STC 177/1999 of 11 October 1999. In STC 2/2003, the Constitutional Court decided to reappraise that solution and to overrule

[1] See Pérez Manzano (2002), pp. 89 ff.; Pérez Manzano (2015), p. 10.

the judgement. In the first place, it maintained that, whichever of the two punitive authorities judges first is a constitutionally relevant issue, because in the Spanish constitutional and legal system, the criminal jurisdiction takes preference. So, the administrative procedure should be stayed until the criminal proceedings have ended and if it is not paralyzed, "*the subsumption of the facts in the administrative offence will violate the principle of sanctioning legality (art. 25.1 SC) and the exclusive competence of criminal jurisdiction to exercise punitive power (art. 25.1 SC in relation to art. 117.3 SC)*".

2.2 The Pre-Requirement of Prohibition: Identity

It is well known that two antagonistic conceptions confront each other in the determination of identity: a *naturalist* (or historical) one, in accordance with which the facts have merely to be individualized on the basis of the place and the time they took place or other natural aspects; and another *normative* one, which takes into account the legal definition of the act, the categorization of the reality described in the norm as well as the disvalue or the detriment assigned to it by the legislator.[2] Although the first concept is usually defended as pertaining to the demarcation of the object of the process, faced with its incapacity to contemplate the singularities of certain cases, such as continuing offences or when the same conduct constitutes several offences (*overlapping offences*), the doctrine, at least partially, accepts a normative understanding, because as Gómez Orbaneja sustained, "*the facts can be identified as procedural objects only if they are contemplated with a sort of legal regard*".[3]

The Spanish Constitutional Court has always defined the required identity in the same way, demanding identity of acts, of person and of rationale. And, although its starting point is to consider the parameters of space and time, it maintains a normative approach, as, on the one hand, it had already affirmed in STC 2/1981 of 30 January 1981 (FFJJ 5 and 6) that in the individualization and comparison of the facts "*it is necessary to take into account criteria of legal assessment*" (FJ 6). Especially relevant in that understanding are the STC 154/1990 of 15 October 1990, relating to the overlapping offences (*concurso ideal*) of robbery together with hostage taking and illegal detention, and STC 204/1996 of 16 December 1996, referring to a crime of professional misconduct for practicing as an optician without a licence. But, also significant in that normative concept is the requirement for identity of rationale,[4] defined as the same perspective of *social defence* (STC 159/1985 of 27 November 1985, FJ 3), the same *legal interest* (STC 234/1991 of 10 December 1991, FJ 2) or the same *legal asset* (STC 270/1994 of 17 October 1994, FJ 8). Finally, even the Constitutional Court's opinion of the identity of

[2]Pérez Manzano (2002), pp. 87 ff. Cancio Meliá, Pérez Manzano (2015) pp. 89 ff.

[3]Gómez Orbaneja (1947), p. 286; De la Oliva Santos et al. (2007), p. 208. Montero Aroca et al. (2016).

[4]García Albero (1995), pp. 64 ff.

subjects, admitting no identity when a physical person and a legal person are both sanctioned, shows evidence of its defence of a normative concept.[5]

This normative conception of triple identity has been maintained and made explicit in STC 77/2010 of 19 October 2010, in which it is literally upheld that: "*the analysis of the concurrency of identity in the acts should not be dominated by a purely naturalistic or arithmetic perspective, but rather, as we previously affirmed in STC 2/1981 of 30 January, 'it is necessary to take criteria of legal assessment into account for the individualization of these facts' (FJ 6). It has necessarily to be so, in so far as what are compared are not mere events, but the description of such events that the legislator has made in the factual situation of the corresponding norm, a description that is inevitably demarcated on the basis of assessable elements and according to the goals that the legislator pursues with his regulation*" (FJ 6).

2.3 The Prohibition on Reiteration and the Discounting of the First Sanction

STC 2/2003 of 16 January 2003, by referring to the ban on dual punishments places emphasis on its link with the principle of proportionality. It therefore affirmed that reiteration is permitted when, with the existence of the required triple identity, steps are taken in the final sanctioning decision to discount the previous sanction and to avoid all of the negative effects tied to the previous sanctioning decision. The reason is that, in such cases, the existence of an excessive punishment, of a disproportionate sanction, may not be affirmed from the strictly material dimension of *ne bis in idem* (FJ 6). Although in that case discounting had affected the economic amount of the fine, the STC 334/2005 of 20 December 2005 (FJ 2) had an occasion to study the constitutionality of the discount in depth, applying it to a case in which it affected sanctions involving deprivation of liberty and prison terms imposed in administrative and criminal-military proceedings for infringements relating to failure to obey orders from a commanding officer. In this case the Court also maintained that there were not any violation of the *ne bis in idem* principle due to the discounting to the first sanction.

3 The Standard of the European Court of Human Rights

3.1 General Features

As previously mentioned, the prohibition on *ne bis in idem* was not recognized in the European Convention of Human Rights (ECHR) until its incorporation in art. 4 of Protocol 7. The essential features of this right, that derive from the case-law of the European Court of Human Rights (ECtHR) and the wording of the above-

[5] Pérez Manzano (2016), pp. 155–166.

mentioned art. 4 are as follows: in the first place, the prohibition is applied in "*criminal*" sanctions or proceedings, which, in line with the ECtHR Judgement, of 8 June 1976, *Engel & Others v The Netherlands*, should be decided in accordance with three criteria: the categorization of the offence in domestic Law; the nature of the offence; and the degree of severity of the sanction. In second place, the regulation of the prohibition requires *a final* judgement regardless of whether it is a conviction or an acquittal, in such a way that it includes both the prohibition on double trial and the prohibition on double sanctions, although it links both to the condition of *res judicata*.[6] This situation has led the Court to sustain that "*the aim of Article 4 of Protocol No. 7 (P7-4) is to prohibit the repetition of criminal proceedings that have been concluded by a final decision*"[7]; and that "*Article 4 of Protocol No. 7 is not confined to the right not to be punished twice but extends to the right not to be tried twice*".[8] Finally, as derived from the second paragraph of art. 4 of Protocol 7, the prohibition has two exceptions: the appearance of new facts or revelations, and the existence of an essential procedural flaw in the first proceeding.[9]

3.2 The Concept of Identity

As highlighted by the Court in 2009 in *Zolotukhin v. Russia,*[10] the case-law of the European Court had until that point been erratic, as different concepts of identity were intermingled within it. In particular, the Court itself mentioned three different concepts, which I would qualify as naturalist, normative, and mixed, respectively. Three very similar cases of punitive duplicity—administrative and criminal—relating to traffic accidents resulting in death or injury are illustrative of the differences in the concepts. A totally naturalist point of view was adopted in *Gradinger v. Austria*. It concerned an accident in which the driver was driving under the effects of alcohol and caused the death of a person. The driver was first convicted in a criminal proceeding of involuntary manslaughter and was then subsequently fined in an

[6]ECtHR Judgement of 10 February 2015, *Kiiveri v. Finland*, par. 38: "*According to the Explanatory Report to Protocol No. 7, which itself refers back to the European Convention on the International Validity of Criminal Judgements, a "decision is final 'if, according to the traditional expression, it has acquired the force of* res judicata. *This is the case when it is irrevocable, that is to say when no further ordinary remedies are available or when the parties have exhausted such remedies or have permitted the time-limit to expire without availing themselves of them'". This approach is well entrenched in the Court's case-law (see, for example,* Nikitin v. Russia, *no. 50178/99, § 37, ECHR 2004-VIII; and* Horciag v. Romania *(Dec.), no. 70982/01, 15 March 2005)*".

[7]ECtHR Judgement of 23 October 1995, *Gradinger v. Austria,* par. 53.

[8]ECtHR Judgement of 29 May 2001, *Franz Fischer v Austria*, par. 22.

[9]See ECtHR Judgement of 13 November 2012, *Margus v. Croatia*. See also Trechsel (1988) pp. 195 ff., Schermers (1987) pp. 601 ff., Specht (1999) and Huerta Tocildo (2014) pp. 399 ff.

[10]Judgement of 10 February 2009.

administrative procedure. The ECtHR upheld the existence of identity and, in consequence, the violation of the prohibition of *bis in idem*, on the understanding that although the offences were differentiated by their denomination, nature, and finalities, and in that the traffic offence only represented one aspect of the crime, nevertheless the same "conduct" was at the root of both sanctions.[11]

On the contrary, in a similar case, *Oliveira v. Switzerland,*[12] the Court concluded the lack of identity of facts. This case also concerned the driver of a vehicle who was sanctioned twice—in criminal and administrative proceedings—. However, on this occasion the first sanction was an administrative fine for failing to control the vehicle, and the second one was a penalty for negligently causing injury resulting from the same traffic accident. When judging the case, the ECtHR affirmed that it was a typical case of *"a single act constituting various offences* (concours idéal d'infractions)", in which it could not be understood that there was identity of offences; to arrive at this conclusion it examined not only the facts from natural parameters, but it also analysed the protected legal interest or assets.[13]

The third approach, recognized by the ECtHR also begins with the natural perspective when comparing the facts, but only requires the identity of the *essential elements of the act* to assert the prohibition. The prototype of this reasoning appears in *Franz Fischer v. Austria*, in which a similar case to the above was judged: driving under the effects of alcohol that was first sanctioned in administrative proceedings and subsequently in a criminal proceeding in which the act was qualified as involuntary manslaughter. The European Court of Human Rights sustained that it was a typical case in which an act constitutes more than one offence: if the offences were only formally different, then the prohibition would be violated; on the contrary, a second trial and sanction would be possible if the overlap between elements of the offenses were slight and it could not therefore be affirmed that the same essential elements were intertwined in both offences.[14]

Faced with this situation of disparity in the concepts of identity, the ECtHR decided to unify its doctrine in *Zolotukhin v. Russia* in 2009. In this decision, it firstly noted the differences in the letter of the international provisions that con-

[11]Par. 55.

[12]Judgement of 30 July 1998.

[13]"*26. That is a typical example of a single act constituting various overlapping offences* (concours idéal d'infractions). *The characteristic feature of this notion is that a single criminal act is split up into two separate offences, in this case the failure to control the vehicle and the negligent causing of physical injury. In such cases, the greater penalty will usually absorb the lesser one. / There is nothing in that situation which infringes Article 4 of Protocol No. 7 since that provision prohibits people being tried twice for the same offence, whereas in cases concerning a single act constituting various offences* (concours idéal d'infractions) *one criminal act constitutes two separate offences*". ECtHR Judgement of 2 July 2002, *Götktan v. France*, par. 50–51; ECtHR Judgement of 24 June 2006, *Gauthier v. France*, par. 2.

[14]See ECtHR Judgement of 30 May, *W.F. v Austria*, pars. 26–28; ECtHR Judgement of 6 June 2002, *Sailer v. Austria*, par. 25–27; Admission's Decisions of 8 April 2003, *Manasson v. Sweden*, par. 5; ECtHR Judgement of 11 December 2007, *Haarvig v. Norwege*.

template the prohibition, and pointed out that use of the term "offence" in Art. 4 of Protocol No 7 would not justify a restrictive interpretation that would only take their legal categories into account, as this interpretation would weaken the scope of the guarantee. Therefore, its inclination was to sustain that "*Article 4 of Protocol No. 7 must be understood as prohibiting the prosecution or trial of a second 'offence' in so far as it arises from identical facts or facts which are substantially the same*".[15]

With regard to the form of determining identity, the Court affirmed that "*Article 4 of Protocol No. 7 becomes relevant on commencement of a new prosecution, where a prior acquittal or conviction has already acquired the force of* res judicata". Therefore, the Court should examine the statements of the facts that figure in these preliminary proceedings, it being irrelevant "*which parts of the new charges are eventually upheld or dismissed in the subsequent proceedings, because Article 4 of Protocol No. 7 contains a safeguard against being tried or being liable to be tried again in new proceedings rather than a prohibition on a second conviction or acquittal*".[16] Since then, the European Court has applied its doctrine on multiple occasions, in which its naturalist method of determination of identity is plain to see.[17]

3.3 The Discounting of the Sanction

It could be inferred from the appraisal of the Court in *Oliveira v. Switzerland* that if two sanctions are not really added together the right would not be violated, even though two proceedings might have been held. However it recognizes that the most correct course of action in those cases is to conduct a single proceeding: "*The fact that that procedure was not followed in Mrs Oliveira's case is, however, irrelevant as regards compliance with Article 4 of Protocol No. 7 since that provision does not preclude separate offences, even if they are all part of a single criminal act, being tried by different courts, especially where, as in the present case, the penalties were not cumulative, the lesser being absorbed by the greater*".[18] After the Judgement of the European Court in the *Zolotukhin* case, it started to be patently clear that the Court had changed its point of view.[19] The clearest case in which the question arise is in *Muslija v. Bosnia & Herzegovina*. In that case, the European Court analysed an initial sanction of deprivation of liberty—imposed in a minor offence procedure

[15]See par. 82.

[16]Par. 83.

[17]For example, in ECtHR Judgement of 25 June 2009, *Maresti v. Croatia*, par. 63; ECtHR Judgement of 18 October 2011, *Tomasovic v. Croatia*; ECtHR Judgement of 14 January 2014, *Muslija v. Bosnia & Herzegovina*, par. 34; ECtHR Judgement of 4 March 2014, *Grande Stevens & Others v. Italia—case FIAT—*.

[18]Par. 27.

[19]See Vervaele (2013), p. 222.

and substituted by a fine—and a second penalty of prison—imposed in a criminal trial—. Despite the legislation provides the first sanction to be discounted in the second conviction when the crime contains some of the elements of the minor offence, the European Court ruled that the convicted person had been tried twice for the same facts, hence Article 4 of the Seventh Protocol should be considered violated.[20]

4 The Standard of the European Court of Justice

The prohibition of *bis in idem* has played a leading role in the case-law of the European Union Court of Justice (ECJ) since its early days as it was recognized as a general principle of Community law in 1966 in *Gutmann v. EURATOM*.[21] Since then, its decisions have mainly been delivered in the framework of two legal sectors. In the first place, within an area where the European Union has punitive competences, which is to say with regard to violations of the rules of free competition; and, in second place, in the framework of judicial cooperation in criminal matters through the interpretation of Articles 54–58 of the Convention Implementing the Schengen Agreement (CISA) of 1985. The leading role of the right to *ne bis in idem* in case-law facilitated its recognition as a fundamental right in art. 50 of the Charter of Fundamental Rights of the European Union (CFREU).

However, this long history of the right in the European Court of Justice has not prevented case-law from presenting some problems of coherency. In fact, the most significant feature of that case-law is the absence of unity in the content of the right in the two fundamental sectors in which it has been developed: free competition and judicial cooperation in criminal matters.[22] In particular, these internal discrepancies are plain to see, both with regard to the use of the concept of identity and with regard to the validity of the discounting technique.

4.1 *Ne bis in idem* and Restrictive Practices of Free Competition

The first pronouncement in which ECJ reflected on this right was in *Wilhelm & others v. Bundeskartellamt*.[23] In this judgement, the ECJ affirmed the compatibility of national and community sanctions and sustained that, although double (national and community) prosecutions might not violate the principle, if the result of that

[20]Par. 39 & 40.

[21]ECJ Judgement of 5 May 1966—Joined Cases 18/65 y 35/65—. See Sharpstin, Fernández-Martin (2008), Satger (2012), Cassese et al. (2013), Klip (2016).

[22]Vervaele (2013), p. 116.

[23]ECJ Judgement of 13 February 1969, (C-14/68).

double prosecution was the imposition of two consecutive sanctions, then a natural requirement of justice demanded that the second decision take into account the first sanction previously imposed. A little later, the ECJ confirmed that the principle of *ne bis in idem* is a general principle of Community law[24] and that the accounting principle is applicable with a general nature, given that its rationale lies in one of the general principles of Community law: the principle of proportionality.

Although the concept of identity that it defended could by then be intuitively seen in these first decisions, it was not until 2004 in *Aalborg Portland & Others v. Commission*, called the "Cement" case,[25] that the ECJ made it expressly clear that the identity required the confirmation of three elements; unity of facts, unity of offender, and unity of protected legal interest. Despite the apparent clarity of that declaration, its application to specific cases is not clear and, above all, it shows that the *ratio decidendi* of the ECJ in these cases has really been the existence or lack of identity in the facts, on the basis of an analysis of such questions as whether the same cartel (the sanctioned firms) had been sanctioned, whether they pursued the same activity, and whether the territory in which the agreement was applied or took effect was the same.[26] What the ECJ model of analysis in this matter shows is that it does not take the facts as an indissoluble unit, but that it dissects them, delimiting those elements of the facts that have specifically been taken into consideration by each sanctioning authority. This form of evaluating the facts hardly matches the concept of identity of the European Court of Human Rights since its judgement, of 2009, in *Zolotukhin v. Russia*, and, as we shall see, neither does it fit in with the pronouncements of the ECJ in the framework of judicial cooperation in criminal matters.

The same incoherency is observed between the model of analysis in these cases and other theses defended in other cases by the ECJ itself. So, it is inconsistent with the idea that the prohibition of double proceedings precedes the prohibition of double sanctions and that the prohibition of double sanctions is only the expression of the general principle of proportionality and is not part of the specific content of the principle of *ne bis in idem*: the strict application of both ideas would have led, in many cases of double sanctions concerning free competition, to the conclusion that two trials had ensued, which in itself violated the right of the offender not to be tried for an act for which he had previously been judged. In fact, the European regulation, which permits supplementary national protection and, therefore, a new national sanctioning proceeding and the application of other sanctions once the Commission has closed its proceeding, can also violate the prohibition of *bis in idem* in its procedural aspect. In these cases, a person whose trial has been finally disposed of, has also been prosecuted, tried and punished a second time for the same acts.

---

[24]See ECJ Judgement of 14 December 1972, Boehringer v. Commission, (C-7/72) par. 2.

[25]ECJ Judgement of 7 January 2004 (Joined Cases C-204/00 P, C-205/00 P, C-211/00 P, C-213/00 P, C-217/00 P and C-219/00 P) par. 398.

[26]Van Böckel (2010), pp. 161 ff., 232.

A paradigmatic example of these problems is the case of *Toshiba Corporation & Others*.[27] In that case, a cartel of which that firm was a member was sanctioned with others for collusive practices by the European Commission and had been sanctioned earlier by the competent court of the Czech Republic turning to the possibility, established in art. 101 of the Treaty of the Union, of the States granting greater protection in the national sphere. Two questions were raised. If, once the Commission had exercised its punitive authority, the States would definitively lose the possibility of sanctioning and, if applicable, within what margin could they sanction without violating the prohibition of *bis in idem*. The interpretation of paragraphs 1 and 2 of art. 16 of Council Regulation (EC) No 1/2003 of 16 December 2002, on the implementation of the rules on competition laid down in Articles 81 and 82 of the Treaty was needed for the solution of the case, and that interpretation was requested.

The ECJ sustained,[28] first, that protection in matters of competition is equally shared between the Member States and the European Union (EU), as the States can offer greater protection; second, that art. 16.1 of the Council Regulation permits the States to suspend the proceeding, while it is brought before the Commission, and that arts. 16.1 and 2 establish that if the national courts pronounce *a posteriori*, they cannot contradict the decision of the Commission, but have to take it into account. It therefore follows that the States do not definitively lose their competence to sanction and can take decisions *a posteriori*, provided that they do not oppose the previous decisions of the Commission.[29] Regardless of the graceful exit in the case of the Court of Justice, it is true that Regulation 1/2003 begins with the possibility of a double prosecution[30] and the—proportional—discounting of the penalty imposed by the Commission, all of which lies uneasily with the thesis of the priority and the autonomy of the prohibition on two trials.

4.2 *Ne bis in idem* and Judicial Cooperation in Criminal Matters

In the context of judicial cooperation in criminal matters, the right to *ne bis in idem* is widely recognized, first through Articles 54–58 Convention implementing the Schengen Agreement (CISA) of 1990,[31] but also in the legislation on mutual

[27]ECJ Judgement of 14 February 2012 (C-17/10).

[28]Par. 84.

[29]Pars. 86 ff.

[30]Also Vervaele (2014), p. 14.

[31]*"Art. 54: A person whose trial has been finally disposed of in one Contracting Party may not be prosecuted in another Contracting Party for the same acts provided that, if a penalty has been imposed, it has been enforced, is actually in the process of being enforced or can no longer be enforced under the laws of the sentencing Contracting Party". "Art. 56: If a further prosecution is*

cooperation in criminal matters, the prototype of which is the Framework Decision relating to the European Arrest Warrant.[32] Likewise, as we already know, it has been recognized as generally applicable in art. 50 CFREU.[33]

4.2.1 Identity[34]

Regardless of its pronouncements in other matters,[35] for the points that are of interest to us here, it has to be highlighted that the Court of Justice has opted for a naturalist concept of identity. The Court has sustained since its judgement in the *Van Esbroeck Case*,[36] that the required identity implies "*identity of the material acts, understood as the existence of a set of facts which are inextricably linked together, irrespective of the legal classification given to them or the legal interest protected*". In case there were any doubts in this respect, in the *Kretzinger Case*[37] the Spanish and German governments held that the criterion of the identity of material acts "*should be applied so as to enable the competent national courts to take account also of the protected legal interest when assessing a set of concrete circumstances*", however, the Court confirmed its thesis that "*the competent national courts [...] must confine themselves to examining whether those acts constitute a set of facts which are inextricably linked together in time, in space and by their subject-matter [...], and considerations based on the legal interest protected are not to be deemed relevant*". Finally, this concept of identity is also

brought in a Contracting Party against a person whose trial, in respect of the same acts, has been finally disposed of in another Contracting Party, any period of deprivation of liberty served in the latter Contracting Party arising from those acts shall be deducted from any penalty imposed. To the extent permitted by national law, penalties not involving deprivation of liberty shall also be taken into account".

[32]Council Framework Decision 2002/584/JHA of 13 June 2002 on the European arrest warrant and the surrender procedures between Member States. "*Art. 3: Grounds for mandatory non-execution of the European arrest warrant. The judicial authority of the Member State of execution (...) shall refuse to execute the European arrest warrant in the following cases: ... 2. if the executing judicial authority is informed that the requested person has been finally judged by a Member State in respect of the same acts provided that, where there has been sentence, the sentence has been served or is currently being served or may no longer be executed under the law of the sentencing Member State*".

[33]"*Art. 50. Right not to be tried or punished twice in criminal proceedings for the same criminal offence: 'No one shall be liable to be tried or punished again in criminal proceedings for an offence for which he or she has already been finally acquitted or convicted within the Union in accordance with the law'*.

[34]A panoramic view in Klip (2016), pp. 293–296; Satger (2012), pp. 132–140.

[35]See Pérez Manzano (2015), pp. 123–153; Pérez Manzano (2016), pp. 176–192.

[36]ECJ Judgement of 9 March 2006 (C-436/04), par. 42; ECJ Judgements of 28 September 2006, *Gasparini & Others* (C-467/04), par. 54 and *Van Straaten* (C-150/05), par. 48.

[37]ECJ Judgement of 18 July 2007 (C-288-05), pars. 32 and 34.

applicable with regard to the ground for refusal to execute the surrender stated in art. 4.2 Council Framework Decision on the European Arrest Warrant.[38]

4.2.2 Discounting

In spite of the fact that the Court of Justice accepted the discounting technique in matters of sanctions for anti-competitive practices, in the context of the interpretation of art. 50 CFREU it must however be understood that the Court has rejected its validity in order to exclude the violation of the right. The question has been raised in the important judgement of *Äkerberg Fransson,*[39] in which the Attorney General Cruz Villalón defended discounting with sensible and well-reasoned arguments.

In that case, Mr. Äkerberg was sanctioned in an administrative proceeding for VAT-related offences of non-payment of tax; in that proceeding, he was ordered to pay two tax surcharges—fiscal years 2004 and 2005—, to which interest was added; these surcharges were not appealed, so that they became final—*res judicata*—. Subsequently, the State Attorney opened a criminal proceeding and the court lodged the preliminary question before the Court of Justice, asking, among other questions, whether the prohibition of *bis in idem* would be applied to the tax surcharge and to the proceeding in which it was imposed. In second place, it asked if it were possible to consider that art. 50 CFREU had not been violated, given that Swedish legislation lays down the *coordination* of the sanctions imposed through both channels—administrative and criminal—, in such a way that the courts can mitigate the sanction that will be finally imposed, by taking into account the surcharges. In other words, it specifically inquired into the efficacy of discounting to exclude the violation of this right.

The first question was answered positively with the indirect application of the "Engel criteria"; and the second one negatively in the framework of the global response that it gave to the second, third and fourth questions.[40] With this tacit response, the Court of Justice lost the opportunity of confirming the opinion of Advocate General Cruz Villalón, who affirmed that "*Article 50 of the Charter must be interpreted as meaning that it does not preclude the Member States from bringing criminal proceedings relating to facts in respect of which a final penalty has already been imposed in administrative proceedings relating to the same conduct, provided that the criminal court is in a position to take into account the prior existence of an administrative penalty for the purposes of mitigating the punishment to be imposed by it*".[41]

---

[38]ECJ Judgement of 16 November 2010, *Mantello* (C-261/09), pars. 40 and 51.

[39]ECJ Judgement 26 February 2013 (C-617/2010). See Vervaele (2013), p. 119.

[40]See par. 32 ff.

[41]See point 96, Opinion of AG Cruz Villalón, delivered on 12 June 2012 (C-617/10).

The pillars of the reasoning behind this conclusion are as follows: in the first place, AG Cruz Villalón began with the possibility and the need to perform an autonomous interpretation of art. 50 CFREU, which should not follow the case-law of the European Court of Human Rights, because there are many different opinions in European states about the scope of the right to *ne bis in idem* as evidenced by the lack of a firm and an uniform application of Protocol No 7 ECHR in which the prohibition on *bis in idem* is expressed; on the other hand, he reasoned that there is no impediment at all in following the interpretation that is proposed in the letter of art. 50 CFREU; finally, he affirmed that, nonetheless, the principle of proportionality and *"the principle of the prohibition of arbitrariness, which is inseparable from the rule of law (Article 2 TEU), requires national law to enable criminal courts to have the power to take into account, by whatever means, the prior existence of an administrative penalty for the purposes of mitigating the criminal penalty"*.[42] This is the reason why the criminal jurisdiction has to take the first sanction into consideration.

5 Comparing European and National Standards

5.1 A More Protective (Higher) European Standard

5.1.1 Summing Up

The presentation of basic patterns of Spanish and European case-law evidences some remarkable differences, both in reference to the concept and the method used when analysing identity, and whether or not the discounting of the first sanction in the second one prevents the violation of the right.

With regard to the concept of identity, we have seen that the Spanish Constitutional Court has used a normative concept on many occasions, while the European Courts have opted for an essentially naturalist concept. In principle, this discordance means that the European standard is more protective (higher) than the Spanish one, because it leads to a statement of the violation of the right in a greater number of cases: if we only compare the facts on the basis of their natural circumstances and space and time, in cases of unity of action, but plurality of affected legal interests—overlapping offences—, identity will have to be affirmed. Driving under the effects of alcohol that has a harmful result, or public disturbance with harmful results that have been judged twice (in administrative and criminal procedures) are examples that have given rise to declarations of the violation of the right following an automatic application of the naturalist concept by the European Court of Human Rights, through the unification of the doctrine in *Zolotukhin v. Russia.*

[42]Point 93.

The same conclusion is reached, if we analyse the decisions of the European Court of Justice relating to judicial cooperation in criminal matters. As we have seen, the Court of Justice coined the naturalist definition of identity of facts that the European Court of Human Rights embraced in 2009 in this sector. Nevertheless, I have also detailed the two concepts of identity and the two different methods of its analysis that exist alongside each other in the case-law of the Court of Justice, because the European Court of Justice uses another concept in the framework of free competition-related sanctions. On the one hand, it accepts the relevance of a normative element, the protected legal interest; and, on the other hand, it selects the factual elements that are taken into consideration for the sanction, in particular the effects and their temporal, spatial and material scope of application.

5.1.2 The Weak Points of Such an Understanding

5.1.2.1 "Essential" Identity, Natural Facts and Legal Detriment; Relevance of the First Punitive Entity

It cannot be left unsaid, however, that the solution to the concrete cases judged by European courts could have been different by applying the same concept of identity of facts. Let us recall that this concept does not require absolute identity, but *essential equality*, and that the identification of such "essentiality" of equality or of difference cannot be automatically derived from the natural event.

The ECtHR declared that *Article 4 of Protocol No. 7 "must be understood as prohibiting the prosecution or trial of a second "offence" in so far as it arises from identical facts or facts which are substantially the same"*. It escapes nobody's attention that the core of the definition lies in how to determine the "substantial or essential identity" to which it refers. From a semantic and logical perspective, there is no more identity than absolute identity, so we may speak of similarity when there is no absolute identity. But beyond this imprecision, it is clearly understood that the European courts seek to affirm that there are factual elements or circumstances that may be different, but that those differences are not of sufficient importance for the purposes of negating the required identity. The problem is that the determination of which circumstances may be relevant to negate the identity is not a neutral question, since the conclusion can vary depending on the methodology that is adopted to compare the facts. In my opinion, the essential or non-essential character of the differences cannot be established without taking into consideration the normative perspective. In other words, it cannot be determined without referring, on the one hand, to the demarcation of the reality by the legislator when including it in a definition of a crime or offence, and, on the other, to the detriment that the legislator has assigned to the act in its configuration in the precept that is applied.[43] In addition, which court has acted first, and which offence and sanction it has applied will all have to be taken into account.

[43] Pérez Manzano (2002), pp. 88–131.

This definition of identity provides, for example, a remarkably different understanding of overlapping offences—*concurso ideal*—, depending on which sanctioning authority has acted first and on the detrimental content of the offence that was applied in the first place. If it is the administrative authority that sanctions driving under the effects of alcohol or without a licence, or disturbance of public order, in the first place, as in many cases that have given rise to ECtHR case-law, the detrimental results (injury, death)—the harm—would not have been covered by the administrative penalty. And those elements, the results, are elements of the natural reality, of the event, that occurred, which arise from the initial action, but that can neither logically nor normatively be identified with it. These harmful results are effects on a human body—bodily harm—and a consequence of the action; they are therefore natural elements that could be taken into consideration to argue that the facts are different. In such a way that although the action and the result have taken place within the same temporal framework, if the result has neither been taken into account nor sanctioned, it could be said that the *facts* sanctioned in administrative and in criminal proceedings are not "substantially or essentially the same". For this purpose, it would be enough to affirm that the natural element, that was not taken into consideration—the harmful result—, was essential. On the contrary, if the criminal jurisdiction were the first to sanction, given that the crime contemplates both the dangerous action and the result, it could be maintained that the sanctioned facts are "essentially the same", even though it may be argued that the caused danger, for example, due to driving under the effects of alcohol, is greater than the danger provoked by the "result" crime (*delito de resultado*) that took place. In this case, if it is the criminal jurisdiction that acted in the first place, given that almost all of the detriment of the administrative offence is integrated in the crime, there would be no space for a new sanction without violating the prohibition of *bis in idem*.

It should be mentioned that this proposal was in the case-law of the European Court of Human Rights prior to 2009, as the difference between the *Gradinger* and the *Oliveira* cases resides in the punitive authority that had acted first, and, therefore, in the nature of the legal qualification and the sanction imposed in the first place. If, in the *Gradinger* case, the criminal jurisdiction acted in the first place, in the Oliveira case, it was the administrative entity. Consequently, in the *Gradinger* case, once the criminal sanction had been imposed, the administrative proceeding violated the prohibition, because there was no space for a new sanction. In the *Oliveira* case, on the contrary, the first penalty—the administrative one—only covered one part of the factual elements, and not the most relevant ones from the perspective of the criminal detriment of the act, in such a way that it could be affirmed that the similarity was partial and that the difference was essential. In other words: the facts were not substantially the same.

But, as we have seen, the European Court of Human Rights, aware of these differences, decided to change track and to adhere to the case-law of the European Court of Justice. In this sense, it is important to point out that the ECtHR now repeatedly sustains that, in the determination of identity, the court will have to examine the presentations of the facts that appear in the preliminary proceedings or judgments, it being irrelevant "*which parts of the new charges are eventually upheld or dismissed in the subsequent proceedings, because Article 4 of Protocol No. 7 contains a safeguard against being tried or being liable to be tried again in new proceedings rather than a prohibition on a second conviction or acquittal*".[44] Accordingly, the determining factor is not which elements of the natural reality have been taken into consideration for their subsumption in the norms (the sanctioned facts), but whether those facts that figure in the preliminary proceedings and decisions (the natural facts) are the same.

The cases that have given rise to the case-law of the Court of Justice in judicial cooperation in criminal matters also show evidence of the shortcomings associated with a naturalist understanding. The crimes and offences are units devised by the legislator delimiting sectors of reality and can consist of either an isolated action or various acts. Illegal detentions, robbery with violence and continuing offences are in fact normative units composed of a plurality of natural actions, so that their disassociation into units of action in space and time would permit the affirmation that there are various facts that may be separately judged and sanctioned in isolation, but this disassociation would lead to unfair results. Even the crime of murder can be broken down into a plurality of natural actions separated by space and time: if someone buys a pistol, the next day approaches his victim, fires a first shot that misses and fires again and finally kills the victim, it could be sustained that there are three separate actions in time and space that could be separately sanctioned. However, there is agreement in that the preparatory act (purchase of the pistol), even the attempt (the first shot), would be subsumed within the consummated crime. Likewise, if someone stabs another 5 times, the fact is qualified as a single offence of bodily harm in which all of effects on personal integrity and health are globally assessed as a single factual unit. The addition of sanctions for each of the natural actions implies a disproportionate—owing to excess—treatment. On the contrary, in cases of overlapping offences (*concurso ideal*) there is agreement, in that they should not be sanctioned as a single offence, in spite of the fact that they are composed of a single and natural action, because they entail various consequences for the legal assets; therefore, to sanction as a single offence when this is the lightest offence constitutes a disproportionate treatment—by default—in itself.

All these questions relating to when unity of act may be established and when one or more offences exist, and in accordance with what criteria they could be determined, constitutes one of the most complex matters, not only of the legal theory of crime but also of the theory of norms; therefore, a simplistic application of the concepts can lead to a casuistry that can soon descend into arbitrariness. In fact, in cases[45] of importing drugs into a European Union country, and their transport and sale in another, it is clear that there are various natural actions that take place at different times and in different territories. If the ECJ sustains, in this case quite rightly, that there is a single act, it cannot ground its conclusion on the idea that

[44]ECtHR Judgement of 10 February 2009, *Zolotukhin v Russia*, par. 83.

[45]See ECJ Judgement of 26 Mars 2006, *Van Esbroeck*, (C-436-04). In general about the concurrency of crimes see Molina Fernández (2016) pp. 395 ff.

these facts constitute a set of acts that are inextricably linked between each other, as this affirmation is nothing more than a *petitio principii*; what it has to justify is why separate actions in time and in territory are "inextricably" linked, and to that end, it can do little more than resort to a normative criterion: the meaning of the offence, the demarcation of the reality defined by the legislator when describing the punishable conduct, and the legal detriment that the behaviour involves.

When the Court of Justice argues, with the principles of mutual trust and freedom of movement as the rationale of its theory, it does not achieve its purpose of basing it on solid pillars, as neither of the two principles excludes the possibility of defending a *normative* concept of identity of facts. This partial normative concept of identity does not require the identity of legal classification, but the essential identity determined from the legal description of the elements of the crime. It would be a matter of comparing the elements of the offences from a legal perspective, in order to conclude whether the differences that exist between them are essential or otherwise. Accordingly, it would not be a question of affirming the relevance of all the differences between the descriptions of crimes and administrative offences in the different States. On the other hand, the objective of ensuring freedom of movement is not achieved through an absolutely naturalist concept of identity of facts. This concept only provides a quite precise delimitation of the unity of acts in simple offences in which the punishable act consists of a single act, or an action and a result that are completed within a short time,[46] in such a way that it generates great insecurity in the rest of the cases and, therefore, a discouraging effect on the freedom of movement that it is intended to protect. In fact, the only thing that could guarantee some legal certainty and sufficient protection of freedom of movement is the harmonization of criminal legislation in the European Union. Until this harmonization takes place, it may not be guaranteed that what is not a crime in one State is a crime in another. And this lack of legal certainty has greater restrictive effects on freedom of movement.[47]

5.1.2.2 The Irrelevance of the Discounting Technique

5.1.2.2.1 Primacy of the Prohibition on Double Prosecution or Trial Over the Prohibition of Dual Punishment

In this context, the irrelevance of discounting is the closing element of the theses of the European Courts. As we have seen, the European Court of Human Rights prioritizes the prohibition on two trials over the prohibition on dual punishments, so that discounting lacks relevance. And in a tacit way, the ECJ applies the same

---

[46]Pérez Manzano (2002), p. 93.

[47]On the negative effects of this understanding in a framework of non-harmonized criminal legislation and with no obligatory criteria for the assignment of competences in criminal matters between the different state jurisdictions, see Vervaele (2013), p. 222; Pérez Manzano (2015), pp. 81, 82.

thesis on judicial cooperation in criminal matters. So, there is no way of avoiding the fact that this point of view is in open contradiction with the reasoning of the Spanish Constitutional Court.

Since the STC 2/2003 of 16 January 2003, the Spanish Constitutional Court has accepted the technique of discounting, both with regard to fines and with regard to terms of imprisonment. And, remaining aware that discounting only circumvented the violation of the prohibition of dual punishments, it completed its reasoning by sustaining that the prohibition of double trials is not always violated when administrative and criminal proceedings concur, but only when the administrative proceeding was as serious for the accused as a criminal trial. This declaration fits with the reasoning of the ECtHR in the *Oliveira* case. Let us recall that, in the aforementioned decision, the European Court of Human Rights maintained that, although opening only one punitive proceeding would have been desirable, nevertheless, as that duality had had no consequences, because it had not resulted in an accumulation of sanctions, the right had not been violated.[48]

At present, it is patent that the ECtHR would not accept the reasoning of the Spanish Constitutional Court, as the Engel criteria will be used in order to determine whether or not art. 4 of Protocol 7 is applicable, and, as we have seen, from among them all, neither is there one that relates to the simplicity of the sanctioning administrative procedure, nor is there one that relates to the special subjection of the accused in a criminal proceeding.

5.1.2.2.2 *Effects on the Spanish Model of Concurrency of Administrative and Criminal Sanctions and on the European Union Regulations That Permit a National Sanction Subsequent to a European Penalty*

This conclusion is, in my opinion, profoundly negative and it distorts European sanctioning systems. In particular, it neither fits in the Spanish model nor permits a fair outcome in the Spanish model, in cases in which the administrative authority does not paralyze the proceeding and sanction in the first place. And neither does it fit with the model that, from my perspective, is the one that best solves the concurrency of administrative and criminal sanctions: a model that entitles the criminal jurisdiction to annul the incorrectly imposed administrative penalty.

The model of the concurrency of administrative and criminal punitive sanctions currently in force in Spain is based on the priority of the criminal jurisdiction, for which reason the administrative proceeding has to be paralyzed and, therefore, if the criminal jurisdiction has declared some facts to be proven, the administrative authority may only determine whether these facts constitute an administrative offence; but it is not allowed to prove the facts once again. This proceeding permits the administrative authority to act after a first criminal decision of acquittal, where the facts do not constitute a crime. It escapes no-one that, in accordance with ECtHR case-law, once the criminal jurisdiction has delivered an acquittal decision,

[48] See par. 27.

because the facts do not constitute a crime, a new administrative procedure, in order to examine whether the facts could be qualified as one of the administrative offences, would hardly be acceptable. Once the criminal nature of the first proceeding has been affirmed and once the first decision becomes a final judgment, there is no room for a new decision.

In this context, one must be aware that the ECtHR has on various occasions expressed an opinion on the proceedings developed in parallel, sustaining that art. 4 of Protocol 7 does not prohibit parallel proceedings, given that it cannot be said that a person has been judged or sanctioned on various occasions in parallel proceedings for an offence *for which he has already been tried*. However, if one of the procedures ends with a decision that becomes *res judicata* and the second proceeding is still open, from that moment in which the first decision becomes a final decision, a violation of the prohibition on *bis in idem* would indeed have taken place.[49] And this thesis has even been upheld when the proceeding is paralyzed and is reopened once the first one is closed.

This same problem is raised in the framework of the legislation of the European Union with regard to the procedure laid down in Council Regulation No 1/2003, because, as we have also seen in matters of sanctions on restrictive anti-competition practices in the European Union, the national sanctioning authorities are allowed to impose a penalty after the European sanction; the requirements are that the second pronouncement cannot contradict the first one and that it must take the previously imposed penalty into account. These requirements safeguard effective judicial protection, as contradictory pronouncements would be intolerable, and the prohibition on dual punishments by permitting a discounted or mitigated sentence. However, they do not prevent the violation of the right not to be judged on various occasions, as once the first decision becomes final, in accordance with the case-law of the ECHR, a further sanctioning proceeding can neither be reopened nor instituted.

Moreover, if, as happened in the cases that gave rise to SSTC 177/1999, 152/2001 and 2/2003, the administrative authority does not paralyze the punitive proceedings and sanctions in the first place, then the criminal jurisdiction has no solution. *Lege ferenda* the only option would be to accept that the criminal jurisdiction is entitled to annul the administrative decisions that would not have paralyzed the sanctioning procedure, in such a way that it would be understood that the administrative decisions would not acquire the status of *res judicata* until the criminal jurisdiction had pronounced on the concurrency or otherwise of the elements of the crime. In this case, given that Articles 4 of Protocol No 7, 54 CISA and 50 CFREU establish as an essential requirement that there is a first decision with the effect of *res judicata*, the debate would shift from the determination of the identity or from the validity of the discounting technique, towards the delimitation of *res judicata* and of the cases of parallel proceedings that can produce the violation of the right. And in this case, as both the ECtHR and the

---

[49]See ECtHR Judgements of 20 May 2014, *Häkkä v. Finland*, par. 48 and *Glantz v. Finland*, par. 59; ECtHR Judgement of 27 January 2015, *Rinas v. Finland*, pars. 55 ff.

ECJ turn to national legislation to know whether or not the first decision has the effect of *res judicata*, it could be argued that, while a—criminal—decision is awaited on the validity of the administrative decision, that decision would lack the force of a final judgment.

5.2 A Less Protective (Lower) European Standard

The discordancies between domestic and European case-law not only mean that in consecuence the Spanish standard is lower than the European standard, but that there are also cases in which the domestic standard is higher than the European standard. This happens in cases in which the prohibition of substantive or punitive *bis in idem* is violated without having instituted two proceedings and without a first decision with the effect of *res judicata*. From the viewpoint of the principle of proportionality, these cases can be especially serious for the citizen given that, as reflected in the case of the STC 154/1990 of 15 October 1990, what the citizen risked was nothing more and nothing less than two prison sentences of 12 years, which had been added to a futher prison sentence also of 12 years.

It is true that in these cases, in the light of positive European law, it appears that there is nothing to do, due to the literal wording of Articles 4 of Protocol No 7, 54 CISA and 50 CFREU. However it should make us reflect on the sense and rationale of the right: would there not be something incorrect in this understanding of the right in which the prohibition on dual trials is prioritized over the prohibition on dual punishments? It is true that such a primacy, in principle, is based on the idea that if the procedural duality is avoided, the sanctioning duality is thereby prevented. And it is also right, from that point of view, that the starting point of identity has to be the unity of natural facts, because to require the identity of legal categories would detract from the full potential of the right, at all times and in any circumstance, given that it would be enough to modify the criminal charges or the administrative offence to open a new route for prosecution and sanctioning of the same facts. However, as I have pointed out, there are other intermediary conceptions that are more precise and that resolve all the cases better, including the "difficult" ones. And in addition, this first delimitation of the right is insufficient and distorts it in many cases. Therefore, the definition of the scope of the right cannot end here.

In my view, the right to *ne bis in idem* should also cover the cases of dual punishment, which can arise within the same trial, as the Spanish Constitutional Court has accepted. In these cases, the identity cannot be determined by spatial-temporal criteria, but by normative ones: one has to begin with the boundaries to natural reality circumscribed by the legislator, to examine the legal detriment of that act and to compare it with the punishable act and the legal detriment of the second offence. And, finally, in my opinion, neither would it be enough to analyse the identity of the facts from the normative perspective, as proposed, to conclude that there had been a violation of the right in these cases, but the reiteration that really occurs will have to be also examined, because it is relevant whether or not legislation permits the addition of the punishments or only provides the imposition of a single punishment (the one foreseen for the most serious crime), but aggravated within the same framework of penalties.

References

Cancio Meliá M, Pérez Manzano M (2015) Principios de Derecho Penal (II). In: Lascuráin Sánchez JA (ed) Introducción al Derecho Penal. Aranzadi, Cizur Menor, pp 89–122

Cassese A et al (2013) International criminal law: cases and commentary. Oxford University Press, Oxford/New York

De la Oliva Santos A et al (2007) Derecho Procesal Penal. Centro de Estudios Ramón Areces, Madrid

García Albero R (1995) Non bis in idem material y concurso de leyes. Cedecs, Barcelona

Gómez Orbaneja E (1947, 1952) Comentarios a la Ley de Enjuiciamiento Criminal de 14 de septiembre de 1882 con la legislación orgánica y procesal complementaria. Bosch, Barcelona

Huerta Tocildo S (2014) El contenido debilitado del principio europeo de legalidad penal. In: García Roca J, Santolaya Machetti P (eds) La Europa de los derechos. Centro de Estudios Políticos y Constitucionales, Madrid, pp 399–427

Klip A (2016) European criminal law. Intersentia, Bristol

Molina Fernández F (2016) Concursos de leyes y de delitos. In: Molina Fernández F (ed) Memento Práctico Penal 2016. Francis Lefebvre, Madrid, pp 395–405

Montero Aroca J et al (2016) Derecho Jurisdiccional III. Proceso Penal. Tirant lo Blanch, Valencia

Pérez Manzano M (2002) La prohibición constitucional de incurrir en bis in idem. Tirant lo Blanch, Valencia

Pérez Manzano M (2015) Sobre la legitimidad y la necesidad de las limitaciones a la prohibición de incurrir en bis in idem en un contexto transfronterizo europeo: a propósito de la STJ 27.05.2014 (Gran Sala), as. Zoran Spasic (C.129/14PPU). Revista Española de Derecho Europeo 54:123–153

Pérez Manzano M (2016) La prohibición de incurrir en bis in idem en España yen Europa. Efectos internos de una convergencia jurisprudencial inversa (de Luxemburgo a Estrasburgo). In: Pérez Manzano M et al (ed) La tutela multinivel del principio de legalidad penal. Marcial Pons, Madrid, pp 149–200

Satger H (2012) International and European criminal law. C.H. Beck/Hart/Nomos, Munich

Schermers H (1987) Non bis in idem. In: Pescatore P et al (eds) Du droit international au Droit de l'Integration: Liber amicorum. Nomos, Baden-Baden, pp 601–611

Sharpstin E, Fernández-Martin JM (2008) Some reflections on Schengen free movement rights and the principle of Ne bis In Idem. Camb Yearb Eur Leg Stud 10:413–448

Specht B (1999) Die zwischenstaatliche Geltung des Grundsatzes ne bis in idem. Zugleich ein Beitrag sur Auslegung des art. 103 Abs. 3 Grundgesestz. Springer, Berlin

Trechsel S (1988) Das verflixte Siebente? Bemerkungen zum 7. Zusatzprotokol zur EMRK. In: Nowak, Steurer, Tretter (eds) Fortschritt im Bewusstsein der Grund- und Menschenrechte. Festschrift für Felix Ermacora. Engel, Kehl, pp 195–211

Van Böckel B (2010) The Ne Bis in Idem Principle in EU Law. Wolters Kluwer, Alphen aan den Rijn

Vervaele JAE (2013) The application of EU Charter of Fundamental Rights (CFR) and its Ne bis in idem principle in the member states of the EU. CJEU judgment (Grand Chamber) C-617/10 of 26 February 2013. Rev Eur Admin Law 6:113–134

Vervaele JAE (2014) Ne bis in idem: ¿un principio transnacional de rango constitucional en la Unión Europea? InDret 1. http://www.indret.com/pdf/1027.pdf

The Principle of Legality in Criminal Law in the Inter-American System for the Protection of Human Rights

Marina Mínguez Rosique

> No one shall be convicted of any act or omission that did not constitute a criminal offense, under the applicable law, at the time it was committed. A heavier penalty shall not be imposed than the one that was applicable at the time the criminal offense was committed. If subsequent to the commission of the offense the law provides for the imposition of a lighter punishment, the guilty person shall benefit therefrom.
>
> **Article 9, American Convention on Human Rights.**

The principle of legality is one of the cornerstones of every criminal law system that traces its lineage from the Enlightenment. It is also an essential principle in the Inter-American system for the protection of human rights: the American Convention on Human Rights (ACHR) provides that Art. 9 can't be suspended under any circumstance.

Its importance has been stressed by the Inter-American Court of Human Rights (IACtHR), which has stated that the principle of legality constitutes one of the central elements of criminal prosecution in a democratic society,[1] given that a fundamental principle of the Rule of Law is to impose limits on the punitive power of the state.[2] Likewise, the Court has substantiated the requirements which comprise this principle: prohibition of *ex post facto* laws (*lex praevia*) or retroactivity, the principle of criminal matters reserved to law (*lex scripta*), the requirement of

---

PhD Candidate at Universidad Autónoma de Madrid.

[1]IACtHR Judgement of 20 June 2005, Case of Fermín Ramírez v. Guatemala, par. 90; IACtHR Judgement of 6 May 2008, Case of Yvon Neptune v. Haiti, par. 125; IACtHR Judgement of 23 November 2012, Case of Mohamed v. Argentina, par. 130; IACtHR Judgement of 22 August 2013, Case of Mémoli v. Argentina, par. 154; IACtHR Judgement of 27 November 2013, Case of J. v. Peru, par. 278; IACtHR Judgement of 29 May 2014, Case of Norín Catrimán *et al.* (leaders, members and activist of the Mapuche indigenous people) v. Chile, par. 161.

[2]IACtHR Judgement of 23 November 2010, Case of Vélez Loor v. Panama, par. 184.

M. Mínguez Rosique (✉)
Universidad Autónoma de Madrid, 28049 Madrid, Spain
e-mail: marina.minguez@uam.es

M. Pérez Manzano et al. (eds.), *Multilevel Protection of the Principle of Legality in Criminal Law*, DOI 10.1007/978-3-319-63865-2_6

legislative precision *(lex certa)*, and the requirement of judicial subjection to law (*lex stricta*).

However, no agreement exists regarding the inclusion of the *non bis in idem* principle as a fifth requirement. In the Inter-American system, this prohibition is covered in another section (Art. 8.4 ACHR); a question that will therefore be dealt with separately.

1 General Approach

The first sentence of Art. 9 ACHR sets forth the general principle of legality in criminal law. This is an adaptation of the aphorism *nullum crimen, nulla poena sine lege*, coined by Feuerbach. The IACtHR has expounded this premise on several occasions, stating that:

> Likewise, and for the sake of legal certainty, it is essential that punitive norms exist and be known, or can be known, before the act or omission that infringes them and is to be punished takes place. The description of an act as wrongful and the formulation of its legal effects must precede the conduct of the individual deemed to be liable for an infringement, insofar as before a form of conduct is described as a crime, it is not considered wrongful in criminal terms.[3]

It indicates that citizens would otherwise be unable to guide their behavior in accordance with a valid and certain legal order.[4]

The Court has also held that, under the rule of law, the aforementioned principle must govern the actions of all the organs of the State, particularly when the exercise of its punitive power is involved,[5] since in this "*[it] manifests with the maximum*

[3]IACtHR Judgement of 2 February 2001, Case of Baena-Ricardo et al. v. Panama, par. 106. In the same vein, IACtHR Judgement of 18 November 2004, Case of De la Cruz-Flores v. Peru, par. 104; IACtHR Judgement of 25 November 2005, Case of García-Asto and Ramírez-Rojas v. Peru, par. 206.

[4]IACtHR Judgement of 2 February 2001, Case of Baena-Ricardo et al. v. Panama, par. 106; IACtHR Judgement of 25 November 2005, Case of García-Asto and Ramírez-Rojas v. Peru, par. 206; IACtHR Judgement of 23 November 2010, Case of Vélez Loor v. Panama, par. 183; IACtHR Judgement of 23 November 2012, Case of Mohamed v. Argentina, par. 132; IACtHR Judgement of 27 November 2013, Case of J. v. Peru, par. 279; IACtHR Judgement of 30 January 2014, Case of Liakat Ali Alibux v. Suriname, par. 60; IACtHR Judgement of 29 May 2014, Case of Norín Catrimán *et al.* (leaders, members and activist of the Mapuche indigenous people) v. Chile, par. 161.

[5]IACtHR Judgement of 2 February 2001, Case of Baena-Ricardo et al. v. Panama, par. 107; IACtHR Judgement of 31 August 2004, Case of Ricardo Canese *v.* Paraguay, par. 177; IACtHR Judgement of 18 November 2004, Case of De la Cruz-Flores v. Peru, par. 80; IACtHR Judgement of 25 November 2004, Case of Lori Berenson-Mejía *v.* Peru, par. 126; IACtHR Judgement of 25 November 2005, Case of García-Asto and Ramírez-Rojas v. Peru, par. 187; IACtHR Judgement of 23 November 2010, Case of Vélez Loor v. Panama, par. 183; IACtHR Judgement of 23 November 2012, Case of Mohamed v. Argentina, par. 131; IACtHR Judgement of 22 August 2013, Case of Mémoli v. Argentina, par. 154; IACtHR Judgement of 27 November 2013, Case of J. v. Peru, par. 278.

strength one of its most serious and intense functions vis-à-vis human beings: repression".[6]

This unconditional guarantee against any exercise of *ius puniendi* has led the IACtHR to establish that the principle of legality is not limited to operating solely in the field of criminal law, but that it also applies where administrative penalties are concerned, stating that such sanctions constitute one more expression of the state's punitive power and are of a similar nature to punishments, since both imply reduction, deprivation, or alteration of the rights of individuals as a consequence of an unlawful conduct.[7] Consequently, the administrative penalty is mentioned explicitly in its explanation of the principle of legality: "*it is indispensable for the punitive rule,* whether of a penal or an administrative nature, *to exist and to be known or to offer the possibility to be known before the action or omission that violates it and for which punishment is intended occurs*".[8] On other occasions, it has adapted the wording of the article, replacing the expression "*act or omission that did not constitute a criminal offense*" by "*an act that, when committed, was not an offense or could not be punished or prosecuted*".[9]

2 The Requirements of the Principle of Legality

2.1 *Retroactivity*

2.1.1 The Principle of Non-Retroactivity of More Severe Criminal Laws

Art. 9 ACHR prohibits the retroactivity of punitive measures that would impose a more unfavourable or harsher penalty than the one applicable at the time the offense was committed.[10]

Although the Court has expressly upheld this prohibition both regarding criminal and administrative sanctions,[11] it has been more precisely specified in the criminal

---

[6]IACtHR Judgement of 2 February 2001, Case of Baena-Ricardo et al. v. Panama, par. 107.

[7]IACtHR Judgement of 2 February 2001, Case of Baena-Ricardo et al. v. Panama, par. 106.

[8]IACtHR Judgement of 2 February 2001, Case of Baena-Ricardo et al. v. Panama, par. 106. In the same vein, IACtHR Judgement of 31 August 2004, Case of Ricardo Canese *v.* Paraguay, par. 176; IACtHR Judgement of 23 November 2010, Case of Vélez Loor v. Panama, par. 183.

[9]IACtHR Judgement of 31 August 2004, Case of Ricardo Canese *v.* Paraguay, par. 175; IACtHR Judgement of 18 November 2004, Case of De la Cruz-Flores v. Peru, par. 105; IACtHR Judgement of 25 November 2005, Case of García-Asto and Ramírez-Rojas v. Peru, par. 191; IACtHR Judgement of 30 January 2014, Case of Liakat Ali Alibux v. Suriname, par. 60.

[10]Art. 9 CADH. In the same vein, IACtHR Judgement of 31 August 2004, Case of Ricardo Canese *v.* Paraguay, par. 175; IACtHR Judgement of 23 November 2012, Case of Mohamed v. Argentina, par. 131.

[11]IACtHR Judgement of 31 August 2004, Case of Ricardo Canese *v.* Paraguay, par. 176.

sphere, requiring that states must not retroactively apply criminal laws that impose heavier penalties, establish aggravating circumstances, or create aggravated forms of the offense.[12]

2.1.1.1 Retroactivity and Permanent Offenses

The interpretation of the IACtHR deserves special attention in those cases involving "permanent offenses": those that do not end with their consummation. A notable example of these offenses is the crime of enforced disappearance.

The regrettable necessity of dealing with such cases has obligated the IACtHR to address two issues: (1) its jurisdiction in trying violations of the American Convention on Human Rights which took place before the Convention's coming into force, but continued after that point; and (2) the creation or (unfavourable) modification of provisions after the consummation of an offense, but before its termination.

Regarding its jurisdiction *ratione temporis*, the Court has determined its own jurisdiction to examine those continuous or permanent violations which began before the activation of the Court's jurisdiction but persist after that date, without thereby breaching the principle of non-retroactivity[13] (as well as, of course, any wrongful event occurring after the date of recognition of jurisdiction). In such cases, the IACtHR argues that violations of the ACHR continue to be committed after its entry into force, adducing that "*stating the contrary would be the same as depriving the treaty itself and the guarantee of protection established therein of its useful effect, with negative consequences for the alleged victims in the exercise of their right to a fair trial*".[14]

---

[12] IACtHR Judgement of 31 August 2004, Case of Ricardo Canese *v*. Paraguay, par. 175; IACtHR Judgement of 18 November 2004, Case of De la Cruz-Flores v. Peru, par. 105; IACtHR Judgement of 25 November 2005, Case of García-Asto and Ramírez-Rojas v. Peru, par. 191; IACtHR Judgement of 27 November 2013, Case of J. v. Peru, par. 279.

[13] IACtHR Judgement of 2 July 1996, Case of Blake v. Guatemala (Preliminary Objections) (1996), par. 40; IACtHR Judgement of 3 September 2004, Case of Alfonso Martín del Campo-Dodd v. United Mexican States (Preliminary Objections), par. §79; IACtHR Judgement of 23 November 2004, Case of the Serrano-Cruz Sisters v. El Salvador (Preliminary Objections), par. 65, 67; IACtHR Judgement of 15 June 2005, Case of The Moiwana Community v. Suriname, par. 39; IACtHR Judgement of 8 September 2005, Case of the Girls Yean and Bosico *v*. Dominican Republic, par. 106; IACtHR Judgement of 26 September 2006, Case of Vargas-Areco *v*. Paraguay, par. 63; IACtHR Judgement of 28 November 2006, Case of Nogueira de Carvalho *et al.* v. Brazil, par. 45; IACtHR Judgement of 12 August 2008, Case of Heliodoro Portugal *v*. Panama, par. 25; IACtHR Judgement of 27 November 2008, Case of Ticona Estrada *et al.* v. Bolivia, par. 29; IACtHR Judgement of 23 November 2009, Case of Radilla-Pacheco v. Mexico, par. 24.

[14] IACtHR Judgement of 23 November 2009, Case of Radilla-Pacheco v. Mexico, par. 24.

Likewise, the Court has ruled that a state's express acknowledgment of events that took place previous to acceptance of the Court's jurisdiction must be interpreted as a waiver of its right to claim any temporal limitation upon the Court, thus recognizing also the Court's retroactive competence over such events.[15]

Surprisingly, this interpretation has been upheld when dealing with the question of the application of unfavorable legal changes during the perpetration of permanent crimes. In such cases, the Court has chosen to overlook its protective case-law regarding the prohibition of retroactivity, holding that the new legal provisions can be applied without any violation of this principle as long as the resulting situation continues under the new regulation.[16]

Before going into depth on this topic, it should be emphasized that, in a literal sense, the Inter-American Convention on Forced Disappearance of Persons uses the terms "continuing offense" *(delito continuado)* and "permanent crime" *(delito permanente)* interchangeably,[17] without realizing the enormous difference between them. While permanent crimes are those in which the extension of the unlawful situation depends on the will of the offender[18] and whose harmfulness intensifies

---

[15]IACtHR Judgement of 27 November 2008, Case of Ticona Estrada *et al.* v. Bolivia, par. 30. In a concurring opinion, Judges García-Sayán and García Ramírez criticize *"the hearing of facts committed beyond the temporal scope comprised by the recognition of competence on the part of the State"* (par. 13), and point out that *"obviously, the Court may not take on, on its own initiative, jurisdiction that has not been conferred upon it"* (par. 10), and that "*the Court may not assume the existence of such recognition, deducing it from isolated, ambiguous or equivocal expressions, to which the State does not clearly ascribe the nature and efficacy of recognition*" (par. 12).

[16]IACtHR Judgement of 26 November 2008, Case of Tiu Tojín *v.* Guatemala, par. 87. Just a few years earlier, [Case of Trujillo-Oroza *v.* Bolivia (Merits; Reparations and costs—2000; 2002)], the IACtHR considered as violations of the right to freedom crimes that might well be included under the offense of enforced disappearance, since in Bolivia, at the time they were committed (1972) there was not any definition for that crime, nor had that country ratified the ACHR or any other international instrument related to the matter. Anyway, since Bolivia acknowledged the facts as well as its responsibility, the case proceeded directly to the reparations stage.

[17]The published English text states: "This offense shall be deemed *continuous or permanent* as long as the fate or whereabouts of the victim has not been determined". E.g. IACtHR Judgement of 24 January 1998, Case of Blake *v.* Guatemala, par. 55 *("continuing or permanent crime*"); IACtHR Judgement of 23 November 2004, Case of the Serrano-Cruz Sisters v. El Salvador (Preliminary Objections), par. 105 ("*continuing crime*"). The domestic law of several signatory states does establish this differentiation. The Penal Code of Peru sets forth what is to be understood by *delito continuado* (Art. 49) and, despite not defining the term *delito permanente*, in Art. 82, regarding limitation periods, it distinguishes expressly between the two categories. The same is true for the case of Guatemala (Arts. 71, 108), while the Penal Code of El Salvador uses *delito continuado* as defined here (and not as used by the Court). On the other hand, Mexico's Federal Penal Code establishes two categories: *permanente* or *continuo* (used as synonyms in Art. 7.I) and *continuado* (art. 7.II). The Bolivian Penal Code makes no distinction at all, although its Constitutional Court has pointed out that enforced disappearance is a permanent crime (*Sentencia Constitucional* No. 1190/01-R).

[18]Berdugo Gómez de la Torre (2010), p. 212; Jescheck (1993), p. 237; López Barja de Quiroga (2010), p. 367, 1155; Mir Puig (2011), p. 234; Roxin (1997), p. 329.

with the passing of time,[19] continuing offenses imply the perpetration of a series of criminal acts with a common link, allowing the consideration of each of them as part of a single (and continual) process.[20] Therefore, they are two totally different types of crime.

The interpretation of the IACtHR—absolutely questionable from the point of view of the principle of legality[21]—is, likewise, revealing of the confusion affecting the Court regarding the term "consummation". There are also discrepancies in academia when it comes to the definition of "consummation", particularly with regard to permanent crimes. On this issue, it has been stated:

- That there is no consummation moment, but a consummation period.[22]
- That a differentiation should be made between "formal consummation" (performance of all the elements that constitute the typified offense) and "material consummation" (phase of harm to the legal interest).[23]
- That consummation is instantaneous and corresponds to the moment when all the elements that constitute the typified offense have been performed.[24] What is permanent, therefore, is not the consummation, but the maintenance of the resulting unlawful situation.

Of these three positions, only the third, with which I am in complete agreement, respects the traditional conception of the term "consummation" as "formal accomplishment of the precisely typified felony",[25] applicable to all offenses, while, on the contrary, the others are manifestly incompatible with this conception, generating constructs that allow the term to be amplified. In my opinion, likewise, this third

[19]Borja Jiménez (1995), pp. 159–160.

[20]Mir Puig (2011), p. 652; Welzel (1956), p. 218.

[21]In the same vein, Guzmán Dalbora, who considers this interpretation to be "*bordering on absolute illegality*", except in those systems whose legislations contemplate it, although regarding it as an exception to their own principles, such as the German Penal Code (§2.2) [(2010), p. 188].

[22]Berdugo Gómez de la Torre (2010), p. 212; Bustos Ramírez (1994), p. 284; Gómez Benítez (1984), p. 168; Gómez Rivero (2010), p. 139; López Barja de Quiroga (2010), p. 367, 1155–1156; Mir Puig (2011), p. 234; Muñoz Conde, García Arán (2010), p. 413; Polaino Navarrete (2000), p. 450; Quintero Olivares (2007), p. 605; Rodríguez Mourullo (1978), p. 128.

[23]Calderón Cerezo, Choclán Montalvo (2005), p. 352; Molina Fernández (2009), p. 100. The latter points out that, although with the first act we are already facing a formally consummated crime, as regards legal interests such as freedom of movement the harm is gradual or progressive ("*material consummation unlimited in time*"). This should not be confused with the use which other authors have made of the term "material consummation", some of them referring to "termination" [Jescheck (1993), p. 468; Roxin (1997), p. 621; Stratenwerth (2005), p. 350] and others to the "attainment of the criminal purpose" [Welzel (1956), p. 191].

[24]Antón Oneca (1986), p. 504, Antón Oneca (1954), p. 2; Bacigalupo Zapater (1999), p. 187; Borja Jiménez (1995), p. 121; Carbonell Mateu and González Cussac (2004), p. 186; Díaz Maroto y Villarejo (1998), p. 44; Jakobs (1997), p. 855; Jescheck (1993), p. 468; Landrove Díaz (1999), p. 67; Mañalich Raffo (2004), p. 12; Lloria García (2006), pp. 105ff.; Luzón Peña (1996), p. 315; Muñoz Conde (2010), p. 170; Roxin (1997), p. 329; Welzel (1956), p. 118.

[25]Jakobs (2002), p. 2; Mir Puig (2011), p. 361; Stratenwerth (2005), p. 350.

position resists—unlike the others—all the criticisms that might be offered, which are explained below.

Thus, in harmony with this conception, it must be stated that the difference between permanent and instantaneous crimes lies neither in the mode of consummation nor in its duration—equal for all crimes—but in the execution or realization of the typified offense: following consummation, a new (criminally relevant) phase opens up, in which the harm done to the protected legal interest is maintained at the will of the perpetrator and which will only come to an end with the cessation of the unlawful situation.[26] This finalizing instant has been denominated "termination",[27] "exhaustion"[28] or "conclusion".[29]

In my opinion, one can neither accept the existence of a "consummative period"—since the idea of prolongation is not compatible with the strict concept of consummation[30]—nor the idea of "constant consummation", since to consider that what is at stake is a succession of consummations through time would imply viewing this legal concept as equivalent to that of a continuing offense (*delito continuado*).[31]

Likewise, this conception respects the traditional differentiation between attempted and consummated crime: an attempted crime is a partial performance of all the elements that constitute the typified offense and, in the precise moment in which the performance is completed, it becomes a consummated one.[32]

This position is shared by most German scholars and dogmatists of Criminal Law, which have set forth:

> "[Unlawful] detention is typically consummated as soon as [the victim's] freedom of movement is eliminated"[33]; "Consummation takes place at the moment when the victim is unable to move from one place to another at will, at least temporarily [...]. [Nevertheless] deprivation of liberty is a permanent crime and only ceases with the end of detention"[34]; "deprivation of freedom is consummated with confinement, but is exhausted only when the imprisoned person regains liberty".[35]

It must be emphasized that this position does not deny the validity of harm caused to the protected legal interest during the "post-consummative phase"

---

[26]Borja Jiménez (1995), p. 123; Lloria García (2006), pp. 105–106, 110.

[27]Borja Jiménez (1995), pp. 99–197; Jescheck (1993), p. 468; Lloria García (2006), p. 100; Mañalich Raffo (2004), p. 14; Roxin (1997), p. 321; Serrano González de Murillo (2008), p. 130.

[28]Lloria García (2006), p. 100; Roxin (1997), p. 321; Serrano González de Murillo (2008), p. 130; Stratenwerth (2005), pp. 350–351.

[29]Borja Jiménez (1995), pp. 121, 149; Serrano González de Murillo (2008), p. 130.

[30]In the same vein, Lloria García (2006), p. 104; Mañalich Raffo (2004), pp. 12–13.

[31]Citing Ragno, Lloria García (2006), p. 104.

[32]Mañalich Raffo (2004), p. 13.

[33]Jakobs (2002), p. 13.

[34]Kindhäuser (2003), pp. 138–139.

[35]Welzel (1956), p. 118.

(i.e. comprised between consummation and termination); during which legitimate self-defense can be exercised.[36]

On the other hand, one of the strongest critiques levelled against this position is the observation that those participating in the post-consummative phase would remain unpunished. This criticism is based on the fact that *"consummation is the limit that represents the instant of termination of a crime; hence it would seem that participation is no longer possible after that moment"*.[37] Nevertheless, it has already been pointed out that the consummation of a crime is not the same as its termination (although this is the case in the majority of crimes); rather, the performance of all the elements that constitute the typified offense does not necessarily imply that this offense is terminated. The typified conduct, although already complete, is prolonged in time, therefore the action continues and criminal participation is possible without forcing the principle of legality.[38]

Less controversial has been the question of determining the *dies a quo* of the limitation period, as there is a generalized agreement locating it at the moment when harm to the protected legal interest ceases.[39]

---

[36]Borja Jiménez (1995), p. 176; Roxin (1997), p. 621; Stratenwerth (2005), p. 197 (*"[...] what is decisive is the harm to the protected legal interest and not the formal consummation of the crime [...]"*).

[37]Molina Fernández (2009), p. 100. This apparent impossibility leads to [an attempt] to solve the problem by establishing the dichotomy of formal consummation-material consummation. Gómez Benítez also states that it is only during that "*period of time in which consummation takes place*" that one can be author or accomplice to a crime [(1984), p. 168].

[38]Borja Jiménez (1995), p. 169 (*"the possibility of appearance of co-authorship or participation at a later time than consummation of the crime can be postulated, as long as this continues in performance of the wrongful act until the moment of termination"*), p. 123 (*"there's a phase following the consummation of the offense that also enters into the sphere of punishability to the extent that the dangerous or harmful progression of the protected legal interest continues, and this phase is covered by the legal crime definition)*. In the same tenor: Calderón Cerezo, Choclán Montalvo (2005), p. 352 (*"It is possible to participate [...], until the point of termination, in those crimes in which a material consummation can be distinguished. Hence, in a permanent crime, participation can take place until the anti-juridical state of affairs ceases"*); Luzón Peña (1996), p. 315 (*"In permanent crimes [...] there is room for participation or co-authorship after consummation while the anti-juridical situation persists"*); Muñoz Conde (2010), p. 212 (*"there is room for participation after a crime has been consummated"*); Roxin (1997), p. 330 (*"In permanent crimes, even after consummation, co-authorship continues to be a possibility (§25) as, likewise, cooperation and complicity (§27) throughout all its duration, as for instance, if someone participates at a later time in the deprivation of liberty"*); Serrano González de Murillo (2008), p. 142; Stratenwerth (2005), p. 351 (*"participation is beyond argument when [...] the performance of the illegal act in effect extends over more of a prolonged period of time"*); Welzel (1956), p. 118 (*"the deprivation of liberty is consummated with the act of confinement, but is exhausted only when the imprisoned person is released; until that point complicity is a possibility. This holds for all permanent crimes [...] as far as the question of participation is concerned, the formal consummation of the fact is of no interest, only the material consummation; in other words, its material exhaustion"*).

[39]Borja Jiménez (1995), pp. 121, 183; Jescheck (1993), p. 823; Landrove Díaz (1999), p. 70; López Barja de Quiroga (2010), p. 367, 1440; Mir Puig (2011), p. 234. This is also established in

Likewise, another equally remediable objection might be raised regarding the criminalization of a hitherto unpunishable conduct. In this case, there is no consummation at all before the entry into force of the precept, since no typified offence has taken place (no elements of any criminal offence have taken place). Once the corresponding statute has come into force, it is possible to speak of consummation, although under the new regulation: only when the consummation has taken place following its entry into force.

In view of the above considerations, it clearly does not seem reasonable to admit the application of an unfavorable normative change introduced after the consummation of the crime, as the Court has indeed considered. Although it might be argued that the subject could adapt his conduct to the new legislation, as I understand it, the motivation of the subject *vis-à-vis* the penal norm is not the same when facing the possibility of committing a crime as against only the possibility of maintaining an extended post-consummative anti-juridical situation: it cannot be assumed that the norm motivates, demands, or influences an individual in the same way considering two such different situations.

Thus, regarding continuing crimes, although it could be argued that typified acts that consummate the offense have been committed after the normative change,[40] what is undeniable is that, under the (strict) principle of legality, no interpretation would justify the retroactive application of a new regulation upon crimes already committed.[41] In the words of Hurtado Pozo, to accept the application of a later law whose entry into force begins while the anti-juridical situation persists would grant the legislator an unlimited freedom to modify the repressive conditions of such offenses in an arbitrary manner.[42]

2.1.1.2 The Ban on Invoking Non-Retroactivity and Statutes of Limitations

The Court has expressly set forth that States may not invoke the statute of limitations, the non-retroactivity of criminal law or the *ne bis in idem* principle to decline its duty to investigate and punish those responsible for serious crimes against humanity.[43]

German legislation (§78a, *"as soon as the criminal offense has terminated"*) and Spanish (Art. 132 CP, *"from the moment when the illicit situation has been eliminated"*).

[40]Thus, the Spanish Supreme Court, which has established that whenever a plurality of acts that might maintain continuity takes place following the normative change (since *"a single act does not constitute the application of criminal continuity"*, STS 2030/2001 of 31 October 2001, FD 1), the application of a later law shall not violate the legality principle (STS 223/2000, of 21 February 2000, FD 4; STS 1548/2005 of 30 December 2005, FD 5; STS 903/2006 of 19 September 2006, FD 3).

[41]Against this position, arguing reasons of criminal policy, Mañalich Raffo (2004), p. 14.

[42]Hurtado Pozo (1987), p. 138.

[43]IACtHR Judgement of 26 September 2006, Case of Almonacid-Arellano *et al.* v. Chile, par. 151; IACtHR Judgement of 29 November 2006, Case of La Cantuta v. Peru, par. 226. This list of unenforceable arguments (normally excepting non-retroactivity) has been reiterated in several

The exclusion of non-retroactivity is not the only one related to the principle of legality: the limitation period is also connected with it. Thus, it has been pointed out that the review of expired limitation periods violates the aforementioned principle, because the author should be able to trust in the continuity of the situation (also indicating that a subsequent consideration that this limitation period has not occurred would suppose a "'re-grounding' of punishability *a posteriori*, in contravention of the principle of legality").[44] According to Jakobs, this principle is also contravened by the extension of existing limitation periods or the facilitation of their interruption, since, by means of such actions, the State broadens its competence to punish retroactively and deliberately.[45]

While one can understand the IACtHR's reasons for adopting this position, given the horrendous nature of the crimes which it is called upon to judge, it must not be forgotten that what the principle of legality sets out to protect (legal certainty and democracy[46]) is also of the greatest importance and, in consequence, its disarticulation may lead to devastating consequences.

In this sense, it is necessary to point out that in recent years the IACtHR has undergone a "*process of punitivization*": it has recognized new rights that were not included in the ACHR (nor derived from it through interpretation) for victims which disarticulate rights, principles and fundamental guarantees of those undergoing criminal process (and which are themselves enshrined in the Convention).[47]

---

judgements: IACtHR Judgement of 14 March 2001, Case of Barrios Altos v. Peru, par. 41; IACtHR Judgement of 3 September 2001, Case of Barrios Altos v. Peru (Interpretation), par. 15; IACtHR Judgement of 27 February 2002, Case of Trujillo-Oroza v. Bolivia (Reparations and Costs), par. 106; IACtHR Judgement of 29 August 2002, Case of the Caracazo v. Venezuela (Reparations and Costs), par. 119; IACtHR Judgement of 18 September 2003, Case of Bulacio v. Argentina, par. 116; IACtHR Judgement of 25 November 2003, Case of Myrna Mack Chang v. Guatemala, par. 276; IACtHR Judgement of 4 May 2004, Case of Molina-Theissen v. Guatemala, par. 83–84; IACtHR Judgement of 8 July 2004, Case of the Gómez-Paquiyauri Brothers v. Peru, par. 150; IACtHR Judgement of 11 May 2007, Case of the Rochela Massacre v. Colombia, par. 194; IACtHR Judgement of 27 November 2008, Case of Ticona Estrada *et al.* v. Bolivia, par. 147; IACtHR Judgement of 22 September 2009, Case of Anzualdo Castro v. Peru, par. 182; IACtHR Judgement of 24 November 2009, Case of the "Las Dos Erres" Massacre v. Guatemala, par. 129; IACtHR Judgement of 24 November 2010, Case of Gomes Lund *et al.* *("Guerrilha do Araguaia")* v. Brasil, par. 148; IACtHR Judgement of 24 February 2011, Case Gelman v. Uruguay, par. 232; IACtHR Judgement of 31 August 2011, Case of Contreras *et al.* v. El Salvador, par. 185.d; IACtHR Judgement of 27 February 2012, Case of González Medina and family v. Dominican Republic, par. 285.e; IACtHR Judgement of 4 September 2012, Case of the Río Negro Massacres v. Guatemala, par. 257; IACtHR Judgement of 24 October 2012, Case of Nadege Dorzema et al. v. Dominican Republic, par. 249.b; IACtHR Judgement of 25 October 2012, Case of the Massacres of El Mozote and nearby places v. El Salvador, par. 296; IACtHR Judgement of 20 November 2012, Case of Gudiel Álvarez *et al.* ("Diario Militar") v. Guatemala, par. 327.b; IACtHR Judgement of 21 May 2013, Case of Suárez Peralta v. Ecuador, par. 175.

[44]Roxin (1997), p. 165; Jescheck (1993), p. 469.

[45]Jakobs (1997), pp. 82–83.

[46]Lascuraín Sánchez (2011), pp. 59–60; Mir Puig (2011), p. 106; Ramos Tapia (2010a), p. 111.

[47]Malarino (2010), pp. 45–46.

As Malarino points out, the violation of human rights is justified in the name of human rights themselves.[48]

2.1.2 Retroactivity of Favorable Laws

Those provisions that are favorable to the defendant are applicable retroactively, since it is irrational to continue to apply a sanction that the legislator regards as unnecessary (or unnecessarily severe). This exception is founded upon the principle of proportionality.[49]

The IACtHR has established a non-exhaustive list of provisions that must always be regarded as favourable penal laws: (1) those that establish a lesser penalty; (2) those that decriminalize behaviours previously regarded as offenses; and (3) those that create new causes of justification or excuses, or an impediment to the effectiveness of a penalty.[50]

Likewise, it has established that the courts have the obligation to compare the most favourable aspects of the penal norms applicable to the case, either upon request from one of the parties or on its own initiative.[51] It has also emphasized that the principle of retroactivity is applicable to laws enacted before the judgement was delivered and during its execution.[52]

Finally, the IACtHR has been keen to point out that the application of the most favorable norm is not only a characteristic of the penal sphere, but one that operates in all spheres related to the protection of rights or freedoms. Hence, if state laws or international treaties grant a greater protection of a right or liberty, or regulate it by giving it a wider scope for enjoyment or exercise, the most favorable norm for the protection of human rights must be applied.[53]

2.1.3 The Retroactive Application of Judicial Decisions

When applying a law, courts interpret and develop it, since the application of law is not a merely logical process, but one that requires the formulation of value judgements by judicial operators.[54] Consequently, they may generate changes in

---

[48]Malarino (2010), p. 48.

[49]Lascuraín Sánchez (2000), pp. 31ff.; Ramos Tapia (2010b), p. 135; Silva Sánchez (1993), pp. 427–428.

[50]IACtHR Judgement of 31 August 2004, Case of Ricardo Canese *v*. Paraguay, par. 179.

[51]IACtHR Judgement of 31 August 2004, Case of Ricardo Canese *v*. Paraguay, par. 186.

[52]IACtHR Judgement of 31 August 2004, Case of Ricardo Canese *v*. Paraguay, par. 179.

[53]IACtHR Judgement of 31 August 2004, Case of Ricardo Canese *v*. Paraguay, par. 180; IACtHR Advisory Opinion OC-5/85, November 13, 1985, par. 52.

[54]Baldó Lavilla (1997), p. 361.

case-law; a situation that could give rise to a weakening of legal certainty and a violation of the principles of legality and equality. Hence, in view of this risk, only two alternatives remain: (1) to prohibit the interpretation of the law by the judges (an impossible option in practical terms that would degenerate into a case-law alien to social reality); or (2) to apply the prohibition of retroactivity to case-law, since, given that Constitutional Courts give flexibility to the requirement of legislative precision (*lex certa*) by appealing to judicial decisions for a further concretion, it would be incoherent to accept the retroactive application of unfavorable changes in case-law on the basis of the argument that the citizen is only subject to the law.[55] Consequently, it can be stated that the prohibition of retroactivity not only applies to the work of lawmakers, but it also operates over the work performed by judges and courts.[56]

The IACtHR has still not pronounced on this question, although—as has been observed in previous paragraphs—it has admitted the retroactive application of its own unfavourable case-law (ratifying on numerous occasions the retroactive application of the interpretation of the Barrios Altos case).[57]

2.1.4 Retroactivity and Procedural Laws

Although the principle of legality applies not only to the offence and to the penalty but also to the penal process, in the procedural sphere the question of retroactivity carries less weight.[58] This is shown by the lack of agreement among scholars: for one sector, the procedural norm is that which is applicable at the moment of undertaking the procedural act, and not the one that is applicable at the time of committing the crime (although the defendant might consider that to be more benign)[59]; for another sector, if the criminal procedure law offers more guarantees to the passive subject, it must be applied retroactively[60]; a third sector inclines towards discerning whether the norms in question are purely procedural or whether, on the contrary, they have a particular relevance to the material circumstance that

[55]Ferreres Comella (2002), p. 199.

[56]Against this, see Roxin, who considers that if the court interprets a norm in a more unfavorable way than had been the case previously, the defendant will have to bear it, since what is at stake is not a retroactive aggravation, but the realization of an intention of a law that already existed, but that so far had not been correctly recognized [(1997), pp. 165–166]. In a similar vein, Jakobs, who points out that the prohibition of case-law retroactivity prevents the amendment of errors and blurs the rule of law and the duty to state the grounds of decisions. He also stresses that it has not been demonstrated that the advantages of principle of confidence compensate the inconveniences arising from case-law immobility [(1997), pp. 126–127].

[57]*Viz*. n. 44.

[58]Fairén Guillén (1992), p. 66.

[59]Lascuraín Sánchez (2011), p. 62.

[60]Fairén Guillén (1992), p. 67.

has generated the proceedings, and thus may have effects on the rights of the defendant and be susceptible to retroactive application.[61]

This divergence of criteria has been highlighted by the Court. On this point, it mentions that, although in the Americas the applicable procedural norm is that in force at the time of the proceedings (understanding that procedural norms are of automatic application, leaving no room for retroactivity),[62] in some countries the application of a subsequent more favorable procedural norm is contemplated,[63] thus accepting the principle of favorable retroactivity for both substantive and procedural laws.[64]

Likewise, the Court has made reference to the position of the ECHR,[65] pointing out that the latter has opted to determine in each case whether the legislative provision includes regulations that affect either the typified offence or the severity of the penalty (that is to say, whether it contains rules of substantive criminal law), in which case Art. 7 ECHR will be applicable.[66]

After setting the context, the IACtHR ruled that the application of procedural norms that enter into force after committing the offense does not violate the principle of legality, since the moment that should be taken as a reference is that of the procedural act.[67] Nonetheless, it has stated that, in the case of procedural norms having an impact on the unfavorable creation or modification of criminal offenses, this position should be reviewed, in order to decide whether it ought to be updated.[68] We shall have to wait, therefore, until a case of such characteristics is examined by the Court, in order to verify whether the Court follows in the footsteps of its European counterpart or whether, on the other hand, it maintains its present position.

---

[61] Maraver Gómez (2011), p. 183. The Spanish Supreme Court has pronounced along these lines when pointing out that "*[...] even though this is a procedural law, it exercises a relevant beneficial effect [...] so that constitutionally, retroactivity is mandatory*" (STS 296/2015 of 6 May 2015), and that "*[...] (when) the norm is not one of substantive criminal law [...] (but it causes) the same effect [...], the retroactivity of the norm is necessarily imposed for basic constitutional reasons*" (STS 297/2015 of 8 May 2015).

[62] Mexico, Brazil, Costa Rica, Peru, EEUU.

[63] Colombia, Argentina, Chile, Nicaragua, Dominican Republic, Venezuela, Uruguay.

[64] IACtHR Judgement of 30 January 2014, Case of Liakat Ali Alibux v. Suriname, par. 67, n. 80–81.

[65] That's not an example of jurisprudential cross-fertilization: the IACtHR replied in those terms to an observation made by the Commission (par. 53) [IACtHR Judgement of 30 January 2014, Case of Liakat Ali Alibux v. Suriname, par. 65].

[66] IACtHR Judgement of 30 January 2014, Case of Liakat Ali Alibux v. Suriname, par. 68, citing ECtHR Judgements Scoppola v. Italy (par. 110–113) and Del Río Prada v. Spain (par. 89).

[67] IACtHR Judgement of 30 January 2014, Case of Liakat Ali Alibux v. Suriname, par. 69.

[68] IACtHR Judgement of 30 January 2014, Case of Liakat Ali Alibux v. Suriname, par. 70.

2.2 The Principle of Criminal Matters Reserved to Law

As was the case with the ECHR, the jurisdiction of the IACtHR has been recognized by states of both civil and common law tradition, hence the interpretation of the principle of legality has had to be nuanced in order to conform to both legal traditions. Accordingly, the aphorism "*nullum crimen, nulla poena sine lege*" has been reinterpreted as "*nullum crimen, nulla poena sine iure*", an expression used more and more in the international sphere.[69]

The IACtHR has pointed out that the principle of criminal matters reserved to law (*reserva de ley/Gesetzesvorbehalt*) must be present in every act that implies an intervention in the sphere of freedom, so that the rights of citizens enjoy untrammeled existence and are legally protected. It has also ruled that the concept of "*law*" is not to be understood as a synonym of just any legal norm, but that it requires the existence of a formal statute: a legal norm generated by the Legislative Power and promulgated by the Executive Branch according to the procedure established by the Law of each state.[70] It has also stressed the need for the existence of a system that guarantees efficacy of application.[71]

Likewise, the Court has pointed out that statutes limiting the enjoyment and exercise of fundamental rights must not only be formal laws but also juridically licit, which means that they must be enacted for reasons of general interest and in accordance with the purpose for which they are established.[72] Thus it has determined that states may restrict a right only when such interventions are not abusive or arbitrary.[73]

In conclusion, "*any limitation or restriction must be both formally and materially provided for by law*",[74] understanding by "law" a "*a general legal norm closely related to the general welfare, enacted by democratically elected legislative bodies established by the Constitution, and formulated according to the procedures set forth by the constitutions of the States Parties for that purpose*".[75]

While the doctrine has assumed that regulations issued by the Executive Branch remain excluded as a source of typified crimes and punishments,[76] the IACtHR has

[69] *Inter alia*, Eser (2009), pp. 172, 176.

[70] IACtHR Advisory Opinion OC-6/86, May 9, 1986, par. 25–27.

[71] IACtHR Advisory Opinion OC-6/86, May 9, 1986, par. 24.

[72] IACtHR Advisory Opinion OC-6/86, May 9, 1986, par. 28.

[73] IACtHR Judgement of 22 October 2001, Case of Artavia Murillo *et al.* ("In Vitro Fertilization") v. Costa Rica, par. 273.

[74] IACtHR Judgement of 2 May 2008, Case of Kimel v. Argentina, par. 63; IACtHR Judgement of 20 November 2009, Case of Usón Ramírez v. Venezuela, par. 55.

[75] IACtHR Advisory Opinion OC-6/86, May 9, 1986, par. 38; IACtHR Judgement of 21 November 2007, Case of Chaparro Álvarez and Lapo Íñiguez *v.* Ecuador, par. 56; IACtHR Judgement of 22 October 2001, Case of Artavia Murillo *et al.* ("In Vitro Fertilization") v. Costa Rica, par. 273.

[76] Mir Puig (2011), p. 107.

not hesitated to subsume these provisions under its notion of "applicable law".[77] This position seems surprising when one takes into account that the purpose of the ACHR is to protect fundamental rights against the arbitrary actions of the state.[78]

During the creation of the ACHR the Colombian delegate proposed an express reference to international law, albeit the Chairman of the Commission considered it to be unnecessary, since that was already implied by the expression "applicable law".[79] The doctrine, in the light of the stipulations of Arts. 10 UDHR, 7 ECtHR and 15 ICCPR, has indicated that, effectively, the expression "applicable law" refers both to national and to international law.[80] It implies that a crime not defined in a state's domestic law can be penalized as long as it exists in international law.[81] This conclusion generates inevitable friction with the pure content of the principle of legality, since it opens the door to custom, one of the sources of international law. Either way, the conflict has been avoided, since the IACtHR has treated the expression "applicable law" solely as in the sense of domestic law.[82]

2.3 *Requirement of Legislative Precision*

Given that criminal law is the most restrictive and severe means to establish liabilities for illicit behavior,[83] the Court has repeatedly insisted that, when drawing up a criminal offense, strict and unequivocal terms must be used to narrowly define the punishable conduct, establishing its elements and the factors that distinguish it from behaviors that are either not punishable or not penalized by criminal law.[84]

---

[77]The Court said nothing about it in following judgements, whose appellants were convicted by virtue of a Decree-law: IACtHR Judgement of 30 May 1999, Case of Castillo Petruzzi *et al.* v. Peru; IACtHR Judgement of 18 August 2000, Case of Cantoral-Benavides v. Peru; IACtHR Judgement of 18 November 2004, Case of De la Cruz-Flores v. Peru; IACtHR Judgement of 25 November 2004, Case of Lori Berenson-Mejía *v.* Peru; IACtHR Judgement of 25 November 2005, Case of García-Asto and Ramírez-Rojas v. Peru; IACtHR Judgement of 27 November 2013, Case of J. v. Peru. In the IACtHR Judgement of 23 November 2010, Case of Vélez Loor v. Panama, the Court made reference to the administrative character of the Decree-law, but to the effect of pointing out its impact on Art. 8 (judicial guarantees).

[78]Guzmán Dalbora (2010), pp. 178–179.

[79]Inter-American Specialized Conference on Human Rights [OEA/Ser.K/XVI/1.2], p. 206.

[80]Guzmán Dalbora (2010), p. 175; Medina Quiroga (2005), p. 347.

[81]Medina Quiroga (2005), p. 347.

[82]Guzmán Dalbora (2010), p. 176.

[83]IACtHR Judgement of 20 November 2009, Case of Usón Ramírez v. Venezuela, par. 55.

[84]IACtHR Judgement of 30 May 1999, Case of Castillo Petruzzi *et al.* v. Peru, par. 121; IACtHR Judgement of 31 August 2004, Case of Ricardo Canese *v.* Paraguay, par. 174; IACtHR Judgement of 18 November 2004, Case of De la Cruz-Flores v. Peru, par. 79; IACtHR Judgement of 25 November 2004, Case of Lori Berenson-Mejía *v.* Peru, par. 125; IACtHR Judgement of 20 November 2009, Case of Usón Ramírez v. Venezuela, par. 55; IACtHR Judgement of 27 April 2012, Case of Pacheco Teruel *et al.* v. Honduras, par. 105; IACtHR Judgement of 27 November 2013, Case of J. v. Peru,

Art. 9 ACHR, therefore, requires states to define criminal actions or omissions in the clearest and most precise way possible[85]: they must be formulated expressly, accurately, restrictively and previously,[86] and the legal framework shall provide legal certainty to citizens.[87] Any ambiguity in the definition of crimes not only leads to doubts and uncertainty, but also facilitates the arbitrary behavior of authorities: an undesirable consequence when establishing the criminal responsibility of the individual and penalizing the latter with punishments that affect fundamental rights.[88] Thus, citing the UN Human Rights Committee, the IACtHR has observed that one of the purposes of this requirement is, precisely, to avoid conferring unfettered discretion on those responsible for applying the laws.[89]

Despite this apparently unequivocal argumentation, the fact is that the IACtHR has not been so categorical in practice. The case of Peru is worth special mention: this country's case-law is particularly abundant in this respect as a consequence of its counter-terrorist policy between 1980 and 1994. Although the extremely poor legislative technique used was initially condemned by the Court on account of its ambiguity, breadth, and indeterminacy,[90] in later judgements it endorsed this very legislation even though it continued to suffer from the same defects.[91]

---

par. 278; IACtHR Judgement of 30 January 2014, Case of Liakat Ali Alibux v. Suriname, par. 61; IACtHR Judgement of 29 May 2014, Case of Norín Catrimán *et al.* (leaders, members and activist of the Mapuche indigenous people) v. Chile, par. 162.

[85]IACtHR Judgement of 20 June 2005, Case of Fermín Ramírez *v.* Guatemala, par. 90; IACtHR Judgement of 6 May 2008, Case of Yvon Neptune v. Haiti, par. 125; IACtHR Judgement of 30 January 2014, Case of Liakat Ali Alibux v. Suriname, par. 61; IACtHR Judgement of 29 May 2014, Case of Norín Catrimán *et al.* (leaders, members and activist of the Mapuche indigenous people) v. Chile, par. 162.

[86]IACtHR Judgement of 2 May 2008, Case of Kimel v. Argentina, par. 63; IACtHR Judgement of 20 November 2009, Case of Usón Ramírez v. Venezuela, par. 55; IACtHR Judgement of 30 January 2014, Case of Liakat Ali Alibux v. Suriname, par. 61; IACtHR Judgement of 29 May 2014, Case of Norín Catrimán *et al.* (leaders, members and activist of the Mapuche indigenous people) v. Chile, par. 162.

[87]IACtHR Judgement of 2 May 2008, Case of Kimel v. Argentina, par. 63; IACtHR Judgement of 20 November 2009, Case of Usón Ramírez v. Venezuela, par. 55.

[88]IACtHR Judgement of 30 May 1999, Case of Castillo Petruzzi *et al.* v. Peru, par. 121; IACtHR Judgement of 31 August 2004, Case of Ricardo Canese *v.* Paraguay, par. 174; IACtHR Judgement of 25 November 2004, Case of Lori Berenson-Mejía *v.* Peru, par. 125; IACtHR Judgement of 27 April 2012, Case of Pacheco Teruel *et al.* v. Honduras, par. 105.

[89]IACtHR Judgement of 31 August 2004, Case of Ricardo Canese *v.* Paraguay, par. 124, citing the UN Human Rights Committee, *General Coment* No. 27, November 2, 1999, §12–13.

[90]IACtHR Judgement of 30 May 1999, Case of Castillo Petruzzi *et al.* v. Peru, par. 121 (*"Laws of the kind applied [. . .], that fail to narrowly define the criminal behaviors, violate the principle of* nullum crimen, nullum poena sine lege praevia *recognized in Article 9 of the American Convention"*); IACtHR Judgement of 18 August 2000, Case of Cantoral-Benavides v. Peru, par. 153 (*"Both Decree-Laws refer to actions not precisely defined, meaning that it could be considered under either"*). The latter reference had been established by the Court in the IACtHR Judgement of 17 September 1997, Case of Loayza-Tamayo v. Peru, par. 68, although in that case its relevance was to the effects of *bis in idem* (Art. 8.4 ACHR).

[91]IACtHR Judgement of 25 November 2004, Case of Lori Berenson-Mejía *v.* Peru, par. 127; IACtHR Judgement of 25 November 2005, Case of García-Asto and Ramírez-Rojas v. Peru, par. 195. For a more exhaustive analysis, cf. Guzmán Dalbora (2010), pp. 180–184.

2.3.1 Blank Criminal Laws

The term "blank criminal laws" refers to those laws that do not give complete expression to the specific elements of punishable conduct, referring to other legal provisions.[92]

While the IACtHR has established that all limitation or restriction of rights must be clearly provided for in law, it has made no stipulation regarding the possible affectation of the legality principle that could be produced by the referral of such laws to regulatory provisions (thus connecting the requirement of legislative precision and the principle of criminal matters reserved to law).

Although the Court examined a case of those characteristics, in its legal reasoning it did not question in any way the use of regulatory provisions that completed the typified offense.[93]

2.3.2 Principle of Imposition of Punishment for Doing, Not for Being

This principle, which prohibits punishing an individual on account of personal characteristics (character, way of being), is closely linked to the requirement of legislative precision, since it demands a clear definition of punishable conducts.

In the case of Fermín Ramírez *v.* Guatemala, the Commission found that the sentencing court had violated the right to due process by taking certain circumstances as an evidence of the dangerousness of the defendant, although those circumstances were not alleged by the Public Prosecutor in the indictment. Nevertheless, the Court stressed that the use of the criterion of dangerousness implied the exercise of the state's punitive power on the basis of personal characteristics, thus substituting a criminal system based on criminal offenses for a criminal system based on the offenders; a characteristic of authoritarian systems unacceptable from the point of view of human rights.[94]

This criterion adds to the accusation of previously committed acts, the prediction of future acts based on the mere appreciation of the Trial Court, punishing the individual not only for what he has *done*, but also for what the judge considers him to *be*: something manifestly incompatible with the principle of legality.[95]

---

[92]Mir Puig (2011), p. 66.

[93]IACtHR Judgement of 23 November 2012, Case of Mohamed v. Argentina, relating to a case of manslaughter as a result of a traffic accident. The legal definition of this crime, set out in Art. 84 CP, referred to provisions contained in a Decree (which, furthermore, was enacted after the commission of the act). The IACtHR did not go as far as determining whether there had been a violation of Art. 9 ACHR, since it considered that it should be determined by the competent court for appeals (given the fact that a violation of Art. 8.2.h ACHR had been registered [par. 117,140,152]).

[94]IACtHR Judgement of 20 June 2005, Case of Fermín Ramírez *v.* Guatemala, par. 93–95.

[95]IACtHR Judgement of 20 June 2005, Case of Fermín Ramírez *v.* Guatemala, par. 95–96.

This particular ruling constitutes a "guaranteeist" landmark which now becomes particularly important, at a time when, unfortunately, many voices are calling for an intensification and consolidation of the punitivist tendency regarding dangerous offenders; a tendency that puts the liberal guarantees that operate as a limit upon the punitive power of the state in a position of unacceptable risk.

2.3.3 Criminalization of Terrorist Acts

The IACtHR has established that the principle of legality imposes a necessary requirement of distinction between the legal definition of offenses of a terrorist nature and ordinary criminal offenses, so that any individual has sufficient legal elements to recognize when a conduct is punishable under one or the other offense.

The rationale behind this requirement is that terrorist offenses entail harsher punishments and that their investigation has procedural consequences that may include the restriction of certain rights during that stage.[96] It thus sets out to avoid broad interpretations that might lead to subsuming conducts that neither have the seriousness nor entail the punishment of terrorist crimes under terrorist laws.[97]

2.4 *Judicial Subjection to Law*

The Court has established that, when applying criminal legislation, the judge is obliged to adhere strictly to its provisions and observe the greatest rigor to ensure that the behavior of the defendant corresponds to a specific category of crime, so as not to penalize acts that are not punishable by law.[98] Likewise, it has emphasized that the application of punishments materially different from those provided by the law contravenes the principle of legality.[99]

---

[96] IACtHR Judgement of 29 May 2014, Case of Norín Catrimán *et al.* (leaders, members and activist of the Mapuche indigenous people) v. Chile, par. 163.

[97] IACtHR Judgement of 29 May 2014, Case of Norín Catrimán *et al.* (leaders, members and activist of the Mapuche indigenous people) v. Chile, par. 165.

[98] IACtHR Judgement of 18 November 2004, Case of De la Cruz-Flores v. Peru, par. 82; IACtHR Judgement of 25 November 2005, Case of García-Asto and Ramírez-Rojas v. Peru, par. 190; IACtHR Judgement of 27 April 2012, Case of Pacheco Teruel *et al.* v. Honduras, par. 105; IACtHR Judgement of 23 November 2012, Case of Mohamed v. Argentina, par. 132; IACtHR Judgement of 30 January 2014, Case of Liakat Ali Alibux v. Suriname, par. 61.

[99] IACtHR Judgement of 23 November 2010, Case of Vélez Loor v. Panama, par. 187. In this case, it was not possible to apply the precept, because it was stipulated that the penalty (2 years of agricultural work) was to be served in the Penal Colony of Coiba, an establishment that had been converted into a center for ecological tourism. The sentence was commuted to a term of 2 years' imprisonment, and this measure was considered to violate the principle of legality because it was based on an extensive interpretation of criminal law.

The IACtHR has also insisted that, in a democratic system, extreme precautions must be taken to ensure that punishments are applied with strict respect for the basic rights of citizens, and subject to an exhaustive verification of the effective existence of the illicit behavior in question.[100]

Nevertheless, in virtue of its already mentioned process of "punitivization", the IACtHR does not seem to see this requirement as applying to itself, for it has departed from it in order to annul laws of amnesty and provisions of exclusion of responsibility, or through case-law to extend the limitation period *ex post facto*.[101]

3 The *non bis in idem* Principle

There is no doctrinal agreement on the inclusion of this principle as a fifth requirement derived from the principle of legality. While one sector regards it as such,[102] another growing sector has held that its basis lies in the principle of proportionality[103] or in the rationality and the interdiction of arbitrariness of public authorities.[104]

The ACHR includes this prohibition in its Art. 8.4: "*An accused person acquitted by a nonappealable judgement shall not be subjected to a new trial for the same cause*". From this curious wording, several conclusions can be drawn. In the first place, its restrictive sphere of application has been confirmed by the IACtHR, which has reiterated that, in effect, among the elements that make up the situation regulated by this article, is the prior existence of a trial that culminated in a final decision of acquittal.[105] Thus the existence of previous proceedings in which a court has taken cognizance of the facts, circumstances, and evidence, and has ruled to acquit the defendant, prohibits further proceedings.[106] This requirement of an acquittal decision is not common in international instruments: on the contrary, the ICCPR, the ECHR and the Rome Statute use the expression "condemned or absolved".

---

[100] IACtHR Judgement of 18 November 2004, Case of De la Cruz-Flores v. Peru, par. 81; IACtHR Judgement of 23 November 2012, Case of Mohamed v. Argentina, par. 130.

[101] The IACtHR ordered Argentina to proceed with, and conclude, the investigation of acts whose limitation period had past [IACtHR Judgement of 18 September 2003, Case of Bulacio *v*. Argentina].

[102] Carbonell Mateu (2001), p. 130; García Rivas (1996), p. 68 (although he points out that it has more to do with the principle of proportionality); Huerta Tocildo (2000), pp. 52–53; Quintero Olivares (1991), p. 281.

[103] Cano Campos (2001), pp. 192, 202; Lascuraín Sánchez (2009), pp. 24–27; Mañalich Raffo (2014), p. 548.

[104] Arroyo Zapatero (1983), pp. 19–20; Cano Campos (2001), pp. 192, 202.

[105] IACtHR Judgement of 18 August 2000, Case of Cantoral-Benavides v. Peru, par. 137.

[106] IACtHR Judgement of 17 September 1997, Case of Loayza-Tamayo v. Peru, par. 76.

In the second place, this regulation does not respond conceptually to the prohibition against multiple punishment, but only against retrial (after an acquittal). Knowing the scope of the right is relevant to the effects of establishing its basis: while the right not to be multiply punished derives from the principles of legality and proportionality, the right not to be retried for the same acts rests on the right to effective judicial protection.[107]

The use of the expression "same cause" (*mismos hechos* in Spanish) also deserves comment; this contrasts with more specific expressions such as those employed by ICCPR and ECHR ("offense") or RS ("crimes"). The IACtHR has emphasized that the choice of the much broader expression "same cause" is to the benefit of the victim.[108]

In any case, the Court has denied the absolute character of this right. Firstly, it has developed the concept of "fraudulent *res judicata*", which results from a trial in which the rules of due process have not been observed, or in which the judges have not acted with independence or impartiality.[109] Thus, it has established that states cannot invoke, to exempt themselves from their obligation to investigate and punish, any judgement delivered in proceedings that did not comply with the standards of the ACHR,[110] since these decisions do not pave the way to a legitimate *res judicata*.[111] Likewise, the IACtHR has stated that the right to *non bis in idem* is not applicable when (1) the action of the court responded to the purpose of shielding the defendant from criminal responsibility; (2) the proceedings were not conducted in an independent or impartial manner in accordance with due procedural guarantees; or (3) there was no real intention to bring those responsible to justice.[112]

Much more controversial is, in the second place, the declaration of the IACtHR that, even when the case ended in (legitimate) acquittal—i.e., meeting the earlier standards—, the appearance of new facts or evidence that might facilitate the determination of those responsible for human rights violations would permit the reopening of investigations, since the demands of justice, the rights of the victims and the spirit and wording of the ACHR supersede any protection afforded by the right to *ne bis in idem*.[113] Once again, although one can understand the reasons for

[107]Pérez Manzano (2002), p.175.

[108]IACtHR Judgement of 17 September 1997, Case of Loayza-Tamayo v. Peru, par. 66.

[109]IACtHR Judgement of 22 November 2004, Case of Carpio-Nicolle *et al.* v. Guatemala, par. 131.

[110]IACtHR Judgement of 22 November 2004, Case of Carpio-Nicolle *et al.* v. Guatemala, par. 132; IACtHR Judgement of 12 September 2005, Case of Gutiérrez-Soler v. Colombia, par. 98.

[111]IACtHR Judgement of 12 September 2005, Case of Gutiérrez-Soler v. Colombia, par. 98.

[112]IACtHR Judgement of 26 September 2006, Case of Almonacid-Arellano *et al.* v. Chile, par. 154. The IACtHR makes here an express reference to Art. 20 RS, as well as the Statutes of the TPIY (Art. 10) and the ICTR (Art. 9).

[113]IACtHR Judgement of 26 September 2006, Case of Almonacid-Arellano *et al.* v. Chile (2006), par. 154.

this pronouncement, it must be insisted that its assimilation implies a violation of a fundamental right present in every convention on human rights: the elimination of one of the key guarantees of the citizen against the state's punitive power.

4 Conclusions

In view of what has been set forth above, it can be stated that the interpretation and application of the principle of legality carried out by the IACtHR paints a mixed picture: on occasions, it has been far from offering the protection of criminal guarantees that might be expected of an international body set up to watch over the protection and application of that principle.

As has been pointed out, the IACtHR is undergoing a process of punitivization that shows that this tendency is not (unfortunately) the exclusive patrimony of European or US contemporary criminal law. In any case, it is worth reviewing the underlying victimological basis in the Inter-American system. Thus, the IACtHR has neutralized certain fundamental rights, principles, and guarantees enshrined in the ACHR under a double justification based on the severity of the crimes and the need to protect victims. Consequently, such apparently untouchable guarantees, like limitation periods or the principles of non-retroactivity and *non bis in idem*, have begun to fall.

For the moment, one can only wait and see if the recently renewed Court will maintain this tendency or, on the contrary, restore the principle of legality with the privileged protection it should never have lost.

References

Antón Oneca J (1954) Delito continuado. Francisco Seix, Barcelona

Antón Oneca J (1986) Derecho Penal, 2nd edn. Akal, Madrid

Arroyo Zapatero L (1983) Principio de legalidad y reserva de ley en materia penal. Revista Española de Derecho Constitucional 8:9–46

Bacigalupo Zapater E (1999) Derecho Penal. Parte general. Hammurabi, Buenos Aires

Baldó Lavilla F (1997) Observaciones metodológicas sobre la construcción de la teoría del delito. In: Silva Sánchez JM (ed) Política criminal y nuevo Derecho Penal. Libro homenaje a Claus Roxin. Jose María Bosch Editor, Barcelona, pp 357–385

Berdugo Gómez de la Torre I (2010) Curso de Derecho Penal. Parte general, 2nd edn. Ediciones Experiencia, Barcelona

Borja Jiménez E (1995) La terminación del delito. Anuario de Derecho Penal y Ciencias Penales 48:89–186

Bustos Ramírez J (1994) Manual de Derecho Penal. Parte general, 4th edn. PPU, Barcelona

Calderón Cerezo Á, Choclán Montalvo JA (2005) Manual de Derecho Penal. Deusto, Barcelona

Cano Campos T (2001) Non bis in idem, prevalencia de la vía penal y teoría de los concursos en el Derecho Administrativo sancionador. Revista de Administración Pública 156:191–249

Carbonell Mateu JC (2001) Reflexiones sobre el abuso del Derecho Penal y la banalización de la legalidad. In: Arroyo Zapatero L, Berdugo Gómez de la Torre I (coords.) Homenaje al

Dr. Marino Barbero Santos: "in memoriam". Universidad de Salamanca, Salamanca, pp 129–144
Carbonell Mateu JC, González Cussac JL (2004) Delitos contra la libertad (I): detenciones ilegales y secuestros. In: Vives Antón T et al (ed) Derecho Penal. Parte Especial. Tirant lo Blanch, Valencia, pp 179–198
Díaz Maroto y Villarejo J (1998) Delitos contra la libertad. Detenciones ilegales y secuestros. In: Bajo Fernández M (dir) Compendio de Derecho Penal (Parte Especial), Volumen II. Centro de Estudios Ramón Areces, Madrid, pp 37–55
Eser A (2009) Human rights guarantees for criminal law and procedure in the EU-charter of fundamental rights. Ritsumeikan Law Rev 26:163–190
Fairén Guillén V (1992) Teoría general del Derecho Procesal. Universidad Nacional Autónoma de México, México D.F
Ferreres Comella V (2002) El principio de taxatividad en materia penal y el valor normativo de la jurisprudencia (una perspectiva constitucional). Civitas, Madrid
García Rivas N (1996) El poder punitivo en el Estado democrático. Servicio de Publicaciones de la Universidad de Castilla-La Mancha, Cuenca
Gómez Benítez JM (1984) Teoría jurídica del delito. Derecho Penal. Parte general. Civitas, Madrid
Gómez Rivero MC (2010) Nociones fundamentales de Derecho Penal. Parte general, 2nd edn. Tecnos, Madrid
Guzmán Dalbora JL (2010) El principio de legalidad penal en la jurisprudencia de la Corte Interamericana de Derechos Humanos. In: Eisner G, Ambos K, Malarino E (coords) Sistema interamericano de protección de los derechos humanos y Derecho Penal Internacional. Konrad-Adenauer, Montevideo, pp 171–192
Huerta Tocildo S (2000) Principio de legalidad y normas sancionadoras. In: Aa.Vv., Actas de las V Jornadas de la Asociación de Letrados del Tribunal Constitucional. Centro de Estudios Políticos y Constitucionales, pp 11–76
Hurtado Pozo J (1987) Manual de Derecho Penal, 2nd edn. Eddili, Lima
Jakobs G (1997) Derecho Penal. Parte general. Fundamentos y teoría de la imputación, 2nd edn. Marcial Pons, Madrid
Jakobs G (2002) Consumación material en los delitos de lesión contra la persona. Revista Electrónica de Ciencia Penal y Criminología 4
Jescheck HH (1993) Tratado de Derecho Penal. Parte general, 4th edn. Comares, Granada
Kindhäuser U (2003) Lehrbuch des Strafrechts Besonderer Teil I. Nomos, Baden-Baden
Landrove Díaz G (1999) Detenciones ilegales y secuestros. Tirant lo Blanch, Valencia
Lascuraín Sánchez JA (2000) Sobre la retroactividad penal favorable. Civitas, Madrid
Lascuraín Sánchez JA (2009) Sólo penas legales, precisas y previas: el derecho a la legalidad penal en la jurisprudencia constitucional. Aranzadi, Cizur Menor
Lascuraín Sánchez JA (2011) Principios del Derecho Penal (I). El principio de legalidad y las fuentes del Derecho Penal. In: Lascuraín Sánchez JA (coord) Introducción al Derecho Penal. Aranzadi, Cizur Menor, pp 53–79
Lloria García P (2006) Aproximación al estudio del delito permanente. Granada, Comares
López Barja de Quiroga J (2010) Tratado de Derecho Penal. Parte general. Civitas, Madrid
Luzón Peña DM (1996) Curso de Derecho Penal. Parte general I. Universitas, Madrid
Malarino E (2010) Activismo judicial, punitivización y nacionalización. Tendencias antidemocráticas y antiliberales de la Corte Interamericana de Derechos Humanos. In: Eisner G, Ambos K, Malarino E (coords) Sistema interamericano de protección de los derechos humanos y Derecho Penal Internacional. Konrad-Adenauer, Montevideo, pp 25–61
Mañalich Raffo JP (2004) El secuestro como delito permanente frente al DL de amnistía. Revista de Estudios de la Justicia 5:11–33
Mañalich Raffo JP (2014) El principio *ne bis in idem* frente a la superposición del Derecho Penal y el Derecho Administrativo sancionatorio. Política Criminal: Revista Electrónica Semestral de Políticas Públicas en Materias Penales 18:543–563

Maraver Gómez M (2011) Vigencia temporal de la Ley penal. In: Lascuraín Sánchez JA (coord) Introducción al Derecho Penal. Aranzadi, Cizur Menor, pp 171–188
Medina Quiroga C (2005) La Convención Americana: teoría y jurisprudencia. Vida, integridad personal, libertad personal, debido proceso y recurso judicial. Centro de Derechos Humanos, Universidad de Chile, Santiago de Chile
Mir Puig S (2011) Derecho Penal. Parte general, 9th edn. Reppertor, Barcelona
Molina Fernández F (2009) ¿Qué se protege en el delito de blanqueo de capitales? In: Bajo Fernández M, Bacigalupo Saggese S (eds) Política criminal y blanqueo de capitales. Marcial Pons, Madrid, pp 91–123
Muñoz Conde F (2010) Derecho Penal. Parte especial, 18th edn. Tirant lo Blanch, Valencia
Muñoz Conde F, García Arán M (2010) Derecho Penal. Parte general, 8th edn. Tirant lo Blanc, Valencia
Pérez Manzano M (2002) La prohibición constitucional de incurrir en *bis in idem*. Tirant lo Blanch, Valencia
Polaino Navarrete M (2000) Derecho Penal. Parte general. Tomo II: teoría jurídica del delito. Volumen I, Bosch, Barcelona
Quintero Olivares G (1991) La autotutela, los límites al poder sancionador de la Administración Pública y los principios inspiradores del Derecho Penal. Revista de Administración Pública 126:253–296
Quintero Olivares G (2007) Parte general del Derecho Penal, 2nd edn. Aranzadi, Cizur Menor
Ramos Tapia MI (2010a) Límites al poder punitivo del Estado (II). In: Zugaldía Espinar JM (dir) Fundamentos de Derecho Penal. Parte general, 4th edn. Tirant lo Blanch, Valencia, pp 111–131
Ramos Tapia MI (2010b) Límites al poder punitivo del Estado (III). In: Zugaldía Espinar JM (dir) Fundamentos de Derecho Penal. Parte general, 4th edn. Tirant lo Blanch, Valencia, pp 133–143
Rodríguez Mourullo G (1978) Derecho Penal. Parte general. Civitas, Madrid
Roxin C (1997) Derecho Penal. Parte general. Tomo I. Civitas, Madrid
Serrano González de Murillo JL (2008) La participación en el hecho ya consumado por otro, en particular en el delito permanente. Cuadernos de Política Criminal 96:129–149
Silva Sánchez JM (1993) Legislación penal socio-económica y retroactividad de disposiciones favorables: el caso de las "leyes en blanco". Estudios Penales y Criminológicos 16:426–461
Stratenwerth G (2005) Derecho Penal. Parte general I. El hecho punible. Thomson-Civitas, Cizur Menor
Welzel H (1956) Derecho Penal. Parte general. Roque de Palma, Buenos Aires

Part III
Parot Doctrine

The Legal Scars of Terrorism: The Unreasonable Parot Doctrine

Fernando Molina Fernández

A characteristic that makes the democratic state under the rule of Law quite singular is how it confronts those who combat it. With an apparently suicidal strategy in any confrontation, it places limits on its means of defence. In a widely-used metaphor, it fights with one hand voluntarily tied behind its back.[1] But it is victorious in the end, which shows that its apparently mistaken strategy in reality involves a wiser mobilization of ethical forces, which more than compensate for what has been lost by voluntary restriction. Extending the metaphor, for each hand that is freely tied behind its back, the state gains another more powerful one.

It is surprising that such a consubstantial idea to the rule of Law, which should and generally does form part of the basic ideas of legal training, is forgotten with such frequency by the jurists themselves when they give (bad) advice to the legislator or (badly) perform their legal work.

When a society faces a criminal challenge of the first order like organized terrorism, the immediate natural tendency is to free the arm that is tied. It is a temptation that is difficult to ignore. Whoever has no solid legal training, or forgets it for whatever reason, easily succumbs to the simple attraction of mobilizing any means to fight against it. So, the main purpose of explaining the basic principles of criminal Law in a Law School should be to ensure that the students understand that the arm must continue to be restrained.

Terrorism has left deep scars in Spanish society; the main ones, without doubt, on its victims. But the loss of quality of the legal system is also noticeable. In

---

Professor of Criminal Law at Universidad Autónoma de Madrid.

[1]Thus, already in the arguments of the memorable judgement of the Israeli Supreme Court of 06-09-1999, in which the practices of torture ("*moderate physical pressure*" in the terminology employed up until then) were declared illegal in the questioning of detainees.

F. Molina Fernández (✉)
Universidad Autónoma de Madrid, Campus UAM, 28049 Madrid, Spain
e-mail: fernando.molina@uam.es

M. Pérez Manzano et al. (eds.), *Multilevel Protection of the Principle of Legality in Criminal Law*, DOI 10.1007/978-3-319-63865-2_7

criminal Law, in particular, the "terrorist exception" has sadly become habitual. It pervades all sorts of institutions in the general section of the Penal Code and almost monopolizes the chapters of the special part assigned to those offences.

Whether this is an intentionally designed strategy or not, a good part of the terrorist logic consists in delegitimizing the system that it fights, highlighting its internal contradictions. And the provocation of unacceptable responses occupies a non-negligible role in that strategy, that is both legal and of other types.[2] All of that is well known, and the Social and Democratic State has instruments to avoid succumbing to provocation: basically, not departing from its own principles, which in the end may be summarized as respect for fundamental guarantees and rights, and to legislate and to judge with only the appropriate material foundation. Nevertheless, the State does not always achieve this. The so-called Parot doctrine in Spain is a sad example of that situation and it is not the only recent one.

If the analysis that will be done here and that many others have done[3] is correct, then the highest Spanish courts succumbed in the Parot case to the temptation of untying the hand that was bound, and the legislator and the courts themselves have done so again in the parallel case of refusing to take into consideration sentences delivered abroad for the purposes of applying the rules of a single act constituting various offenses.[4] It is a question of two doctrines with serious consequences for those affected, (even although the criminals never awaken our sympathy for so many reasons), but above all of two profoundly erroneous doctrines from the perspective of good Law. It has, fortunately, been possible to reverse the damage occasioned by the first, thanks to the European Court of Human Rights; the reversal

[2]The clandestine formation of the so-called GAL (Grupos anti-terroristas de liberación) [Anti-terrorist liberation groups], which fought a dirty war on the side of the State against the terrorist organization ETA, and the damage it inflicted on the cause of anti-terrorism is well known.

[3]There are many observations that this doctrine has deserved, for the most part very critical, although a large part of them affect the question of retroactivity, which was finally decisive for its annulment and less attention is usually lent to the questions of ordinary legality. Among the comments, the following may be cited: Alcácer Guirao (2012), Cuerda Arnau (2013), Cuerda Riezu (2006), García Amado (2013, 2014), Gómez Benítez (2013), Hava García (2014), Landa Gorostiza (2012), Llobet Anglí (2011, 2015), Manzanares Samaniego (2011), Nistal Burón (2013), Orts Berenguer (2009), Rodríguez Horcajo (2013), Rodríguez Montañés (2014), Savater (2013a, b), Vives Antón (2006, 2013). A more complete bibliographic list may be seen in Llobet Anglí (2015), pp. 24–30.

[4]With regard to the clear inspiration of "Council Framework Decision 2008/675/JHA of 24 July 2008 on taking account of convictions in the Member States of the European Union in the course of new criminal proceedings", incontrovertibly in favour of the harmonization of the punitive system in Europe–"The principle that the Member States should attach equivalent effects to a conviction handed down in other Member States to those attached to a conviction handed down by their own courts in accordance with national law should be affirmed, whether those effects be regarded by national law as matters of fact or of procedural or substantive law"–, the first Spanish law—LO 7/2014–, and the Supreme Court afterwards—STS 874/2014 of 27 January 2015–, have once again established the terrorist exception to avoid taking into account, by application of the limits of real concurrence of crimes, other earlier convictions in other countries to reduce the punishment to be imposed in Spain.

of the second is still awaited. I shall only discuss the first here; the unreasonable Parot doctrine, an unmistakable example of the corrupting effect of terrorism on justice. Except as a future example of how not to proceed, for use in the Faculties of Law for the training of young jurists, it is difficult to draw out something positive from this doctrine, which created a problem where there was none, and settled it in the worst possible manner. Nevertheless, its annulment by the Grand Chamber of the European Court of Human Rights, without doubt great news for the Law, provoked something akin to a cataclysm in Spain, where not only was it headline news in the media, but the object of a fierce debate in which arguments were prodigiously wielded that in some cases were verging on the absurd.

There are various legal reasons that make this a bad doctrine. Public attention, between jurists and non-jurists has centred more on some than on others and specifically on what was in the end definitive for its annulment: its retroactive application. Faced with that situation, less attention has been paid to the question that should, theoretically, be of greater interest to jurists: the ordinary unlawfulness of the Parot doctrine with regard to its central argument.[5]

I believe that there are two reasons that explain this relative silence:

1. The first is the belief, which has been opportunely supported from the sectors in favour of it, that the Parot doctrine was a *possible* interpretation, among others, of the law currently in force. Certainly, not the one that had been followed up until then (nobody denies that there was a profound doctrinal change here), but ultimately a possible one.
2. The second is the assertion that the legislator himself would have supported the legality of this doctrine accepting it into successive reforms of the Penal Code.

Both affirmations are incorrect. The second in absolute terms; in his reforms, the legislator not only gave no support to the Parot doctrine, but expressly rejected it. It was therefore not applied to acts committed under the new Spanish Penal Code of 1995. It is true that the legislator agreed in part with the politico-criminal line that lies behind this doctrine, but at the same time gave an outright 'no' to the core formulation of the doctrine.

With regard to the first, only if the "possible interpretation" is understood as an interpretation within the limit of the possible meaning of a text, can it be said that it was possible. However, art. 3 of the Spanish Civil Code establishes various cannons of interpretation, and common sense dictates that there are unreasonable and even extravagant interpretations, and therefore unlawful ones, which despite everything fit into the literal tenor of the law. In this sense, unreasonable interpretation should not only be understood as that which is contrary to the literal tenor of the text, but also as that which, not being so in some of its possible meanings, is contrary to the rest of the canons of interpretation. To conclude that men can only commit the

[5]However, an excellent analysis of the unreasonableness of the argumentation followed in the Supreme Court judgement that placed the Parot doctrine in the limelight may be seen in Llobet Anglí (2015), pp. 6 and ff.

crime of murder because art. 138 of the Penal Code states "*El que matare a otro*" [literally: He who killed another] is an outrageous interpretation, if heedful of the usual meaning of the words, but it is still possible in the literal sense.[6]

In this work, I will occupy myself solely with the question of ordinary legality and its material background.[7] If I am right, the Parot doctrine should never have been formulated, because it contradicts basic principles and institutions of criminal law (teleological argument), and it was also contrary to the law (argument of legality).

In the analysis, I will first set out the background problem, then the material reasons that support the different possible solutions, in order subsequently to examine what the law says and what the case-law says. I will, lastly, finish with some final observations.

1 The Problem

The theoretical problem is relatively simple: it has to do with the criminal treatment of real concurrence of crimes: those situations in which an offender has performed various actions that give rise to various offences that are or could have been judged at the same time. The rule for resolving real concurrence foreseen in art. 73 of the Spanish Penal Code is to accumulate the different punishments that correspond to each separate crime, so that the accused serves them concurrently, if it were possible (for example, a prison term and a fine), or successively (for example, two prison terms).

However, as linear accumulation can lead to the imposition of extremely serious sanctions, two additional questions are raised: the first is to determine whether it is convenient to place *limits* on that accumulation—should there be a maximum sentence to serve, whatever the accumulated offences and however many there are?–; the second, if the response to the first question is affirmative, is whether this limited punishment should be the one that is taken into account for the concession of *prison benefits* that permit a percentage of the sentence that is delivered to be served, such as access to the status of a category three prisoner (semi-freedom) and release on temporary licences, or, formerly, remission of sentences for prison work.[8] In other words, it is a question of determining whether the limits on real concurrence of crimes involve a genuine consolidation of the previous convictions in a new one, to which the prison benefits would then have to be applied (traditional

[6]A similar example is used in Llobet Anglí (2015), p. 11.

[7]The questions of retroactivity, in general, have been studied much more by the doctrine in the wake of the ECtHR judgement in the case of Del Río Prada v. Spain. Above all, among many others, Alcácer Guirao (2012), pp. 938 and ff.; Cuerda Arnau (2013), pp. 52 and ff.; Rodríguez Horcajo (2013), pp. 280 and ff.

[8]This category, which is no longer in the current Penal Code in Spain, permitted a reduction in the time of imprisonment proportionate to the work done in prison.

position in Spanish doctrine and case-law), or whether the previous convictions should retain their individuality and continue to be the basis for access to prison benefits (as in the Parot doctrine).

The Parot doctrine solely impacts on this second question, because the response of the Spanish law to the first is incontrovertible: art. 76 PC expressly foresees such limits (the punishment may neither surpass an absolute maximum, which is defined according to the duration of the accumulated punishments, nor may it be more than three times the most serious punishment among those imposed). But it is also interesting to analyse, albeit briefly, the first question, as both of them are closely related. In fact, it is not easy, without incurring in a contradiction, to uphold the valuative reasons that support the existence of limits and then to deny that those may be applied in one of the most relevant fields of the sanction, which is the application of prison benefits.

2 The Reasons

The possible theoretical responses to both questions are basically three:

- A reply in the negative to the first question and to deny any limitation to the accumulation of punishments in the case of real concurrence of crimes. In this case, the second question no longer makes sense.
- Respond positively to the first question, accepting limits to the accumulation, and negatively to the second, maintaining the independence of the concurrent convictions (Parot doctrine).
- Or to answer both questions in the affirmative, accepting the limits for the effects of both the punishment and the benefits, upon the basis of a genuine consolidation of sentences (traditional position in case-law).

2.1 No Limits to the Accumulation

The first answer is the harshest for the convicted prisoner. An argument is presented in his favour, the effect of which in the end is only very limited, but it can appear convincing when it is advanced: apply to each act the punishment that the legislator decided was the most adequate for its detriment, and by doing so, apparently, maintain parity between the seriousness of the facts as a whole and the punishment that is applied to them (with due respect—apparently—for the principle of proportionality). But there are two arguments against it of far greater weight, which explain why this first option has never been welcomed by the law: it is contrary to a clear understanding of proportionality and can mean that rehabilitation becomes quite impossible.

The supposed advantage is ineffective for two reasons. First, because even if it were true that proportionality is thus maintained, it would only be so up until a certain time, due to the factual limitations on the linear accumulation of punishments in a human lifetime that is necessarily finite. Second, because this solution arises from an erroneous concept of proportionality.

With regard to the first, some of the arguments brandished in favour of the Parot doctrine and against accumulation, which are also completely applicable to the analysis of this first option, came to uphold that committing one murder cannot be the same as ten or one hundred murders.[9]

This analysis is unquestionably so and anyone can understand it. For certain purposes, it is not the same thing. But it is simply false for others. When it is a matter of very serious offences, sanctioned with severe punishments, the linear effect of aggravation that comes from the accumulation of punishments disappears immediately, and it could not be otherwise.[10] In a life that is necessarily conditioned by death, it is almost impossible to accumulate more than three sentences for murder, or directly impossible to accumulate more than one when the new permanently revisable prison sentence is applied. The remainder of the offences, punished with sentences that cannot really be enforced, turn out to be literally free. And that is so in any part of the world and in any imaginable world in which the duration of human life is limited, without us being able to do anything to avoid this effect.[11] And the more severe the punishment of the initial offence, the more this effect occurs. In fact, in crimes that are punishable by the death sentence (in those countries that permit it), or total life imprisonment, the effect is absolute: the first crime provokes all the punishment that is imaginable, and the others go free. It is surprising that the same government that brandished this false argument in favour of the Parot doctrine is the one that has introduced the permanently reviewable prison sentence in the Penal Code, which collides head on with a linearly ascendant system of punishments.

---

[9]The Parot judgement itself echoes this argument to justify its position (Pt. of Law 3). Along the same lines, very clearly Savater, who understands that the judgement from Strasbourg has not affected the legality of the doctrine in any way, but only its retroactive application (Savater (2013a). Certainly, the sentence does not cover questions of ordinary legality, but that does not mean that the Parot doctrine was not unreasonable, and therefore unlawful. Veraciously critical with the arguments of Savater, Díez Ripollés (2013), who considered that "*what really resides in that criticism is insatisfaction, because the life of a person cannot be sufficiently lengthened so that the person is fully answerable for all the evil that is done*".

[10]As Savater himself recognises, nobody can spend a thousand years in prison, such that, in his opinion, the finality of the doctrine is to prevent premature release from prison (Savater 2013b). It is evident that that was the finality of the Parot doctrine, but the important thing in law is whether such a finality was sought through lawful means, as Savater believes, or unlawful means, as is the opinion of a significant part of the criminal doctrine.

[11]At least hardly reasonable. We could, quite clearly, conceive of an ever increasing system of punishments—to continue cutting off fingers as the offences increase?–, but aside from the fact that even this approach would have a limit—the absolute quantity of pain that a person can suffer is limited–, it is enough to set out such a punitive system to perceive its radical implausibility.

It is a very similar argument that was also brandished in favour of the Parot doctrine, and which consists in calculating how little a multiple offender would pay for each of his crimes in a non-Parot system. For example, in the known case of the terrorist Inés del Río, who had played a part in multiple murders, it was pointed out that she had spent no more than 1 year in prison for each murder.

That much is also true in such a peculiar calculation. If we divide the total time in prison by the number of crimes, it gives us that result. But could it be any other way? Let us imagine that this strange logic was applied to a person judged in Spain, convicted of the terrorist attack of 9/11 on the Twin Towers, and that we also applied the Parot doctrine—the alleged cure for the above-mentioned problem—and that we also eliminated art. 75 PC, which sets the limits of accumulation. Even if the result of all that were a term of life-imprisonment, in the most extreme case, a person convicted to 25 years would not spend much more than 60 years (no more than 70 if he were very long lived and our prison system were a harsh one). But supposing that he had committed over 3000 murders, he would hardly have served seven days for each one. An insignificant amount, that is no longer insignificant when it is clear that such a criminal would have spent all of his life in prison. Thus, to divide the effective sentence on a pro-rata basis to ridicule those who oppose the Parot doctrine is an emotional but a completely false argument. No imaginable doctrine is capable of overcoming that "inconvenience". Such an argument being raised, shows up to what point other more solid ones are missing.

And laying bare these types of arguments leads us precisely to the second and decisive objection against the limitations on the accumulation of punishments: it is a serious distortion of values to understand proportionality in a linear sense. As with so many other things in life, its structure is precisely non-linear: deservingness of punishment (retribution) and its necessity (prevention) maintain no direct relationship with the increase in the seriousness of the crime, but continue progressively to decrease until they reach a limit of saturation, which I have called elsewhere the *principle of sufficient punishment.*[12] This principle complements the basic principle of proportionality, which in matters of concurrency may be expressed in the following manner: concurrent crimes are settled on the basis of concurrent norms that, in principle, establish proportionate punishments, but, once the concurrence is resolved, the final resulting punishment should also be proportionate to the complexity of the act that is assessed; that is, "*the most similar to the sanction that would be imposed if, hypothetically, the set of concurrent cases were valued unitarily and settled with a special norm*".[13]

Therefore, if the proportionality clearly understood as such involves no linear accumulation of sanctions, the characteristic limits of the real concurrence of crimes acquire their full meaning, and they oblige this first option to be discarded.[14]

[12]Molina Fernández (2015a), p. 411.

[13]Molina Fernández (2015a), p. 411.

[14]This idea is accurately highlighted by Manzanares Samaniego (2011), p. 1.

However, this is not the only reason for its rejection. As important as that is a second argumentation that is also obvious. If, in accordance with the Spanish Constitution, punishments involving deprivation of liberty should be oriented towards rehabilitation, then the linear sum of convictions in many cases prevents this objective from being reached at all, or at least prevents a space opening up from which to reach it. The argument is so incontrovertible, and it affects a question of such importance, that it is not surprising that this first option has not been defended, and that the Penal Code has always maintained limitations on the accumulation of punishments.

2.2 Parot Doctrine

The second option is precisely the one that the Parot doctrine underscores: the limitations on the accumulation of punishments are accepted—grudgingly–, but not so the application of the benefits of remission of sentences for prison work.

If the criticism of the earlier position is considered, this option can fare no better.

Starting at the end, rehabilitation sees itself truncated in the same way, and precisely when applying institutions, such as prison benefits, directly oriented towards that end. It is impossible to conciliate the clear constitutional message that, with all the nuances and the discounts one might wish, continues firmly to say under article 25.2 that "*Punishments entailing imprisonment and security measures shall be aimed at rehabilitation and social reintegration*", and a doctrine that directly prevents in a large number of cases—certainly those in which it is more necessary-, such social reintegration. The Parot doctrine sends out a message that is no less clear than that of the Constitution. Paraphrasing this message, might be: "*the punishments that entail imprisonment of multiple re-offenders are oriented towards preventing rehabilitation and social reintegration*". Although few things can now surprise us on this matter, it is difficult to understand that the Constitutional Court itself, the custodial organ of the Constitution, may have demonstrated such little sensitivity towards one of its articles when it lent its support to the doctrine in its plenary judgement STC 40/2012 of 29 March 2012.

With regard to proportionality, although it is respected here at least in one of its basic aspects, which is the theoretical measurement of pain, it is undone in its practical application: the damage that punishment inflicts does not depend solely on its duration or amount, but also on the way it is executed. And when the prison benefit affects the duration of the punishment, which was the case of the remission of sentences for prison work, the objections seen in the preceding section re-emerge with all their force. Proportionality affects the whole process of the imposition of the punishment, not only its initial definition in the sentence.

2.3 *Non-Parot Doctrine*

In opposition to that, the third option has all the advantages: it opens a window to social reintegration, and respects the principle of proportionality in all of its aspects: when defining the punishment in the sentence and its execution.

In summary, by application of basic principles of criminal Law, the third option is clearly better. The first should always be discarded and it is directly incompatible with our system of values. But the second could be a possible, although clearly a sub-optimum option. The question now is to inquire into what the legislator has decided in this alternative.

3 The Law

Spanish law has developed on this point, in which three phases may be distinguished:

3.1 *Earlier Spanish Penal Code (PC73)*

The earlier Spanish Penal Code (PC73), at the same time as accepting limits to the accumulation of sentences, thereby discarding the first option, in no way expressly opted between the other two. This is precisely one argument insistently upheld in favour of the plausibility of the Parot doctrine. But it does not mean that the two interpretations had identical arguments in their favour. If the grammatical interpretation could not decide it, the systematic and the teleological arguments were markedly inclined towards the third option. And it cannot be forgotten that the Spanish Civil Code set out four canons of interpretation that obliged the judge to select the best response that resulted from their joint application. As the second option offered no data in its favour, the third option should have prevailed, which in its favour was seen as the most respectful towards the principle of proportionality and social reintegration. And, as we shall go on to see, it was in this way completely passive in the case-law during the period of validity of the earlier Code: the convictions were consolidated in a new one to which the prison benefits were applied, very specifically the remission of punishments for prison work. It afforded any convicted person the possibility of improving his situation in prison, if he met the requirements for social reintegration.

3.2 *Original Penal Code of 1995*

With the entry into force of the Penal Code of 1995, the situation changed slightly when a new provision under art. 78 was included in its original draft, prior to the reform of 2003. This article was a novel provision, which partially broke with the earlier tradition in the matter, and which favoured penal pressure to the detriment of social reintegration, because it amounted to accepting in a clear way an exception in the regime of application of prison benefits. Such an exception consisted of accepting that the courts could do what up until then they had never done (because they interpreted, correctly, that the law prevented them from doing so): computing the periods for the prison benefits taking as a reference the original convictions and not the punishment limited by the rules of real concurrence of crimes. Said in even clearer terms, it accepted for the first time, as an exceptional possibility, the central argument of the Parot doctrine.

It is very important to highlight two ideas, for a correct interpretation of this questionable legislative step:

- First, that at least in its original formulation, it was only a timid step in that direction, as although it establishes an exception to the ordinary regime, at the same time it permitted the judge responsible for the execution of sentences to return to the general regime of enforcement, which, as will be seen, in practice implied no relevant changes.
- Second, and especially important in the whole debate, which, against an argument that has insistently been brandished in support of the Parot doctrine, the new Code in no way expressed such a doctrine, but it expressed the one that was conceived as *exceptional*, recognizing that the general regime was precisely the contrary. I will return to this essential point later on.

3.3 *Penal Code of 1995 After Organic Law LO/72003*

The third stage of the process was opened after Organic Law LO 7/2003, *de medidas de reforma para el cumplimiento íntegro y efectivo de las penas* [on reform measures for the full and effective enforcement of sentences]. The title of the provision already gives a clear idea of its purpose. Technically, the new article 78 is structured through a system of successive rules and exceptions. Thus, maintaining in this the earlier regulation, paragraph 1 provides that "*[i]f as a consequence of the limitations established in section 1 of art. 76 the sentence to be served were less than half of the sum total of those imposed, the sentencing judge or court may agree to refer the prison benefits, the licenses for release, the third category of prisoner,*[15] *and the calculation of the time for conditional freedom to the totality of the punishments imposed in the sentences"*.[16]

Almost certainly, the legislator included the provision of the first sub-section of art. 78.2, because he was aware of what that implied from a constitutional perspective, according to which, *"[i]n these cases, the judge responsible for the execution of sentences, following an individual assessment, favourable to social reintegration, and assessing, if applicable, the personal circumstances of the prisoner and the evolution of the reeducative treatment, may agree, in a reasoned opinion, having heard the Office of Public Prosecution, Prison Institutions and other parties to the application of the general regime of compliance"*.

A second paragraph is added to it, which establishes an additional, and now definitive exception to the earlier one, according to which, *"[i]f it were a matter of crimes referring to terrorist organizations and groups and crimes of terrorism [...], or committed within criminal organizations,*[17] *and in relation to the sum total of the punishments that were imposed, only the earlier possibility will be applicable: a) to category-three prisoners, when a fifth part of the maximum sentencing term remains to be served; b) To conditional freedom, when an eighth part of the maximum sentencing term remains to be served"*.

The first sub-section, similar to situation before the reform of 2003, establishes a general exception to the exceptional restrictive regime that art. 78 imposes, and means that, in the majority of cases, things practically return to the way they were. By conditioning the application of the general regime of compliance to the same requirements that this foresees—attending to reintegration–, the result will be that, if things are done well, the occasion will never arise to apply the first section of the aforementioned article, which would be nothing other than a new manifestation of symbolic criminal Law, in this case with its *double-entendre*: directed at public opinion and without real effects on the punishment.

In fact, the sole difference in the regime of execution that is introduced in section 1 of art. 78 is none other than institutionalizing the *prima facie* intervention of the sentencing court in the phase of serving the sentence in prison, permitting or obliging it to impose exceptions to the regime of enforcement, which the judge responsible for the execution of sentences will then have to remove, if the conditions of the general regime arise. As, in any case, those conditions should always be

[15]In Spain, three prison categories are applied to prisoners: (a) prisoners subject to the most restrictive security measures; (b) prisoners subject to ordinary security measures; and, (c) prisoners under any of the modalities of open prison. The final point in this progression would be the license for conditional release.

[16]Up until Organic Law 1/2015, on the reform of the Penal Code, art. 78 established in addition that "*such an agreement will be mandatory in the circumstances envisaged in paragraphs a), b), c) and d) of section 1 of article 76, provided that the sentence to be served is lower than half of the sum total of those imposed*". The reform has fortunately suppressed this reference, which was at an extreme of the punitive scope of the precept.

[17]Before the reform of Organic Law 1/2015, on the reform of the Penal Code, criminal groups were also included, which are now excluded from this severe rule.

examined by the judge for progression to a less restrictive prison category and to obtain the licenses, the effect of the restriction on the sentence is purely symbolic: finally, everything would strictly speaking be decided in the enforcement phase.

The last paragraph, however, deserves further commentary. Here the restriction is a real and not a symbolic one. Directly, with no exception at all, those sentences imposed for crimes of terrorism or committed within the heart of criminal organizations are removed from the general regime of serving sentences. Additional requirements are established for the categorization as a third level prisoner that do not concur in any other case, introducing a restrictive criterion for the enforcement of sentences completely alien to its own dynamic, and by doing so contravening the principle of equality in relation to principle of social reintegration. It is, therefore, a regressive provision and of doubtful constitutionality.

But, neither is there support for such a doctrine, even with this additional step inspired along the lines of the Parot doctrine. The very law that defines itself as a law directed at "*cumplimiento íntegro y efectivo de las penas*" [full and effective enforcement of sentences], still recognizes that the ordinary regime is precisely contrary to the Parot doctrine, and only exceptionally, and with important limitations, does it allow its application in certain cases.

The conclusion of this section could not be clearer:

- With regard to the first question that is raised—should limits be placed on accumulation?—the response, never questioned by anyone, has always been the same: yes, there should be limits, which are fixed in art. 76 PC.
- With regard to the second question—should prison benefits be applied to the limited sentence (traditional position) or to the original sentences (Parot doctrine)?–, the law has undergone a development. In the abrogated Penal Code (PC73), there was no express decision of the law on the second question, but, *prima facie*, the teleological and systematic interpretation strongly supported the first alternative (in what follows we shall see a new systematic-historic argument that is even more decidedly in favour of this thesis). On the contrary, in the new Code, both before and after 2003, the response is clear: the normal regime of enforcement is indisputably to apply the benefits to the limited sentence (a non-Parot regime), and only exceptionally can it or should it be done to the original sentences.

4 The Interpretation in Case-Law

With regard to the position of case-law, there has also been a development here, but rather than in parallel to the legal changes, marked by its own dynamic. Three phases may be distinguished[18]:

---

[18] A detailed analysis of the development of case-law can be seen in the works of Alcácer Guirao (2012), Cuerda Arnau (2013), Nistal Burón (2013), and very especially, Rodríguez Horcajo

4.1 Period Before the Judgement of 28 February 2006 (Parot Case)

Both under the validity of PC73 and afterwards, with art. 78 of the present Code in force, case-law has practically been invariable in its preference: it has chosen without further discussion to apply the benefits to the limited sentence.[19] The sentences were consolidated in one, in accordance with art. 76, to which the benefits were applied. In the new Code, it was derived directly from the law, in which this system was described as the ordinary one, but the matter was no different in the abrogated Code. As the Supreme Court was still saying in 2005, 10 years after the approval of the new Code, the accumulated sentence now served as a new and independent penalty, and the benefits granted by the law, which are conditional freedom, and licences for release (STS 1003/2005 of 15 September 2005) have to refer to it.[20] In accordance with that, systematically, the old remission of sentences for prison work was applied to the consolidated sentence. The possibility was only accepted under the validity of the new Code, to impose the exceptional regime of enforcement, which takes the totality of the sentences that are imposed as its basis, in the cases foreseen in the new art. 78.

4.2 Period Following the Parot Judgement

The situation changed radically in 2006, after the STS 197/2006 of 28 February 2006 (Parot case) that established that the limit of 30 years was not converted into a new punishment, different from those successively imposed on the prisoner, nor therefore in another resulting from all of the earlier ones, but that such a limit represented the maximum term of imprisonment of the convicted person in a prison centre. Adding afterwards that the term "*refundición de condenas*" [consolidation of convictions] is greatly mistaken and inappropriate (FD 4). In consequence, it held that the benefits should be applied to each of the convictions that were imposed, and not the one resulting from the limitation: the convicted person should serve the punishments that were imposed in the different proceedings and successively, calculating the prison benefits with respect to each one of them individually, each with a maximum term of 30 years (FD 5).

It is very important, for the correct interpretation of this judgement, to highlight three questions: its date of issuance; the general nature of its doctrine; and its limited actual application to acts committed under the former Penal Code.

(2013), pp. 253 and ff., which conducts an extraordinarily minute analysis of all the antecedents and consequences of the Parot judgement.

[19]Thus, specifically, Rodríguez Montañés (2014), p. 139.

[20]Also, a lot earlier, in cassation of a previous judgement of the provincial court, STS of 8 March 1994.

The judgement was delivered in 2006. It was 10 years since the old Penal Code (PC73) had been repealed, and, however, what was being done was a retroactive interpretation of that Code. Due to the time that had elapsed, only very serious offences remained to be tried for which their perpetrators had not been detained: the murders committed by terrorists who had fled Spain under the earlier Code, or the very serious sexual attacks (rapes) by perpetrators up until then hidden, were the ideal candidates for this doctrine. Not so subsequent ones, simply because the exceptional regime foreseen by that time could be applied to them directly. In addition, the earlier Code contemplated the remission of sentences for prison work, and this was a legal measure, compliance with which was obligatory, which meant that the sentences of these criminals were much shorter than many considered acceptable.

The principal problem was that, unlike the situation after the new Code, the earlier one made no distinction between an ordinary and an exceptional regime. It did no more than remain silent on what to do. It meant that, if it were wished to apply through interpretative channels what would later be expressly considered by the law as exceptional, there was no other remedy than to turn it into the *ordinary* regime of the earlier Code, applicable to all those crimes in all situations of a single act constituting various offences. Only in this way could the suspicion or the certainty that it was an *ad hoc* formulation to keep terrorists in prison, whatever the law might say, be distanced from that doctrine. And the Supreme Court had no doubts over taking this surprising step in its judgement: although it is a question that has not been sufficiently highlighted, it is essential to underscore that the Parot judgement made a general interpretation—that is, *always* applicable—of real concurrence of crimes in the repealed Penal Code. And here resides its profound extravagance: using the pretext of the silence of the repealed Code, it interpreted that the ordinary system of application of prison benefits in that code was the one that the court had up until then rejected without any doubts. And, what is almost phantasmagorical, that it was the one that the new Code, in force for over 10 years, and the law that reformed it in 2003 with the unmistakable name of a law "to ensure the full and effective enforcement of sentences", had declared as exceptional. In doing so, in a pirouette that is difficult to surpass, it managed *de facto* to convert the new regulation into a reform for the "full and effective non-enforcement of sentences" except in special cases. This is so, because if, according to such a peculiar interpretation, the ordinary regime before the reforms was then expressly defined as exceptional, the effect of the reform could be none other than to separate the majority of offences from full and effective enforcement of the punishments. If this is not an unreasonable interpretation of the silence of the law, it is difficult to know what might come under this heading. And if it is, in addition, noted that this interpretation came 10 years after the legislator had specifically discounted it, except in exceptional cases, the perplexity moves up a notch.

If I am not mistaken, this systematic-historic argument by reduction to the absurd shows up to what point the Parot doctrine was not a possible interpretation of the silence of the earlier Code, according to the classic canons defined in the Civil Code. It is not possible in truth to think that the will of the legislator when incorporating art. 78 in the new Penal Code, and then reinforcing it in 2003, was to *attenuate* the rigour of full enforcement of the sentences. But it is what one would tacitly have to deduce from the doctrine. That the Supreme Court in its judgement of 2006 (fortunately with three extraordinarily critical dissenting opinions, which do honour to their authors and to the institution, to which a fourth was added in STS 734/2008 of 14 November 2008) gave its positive approval to this interpretation, and convinced a large part of society, including many notable jurists, that it was not only possible, but also lawful,[21] and that subsequently, the Constitutional Court would support it (STC, plenary session, 40/2012 of 29 March 2012, 41/2012 of 29 March 2012, 57/2012 of 29 March 2012, 68/2012 of 29 March 2012, 114/2012 of 24 May 2012, although once again fortunately with various particular dissenting opinions) is something that is still very difficult today to understand for anyone who appreciates legal science.

That the law was in addition retroactively applied is almost anecdotal, although, in a happy ending, its retroactive application was what would prove its demise in the end.[22]

4.3 *Intervention of the ECtHR*

The final and definitive phase of this process, as is well known, was marked by two judgements from the European Court of Human Rights: first in the ECtHR Judgement of 10 July 2012, c. Del Río Prada v. Spain, and then, definitively, in the ECtHR (GC) Judgement of 21 October 2013, c. Del Río Prada v. Spain. They both determined that articles 5.1 and 7 ECHR had been violated by applying a change of case-law doctrine retroactively that was not reasonably foreseeable for those it concerned at the time of committing their crimes.[23] From the perspective of a State under the rule of Law, this judgement should be unreservedly applauded, although the sad thing is that has been necessary to arrive at that point, and that the annulment

[21]The judgement was right in only one aspect. The traditional criteria for the consolidation of sentences that are imposed cannot make us forget that these maintained their independence for certain purposes. They maintain it completely with regard to everything that has to do with individual responsibility for each of the offences. If new evidence shows that the convicted person did not commit an offence, the review of the sentence only affects, as is obvious, the punishment of that offence, and not all of them. For the same reason, if a pardon is linked to a concrete act, only the punishment concerning that act is extinguished—the judgement was right on that point-. The same would happen with the pardon for the offender, if, as earlier, it were granted after the judgement, etc. In reality, the consolidation only influences those effects that justify the existence of limits to a crime involving more than one offence: to favour social reintegration. The reasonable criteria, for everything that has to do with this question, is on the basis of the limited penalty. Precisely the contrary to what the Parot doctrine proposed (Molina Fernández 2015b), p. 597.

[22]Llobet Anglí (2015) qualifies this torturous process as a "*sad legal saga with a happy ending*", p. 2.

[23]The Supreme Court assumed the judgement through its Agreement of 12 November 2013.

hinged on the question of retroactivity, and not also, and beforehand, for reasons of ordinary legality of the doctrine.[24] In fact, if the European Court of Human Rights had no doubts over the unforeseeableness of case-law changes, it was very likely because both the constant case-law up until then, as well as the most elemental interpretation of our legislation, signposted a different path to that followed by such a doctrine, which made itself completely unpredictable in that way, and that, as the voice of a dissenting magistrate of the Supreme Court said, may be qualified as "*profoundly incorrect*" (personal dissenting opinion to STS 734/2008 of 14 November 2008.

5 Some Final Remarks

The Parot doctrine has left damaged people and scars of different sorts in its wake. Having stoked social conflict a little more may for the meantime be added to its debt, on such a sensitive theme as the treatment of the criminal, especially of the terrorist criminal. But, in addition, it has certainly inflicted serious damage on the victims. One might say that it is not the Parot doctrine that has damaged them but the terrorists, rapists, etc., and that is so evident that it requires no further commentary. Or it has been those who have criticized and finally annulled this doctrine. But, in a State under the rule of Law, any other attitude against something unlawful is impossible. On the contrary, those who led society and the victims to believe that such an interpretation was possible and lawful should be the target of legitimate criticism. The victims know, and certainly many to a great degree accept that the Law should place limits on the retribution that falls on the criminal to avenge the crime, and that not everything is valid to satisfy their legitimate desire for justice. But if the Supreme Court and then the Constitutional court endorsed with a new doctrine keeping whoever inflicted such pain in prison, it is normal that the victims would then feel defrauded and resentful towards whoever, doing the right thing, brought that doctrine to an end. Upholding that belief, the Spanish courts contributed to making many people think that the release, as a consequence of the ECtHR judgement, was a victory for the murderers, and not the normal enforcement of the law, which at all times and in all places frees those who have served out their conviction, regardless of what they have done.

No less so, although certainly more difficult to appreciate for lay persons, is the damage that it has caused to the rule of Law. As highlighted very accurately by Vives Antón, the supposed novel interpretation of the Parot doctrine "*does not appear to be a victory of the Democratic State under the Rule of Law, but more so a*

[24]It never ceases to shock that the argument of ordinary legality against the Parot doctrine, which in my opinion is undisputable, had passed by relatively unperceived, while the violation of the principle of retroactivity was decisive in the end, even though from a theoretical point of view it is somewhat more delicate, as García Amado (2013, 2014) has highlighted.

serious abdication of it".[25] That the victims of society prefer solutions to immediate justice, without placing too much attention on the importance of respecting the proper guarantees of a State under the rule of Law is understandable. That our highest courts do so and that so many have applauded it is more than worrying.

It is difficult to draw something positive from the Parot doctrine, except perhaps experiences, so as not to repeat similar errors in the future and a good example for teaching, which can help young jurists to understand the subtleties of the canons of interpretation, the material problems of retroactivity, the pressure that society exerts on the courts and, therefore, the importance of carefully selecting whoever is to sit in judgement, and, in general the importance of the Democratic State remaining at all times faithful to its principles.

References

Alcácer Guirao R (2012) La Doctrina Parot ante Estrasburgo: Del Río Prada c. España (STEDH 10.7.2012, N° 42750/09). Consideraciones sobre la aplicación retroactiva de la Jurisprudencia y la ejecución de las Sentencias del TEDH. Revista de Derecho Comunitario Europeo 43:929–952

Cuerda Arnau ML (2013) Cambios jurisprudenciales y retroactividad desfavorable (a propósito de la STEDH Del Río Prada c. España). Revista Penal 31:52–69

Cuerda Riezu A (2006) El concurso real y la acumulación de penas en la Sentencia del Tribunal Supremo 197/2006, de 28 de febrero, relativa al caso Henri Parot. Observaciones legales y constitucionales Cuadernos de Derecho Judicial 7:215–296

Díez Ripollés JL (2013) Los límites a las penas máximas. Diario El País, November 12

García Amado JA (2013) La sentencia del TEDH sobre la "doctrina Parot". Consecuencias para el principio de legalidad penal Dura Lex Política, Derecho, sociedad Y algo de otras cosas [Blog], Entry from March 21, available at: http://garciamado.blogspot.com.es/2013/10/la-sentencia-del-tedh-sobre-la-doctrina.html

García Amado JA (2014) Sobre algunas consecuencias de la sentencia del TEDH en el caso Del Río Prada contra España: irretroactividad de la jurisprudencia penal desfavorable y cambios en las fuentes de producción del Derecho penal. El Cronista del Estado Social y Democrático de Derecho 41:54–63

Gómez Benítez, JM (2013) El final de la doctrina Parot. Diario El País, October 21

Hava García E (2014) Antes y después de la doctrina Parot: la refundición de condenas y sus consecuencias. Eunomía, Revista en Cultura de la Legalidad 6:153–173

Landa Gorostiza JM (2012) Ejecución de penas y principio de legalidad ante el TEDH. InDret 4:1–25

Llobet Anglí M (2011) Caso Parot. In: Sánchez-Ostiz Gutiérrez P (coord) Casos que hicieron doctrina en Derecho Penal. La Ley, Madrid, pp 895–910

Llobet Anglí M (2015) No sólo imprevisible, también irrazonable: otra vez sobre la "doctrina Parot". Indret 2:1–32

Manzanares Samaniego JL (2011) Reflexiones sobre el caso Troitiño, la doctrina Parot y los vaivenes jurisprudenciales en materia de terrorismo. Diario La Ley 7654

[25]Vives Antón (2006). Equally, in the opinion of Rodríguez Montañés (2014, p. 151), with the annulment of the Parot doctrine "*a dark chapter in our democracy and our State under the rule of Law*" ended.

Molina Fernández F (2015a) Concursos de leyes y de delitos. In: Molina Fernández F (coord), Memento Práctico Penal 2016. Francis Lefebvre, Madrid, pp 411–422
Molina Fernández F (2015b) Reglas de determinación de la pena. In: Molina Fernández F (coord) Memento Práctico Penal 2016. Francis Lefebvre, Madrid, pp 577–612
Nistal Burón J (2013) El controvertido periplo judicial de la "doctrina Parot" (De la Sección 1ª de la Sala de lo Penal de la Audiencia nacional al Tribunal de Estrasburgo). Diario La Ley 8068
Orts Berenguer E (2009) Comentarios a la Sentencia de la Sala Segunda de lo Penal del Tribunal Supremo 197/2006, de 28 de febrero (caso Parot). Revista de l'Institut Universitari d'Investigació en Criminologia i Ciències Penals de la Universitat de Valencia 1:27–43
Rodríguez Horcajo D (2013) Nulla poena sine lege y retroactividad de cambios jurisprudenciales: modificaciones tras la STEDH as. Del Río Prada c. España (21/10/2013). Anuario de Derecho Penal y Ciencias Penales 66:252–292
Rodríguez Montañés T (2014) Doctrina Parot: claves para entender las sentencias del TEDH en el caso Del Río Prada c. España Eunomía 6:137–152
Savater F (2013a) Fuera del área. Diario El País, October 25
Savater F (2013b). Penalty. Diario El País, October 30
Vives Antón T (2006) Una sentencia discutible. El País, March 11
Vives Antón T (2013) ¿Estado de derecho a la carta? El País, October 26

The Annulment of the Parot Doctrine by the European Court of Human Rights. ECtHR Judgement of 21 October 2013: Much Ado Over a Legally Awaited Judgement

Susana Huerta Tocildo

1 Origin and Meaning of the So-called Parot Doctrine

Henri Parot, convicted of crimes of terrorism, was the direct protagonist of the doctrine established under his name by the Supreme Court (SC) in its STS 197/2006 of 28 February 2006 (hereinafter: STS 197/2006). Curiously, he was not the principal character in its definitive annulment by the European Court of Human Rights (ECtHR), dated 21 of October 2013, because his appeal for "*amparo*" (relief) before the Spanish Constitutional Court (hereinafter SCC) was turned down in the decision of that Court in ATC 1979/2010 of 29 November. A decision that was due to the absence of the formal requirement of having exhausted all possible remedies of appeal before the ordinary jurisdiction, thereby definitively closing the door to any appeal to the European Court at Strasbourg. The doctrine contained in STS 197/2006—that had been retroactively applied to deny him the release from prison that he had sought on the grounds of having served his sentence—did, however, leap over all the barriers and was brought before the European court[1] in the course of the appeal presented by another prisoner convicted

Former Law Clerk at the Spanish Constitutional Court (1991–1997; 2002–2006). Former Jurist-Reviewer to the European Parliament (1988–1991). Former Jurist-Linguist to the Court of Justice of the European Union (1986–1988). Former Professor of Criminal Law, Universidad Complutense de Madrid. The present article was originally published in the Revista Jurídica de Catalunya 113 (2014):11–37. The notes of the author to the last version of her article "El contenido debilitado del principio de legalidad penal (Art. 7 CEDH y art. 4 P7)" have been updated.

[1]Hence the title of the article published by Díaz Crego (2013), "Cuando Parot llegó a Estrasburgo", although it was not Parot who would get there but the doctrine that had emerged as a result of the presentation on his behalf of an appeal for cassation before the Supreme Court.

S. Huerta Tocildo (✉)
Universidad Complutense de Madrid, Ciudad Universitaria, 28040 Madrid, Spain
e-mail: mercedesp.manzano@uam.es

M. Pérez Manzano et al. (eds.), *Multilevel Protection of the Principle of Legality in Criminal Law*, DOI 10.1007/978-3-319-63865-2_8

of terrorism, Inés del Río Prada, to whom the doctrine had likewise been applied with the same effects but, unlike Parot, her appeal had met the formal requirements of the Constitutional Court, although as will be seen later on, she too would be denied the relief she sought.

We could, in consequence, refer to the annulment of the Parot doctrine by the Del Río Prada doctrine laid down by the ECtHR; however, given the constant references in legal and media circles to the first of those two doctrines, she will also be referred to throughout this work for the purposes of greater expositional clarity. But, what was the content of the so frequently cited and now annulled Parot doctrine? I will not go on at great length here in detailing it, because it has been the object of various commentaries.[2] Instead, in the course of an essential summary to approach its study, it may be affirmed that the doctrine basically consisted of applying the calculation of the benefits of remissions of sentence for prison work, repealed in the Spanish legal order following the entry into force of the Penal Code of 1995 (PC95), not to the maximum sentencing limit set at 30 years by article 70.2 of the aforementioned Penal Code, as had been the standard practice of the courts, but to each penalty that had been imposed. So, in cases of conviction to lengthy terms of imprisonment, in reality it implied the non-application of any remissions of sentence due to that benefit and, in consequence, the effective enforcement of that maximum limit.

What was the reason for such a sharp and surprising change of paradigm? It is, in my opinion, necessary to examine the socio-political context in which the above-mentioned change took place, in order to ascertain that reason: the Parot doctrine emanates from a Judgement of the Supreme Court in 2006, at a time when numerous releases of prisoners were about to take place. They had been sentenced to very much higher terms of imprisonment than 30 years for acts of terrorism that occurred during the 1980s. However, with the limitation of article 70.2 PC73 and the retroactive application of that text as a more favourable Law, according to the interpretation that up until that date the courts had generally applied to the benefits of remissions of sentence for work, these sentences would have been reduced by approximately one third of their duration; the equivalent, in consequence, to 20 years of effective deprivation of freedom. However: in the above-mentioned context there was certainly a clear political will, even expressed in public by some members of the government, that the release from prison should not take place "*en masse*", which I understand was a decisive factor in the legal search for a new interpretative criteria of articles 70.2 and 100 of PC73.[3] A new interpretative criteria is evidently expressed in STS 197/2006, previously criticized in its day by numerous jurists, on account not only of its retroactive, but also its

[2]Vid., among others, Díaz Crego (2013), Alcácer Guirao (2012), Cuerda Arnau (2013), Landa Gorostiza (2012). It has to be noted that unlike the present work, all of the above works refer exclusively to the ECtHR Judgement of 17 July 2012, the first of those delivered by the ECtHR, nonetheless they have not lost relevance today as the criteria upheld in the first instance and on appeal coincide.

[3]Cfr., in the same sense: Rodríguez Montañés (2013).

extemporaneous nature, as that interpretation was based on nothing less than a set of provisions abolished 10 years earlier.[4]

The effects of the Parot doctrine were not long in coming. As said, to begin with in practice, it meant the non-application of the benefit of remissions of sentence for work to inmates, who had been sentenced to accumulated penalties of well over 30 years of prison. It implied a significant rise—by approximately one third—in the effective time of imprisonment that had been imposed. But, in addition, the retroactive application *in malam partem* of the "Parot doctrine" to prisoners convicted in accordance with the provisions of the 1973 Penal Code constituted a highly incongruent decision with the mandate of determining which law was most favourable when taking into account the benefits of sentence remission for work: whether it was the regulation foreseen in PC73, in force at the time the acts were committed, or the criteria established in PC95 that had replaced the former, in which the aforementioned benefit had been suppressed. Finally, it hardly has to be said that the outcome of this "novel" legal interpretation was the paralysation of the prison releases that were underway, which had as an additional consequence, the appearance of patent inequalities in the application of the law, given that many prisoners in the same situation had already been released before the aforementioned change in paradigm. However, it has to be recognized that the abundant reasoning contained in the Supreme Court Judgements to justify this change of paradigm made the claim of a violation of article 14 Spanish Constitution (SC) quite impossible, given the restrictive doctrine set down in this respect by the SCC.[5]

2 The Point of View of the Spanish Constitutional Court on the Application of the Parot Doctrine

In view of all these problems—some of which are irredeemable, as I will have the opportunity to express in these pages, given their evident confrontation with some of the requirements of the principle of criminal legality–, the question that we shall now ask is the following: why did the SCC, to which various inmates affected by the Parot doctrine had turned for *amparo*, not take steps to abolish it, without them having to seek, as a final resort, the protection of the ECtHR?

As has been said, the petition for constitutional protection presented by Henri Parot was not admitted, due to his not having exhausted all remedies for appeal

[4]Vid., for example: Vives Antón (2006), Cuerda Riezu (2006), García-Pablos de Molina (2006), pp. 192 and 206; Muñoz Clares (2006), Llobet Anglí (2011).

[5]Which is clearly confirmed in view of STC 39/2012 of 29 March 2012, FJ 3, in which it is affirmed that *"[. . .] neither selective voluntarism may be appreciated, nor unreasoned distancing from the criterion that has been applied, consolidated and maintained up until this point by the court, the decisions of which are challenged, which constitutes the essence of the application of inequality according to our case-law"*.

through ordinary legal channels, insofar as the applicant had not lodged the obligatory appeal for the nullification of STS 197/2006, based on the inconsistency *of extra petita partium,* having taken cognizance in that decision of a question—the calculation of the benefit of sentence remission for work—that nobody had raised. The remainder of the appeals that had been submitted were for the most part accepted for review by the court, giving rise to a battery of decisions of different types: it was a question, for the most part, of unfavourable Judgements, in which the claim relating to the violation of a fundamental right to legality arising from the retroactive application of new unfavourable case-law was rejected outright[6]; in very few cases were the *amparo* appeals in question upheld. Where they were upheld, it was not because of a violation of article 25.1 SC, but because of the violation of the principle of intangibility of *res judicata*, integrated in the framework of the protection of the fundamental right to effective judicial protection (article 24.1 SC), in connection with the violation of the right to personal freedom (article 17.1 SC).[7]

In relation with the absence of any appreciation of a violation of the right to legality in the judicial decisions to which the Parot Doctrine was applied, the Constitutional Court basically developed for the first time, in STC 39/2012 of 29 March, the following arguments:

1. The new doctrine on the method for the calculation of the benefits of remissions of sentence for prison work is not a question that affects the sentence that is imposed, but the enforcement of the sentence, so it therefore remains outside the scope of the fundamental right to criminal legality recognized in article 25.1 SC.
2. The case-law of the ECtHR has frequently declared that the questions relating to sentence enforcement are not integrated in the content of article 7 ECHR, although they can affect the right to freedom.
3. Neither serving a longer term of imprisonment than is foreseen for the criminal offences under reference nor exceeding the maximum of 30 years established in article 70 PC73 are derived from the application of the controversial judicial doctrine.
4. The right to criminal legality does not include a right to the non-retroactivity of changes in judicial interpretation that may be unfavourable.

As previously said, some, –comparatively few[8]—of the *amparo* appeals presented by prisoners convicted of crimes of terrorism, whose release from prison had been turned down on account of the retroactive application of the Parot

[6]Vid. SSTC delivered on 29 March 2012, under the following references: 40, 41, 42, 43, 44, 45, 46, 47, 48, 49, 50, 51, 52, 53, 54, 55, 56, 59, 61, 64, 65, 66, 67, 68 and 69; vid. likewise, SSTC 108/2012 of 21 May, and 114/2012 of 24 June.

[7]Vid. SSTC 39/2012 and 57/2012 of 29 March; 113/2012 of 24 June.

[8]Specifically, those that gave rise to SSTC 39/2012 and 57/2012 and 62/2012, of 29 March and 113/2012, of 24 June.

doctrine, resulted in favourable Judgements, because the Constitutional Court considered that such a decision contradicted the fundamental right to effective judicial protection when it contradicted the content of an earlier judicial decision that had acquired the status of a final judgement on the remission of a sentence.

Succinctly expressed, the reasoning that the Constitutional Court advanced in these cases follows the pattern laid down by the State Attorney in its report on the appeal for *amparo* that led to STC 39/2012, in which it considered: "*it is not acceptable that, certain criteria of normative interpretation established in a judicial decision to set the remission of a sentence [. . .], [. . .] may vary on the basis of a new interpretation of the applicable norms [. . .], the application of which to the present case violates the right to the intangibility of final decisions ex art. 24.1 SC*".

In STC 39/2012 of 29 March, a violation is also appreciated of the right to personal freedom (art. 17.1 SC) in close connection with the right to the intangibility of judicial decisions that were likewise considered violated.[9] On the contrary, in STC 40/2012 of 29 March, the violation of the right to personal freedom was excluded, as the above-mentioned principle of intangibility. In this case, the reasoning was as follows: "*it may be concluded that, in the present case, there has neither been a violation of the right to effective legal protection in its aspect of intangibility of final judicial decisions (art. 24.1 SC) nor, in this cause, a violation of the right to personal freedom (art. 17.1 SC). In effect, neither may the existence of a final judicial and intangible decision be affirmed from which the application of a doctrine to the case is derived for the calculation of remissions of sentence for work other than that applied in the decision that is appealed against, nor may it be affirmed that the appellant had a legitimate and solid expectation, derived from the previous actions of the courts in the present enforceable judgement, of achieving his release at a time other than that arising from the judicial decisions that are appealed against*" (FJ 10).

In summary: the Constitutional Court in no way upheld the presence of an autonomous violation of the right to personal freedom, but instead made it dependent on the previous affirmation of the existence of a violation of the right to

---

[9]The reasoning that was upheld in this regard in STC 39/2012, FJ 8 is as follows: "*[. . .] in application of the existing legal framework at the time of committing the criminal act and calculating the remission of the sentence for work in accordance with the firm and intangible doctrine established by the court responsible for its enforcement, the applicant has already served the sentence that had been imposed upon him. Therefore, and although the applicant was legitimately deprived of his liberty, having served the sentence in the terms previously set out, we are confronted a case of deprivation of liberty beyond those cases envisaged in the law, because the law that legitimized it is now repealed. Therefore, the excess time spent in prison constitutes a privation of liberty lacking any legal basis and in breach of the fundamental right to freedom enshrined in art. 17.1 SC (STC 322/2005, of 12 December, Pts. of Law 2 and 3; and ECtHR of 10 July 2003, Grava v. Italy §§ 44–45). Under the Rule of Law, the deprivation of liberty of a person who has already served the conviction imposed upon him in its day cannot be prolonged, hence the ordinary courts have to adopt, as swiftly as possible, the relevant decisions, so that the violation of the fundamental right to liberty is ended and steps are immediately taken to release the applicant*".

effective legal protection. It has therefore to be supposed that following this same logic, had a breach of the right to criminal legality been appreciated, then the Court would likewise have pronounced in favour of a violation of article 17.1 SC. But, as has already been seen, it did no such thing, the appreciation of the aforesaid violation remaining, in consequence, limited to the few circumstances of favourable Judgements, due to a violation of article 24.1 SC.

3 The Evaluation of the Parot Doctrine by the ECtHR

In this way, we arrive at the heart of the question that is the principal object of this work, relating to the very controversial—although, as a general rule, in areas that are not representative of strictly legal thought processes—repeal of the Parot Doctrine by the ECtHR, through the decision on the appeal presented by one of those its application affected: Inés Del Río Prada.

In relation with that appeal, two successive judgements were handed down from the ECtHR –10 July 2012 and 21 October 2013. The latter was heard before the Grand Chamber on appeal by the Kingdom of Spain against the judgement mentioned in the first place—in which violations of both the principle of legality and the right to liberty were appreciated as a consequence of the Parot doctrine. The arguments developed on both sides are practically coincident, although greater care in their defence is observable in the judgement adopted by the Grand Chamber. Linked to the knowledge that the judgement pronounced in the first instance had previously been the object of numerous doctrinal commentaries will, for reasons of conciseness and the inherent limits on the length of a paper of this type, mean that I will centre my analysis on the contents of the ECtHR Judgement of 21 October 2013, c. Del Río Prada v. Spain.

3.1 The Motives of the Appeal Presented Before the ECtHR

I will start by referring briefly to the criminal situation of the applicant and the reasons for her appeal before the Court at Strasbourg. It was a matter of a conviction for various crimes of terrorism (murder) with very high prison terms that when added up amounted to no less than 3000 years of prison, but they were subject to the maximum limit of 30 years established at the time in article 70 of the 1973 Penal Code. By application of the benefit for remission of sentence through prison work, applicable to her, because it constituted—precisely because of its existence in that earlier Penal Code, prior to its effacement in the one that came to substitute it—more favourable criminal law, in accordance with reiterated case-law, she would have been released on 3 July 2008. Such an expectation for release was nevertheless cut short when the Parot doctrine was applied to her with the consequence that, by decision of the Audiencia Nacional of 15 February 2001, confirmed in a further Court Order of 23 June 2008, a new date for the completion of the sentence was set at 27 June 2017, which implied a considerable increase of almost 9 years over and above her initial expectations for compliance with the sentences imposed on her.[10]

An *amparo* appeal presented against the decision to extend her sentence was rejected in the Decision of the SCC of 17 February 2009, because the applicant had not justified the constitutional significance of her complaints, referring principally to the violation of the principle of non-retroactivity of unfavourable criminal norms (enshrined in both article 25.1 SC and in article 7 ECHR) and of her right to personal freedom (article 17.1 SC and article 5.1 ECHR).

These two submissions were reiterated before the Court at Strasbourg and both were upheld in accordance with the arguments that will be explained in this section. Leading up to this explanation, I think it will be convenient, however, to highlight the principal aspects that the conformation of the main principle of legality of article 7.1 ECHR presents in the case-law of the ECtHR, so that, far from what some have affirmed with astounding frivolity or lack of rigour, it may be clearly confirmed that the judgements of the ECtHR delivered in the Case of Del Río Prada have not only not distanced themselves one iota from that case-law but, quite on the contrary, have continued to apply it in an absolutely foreseeable manner.

3.2 *The Elements of the Principle of European Legality (Art. 7.1 ECHR)*

With regard to the principle of criminal legality, the ECtHR has, especially over these past few years, been developing a consolidated doctrine, the principal features[11] of which could be summarised in the following way:

[10] I must add that Del Río Prada was definitively released on 22 October, 2013, by Order of the Criminal Chamber of the *Audiencia Nacional* [Spanish High Court], delivered in application of the Judgement pronounced by the ECtHR the previous day, which meant she had effectively served a prison sentence of approximately 26 years. A term that might appear short to some—of course, it appeared so to certain associations of victims of terrorism and, what is criticizable from all sides, to some governmental bodies that forgot the fundamental role that the ECtHR plays in our legal system in accordance with the Treaties to which the Kingdom of Spain has subscribed and our own Constitution–, but from strictly penological points of view it greatly exceeds what is generally established as a limit so that the principle of resocialization—in its purest meaning of the reintegration of the ex-criminal so that he can develop a life in freedom in a more or less normal way—can be of some efficacy. In this sense, although the pain of the victims, who would have preferred them to stay in prison for as long as possible, appears understandable to me from all points of view, I consider some of the comments that appeared in the communications media, in which it was maintained that the terrorists had "got away with it", quite unacceptable.

[11] For a more detailed description of this conformation of the principle of legality by the ECtHR, vid. Huerta Tocildo (2014), *passim*.

1. In accordance with the aforementioned text of article 7 ECHR, the regulatory sources of Criminal Law are not limited—as happens in positive Spanish Law—to the law understood in the formal sense, but are enlarged in accordance with the special characteristics of a system that aspires to be applicable to countries with different legal regimes, to case-law, custom and the general principles of Law.
2. The role attributed to case-law by the ECtHR stands out especially, as an instance with more than a merely interpretative function of criminal offenses, but one that even defines them or is complementary to them.
3. In any case, so that this broad concept of the law can be fitted into the limits of article 7, the ECtHR demands that it must necessarily meet the requirements of accessibility and foreseeability.
4. The bundle of guarantees specific to the aforementioned principle coincide with the guarantees traditionally attributed to the same principle in the Spanish legal order, having to highlight the recent incorporation in its content of the right to the retroactivity of a more favourable criminal law.
5. The concept of the penalty in article 7 ECHR is an independent concept of the Convention, determined in each case by the ECtHR in accordance with the concurrent circumstances.

All of these elements are present in the ECtHR Judgement of 21 October 2013,[12] highlighting those elements in its analysis that relate to the necessary foreseeability of criminal law (both with regard to the description of the offence and with regard to the foreseeable penalty) and the prohibition on the retroactivity of unfavourable criminal law.

With regard to the first of these requirements, the Grand Chamber concluded, as it had previously done in the ECtHR Judgement of 10 July 2012 delivered in the first instance, that, given the concurrent circumstances in this case, "*it had been difficult, or even impossible, for the applicant to imagine, at the material time and also at the time when all the sentences were combined and a maximum term of imprisonment fixed, that the Supreme Court would depart from its previous case-law in 2006 and change the way remissions of sentence were applied, that this departure from case-law would be applied to her case and that the duration of her incarceration would be substantially lengthened as a result*" (par. 60).

The requirements of accessibility and foreseeability of criminal law are a constant theme in the case-law of the ECtHR on article 7.1 ECHR, although it is true that the precisions made to date, with regard to the latter, are not excessive. The case-law limits itself to specifying that its scope depends, in large part, on the content of the text that it concerns, on the scope that it covers, as well as on the number and quality of the people it addresses.[13] It should nevertheless not be understood as incompatible with the necessity that the affected person may have

[12]Vid. par. 78 and section D.1.b.

[13]Vid., for example, ECtHR Judgement of 22 October 1996, c. Cantoni v. France.

of seeking clarificatory advice to evaluate up to a reasonable degree, given the circumstances, the consequences that may arise from a particular act.[14]

With regard to the role that case-law plays, it is quite clear from the text of article 7 ECHR that this role is superior to and not coincident with the role that it is given, in criminal law, in countries with traditional types of legal systems, since it is elevated to nothing less than a normative source of law in that precept. Nothing else may, in fact, be inferred from the interpretation given by the ECtHR to the terms "*law*" and "*droit*", respectively used in the English and French versions of the aforementioned precept, in the sense of considering that they both refer to a "*concept which comprises statute law as well as case-law*",[15] and that is regardless of its written or non-written nature.[16]

The admission of case-law as a source of criminal law implies that case-law, to consider it compatible with the guarantees of article 7 of the Convention, meet the same requirements of accessibility and foreseeability that are required from the law understood in a formal sense. The ECtHR interprets it in this way when it states that, to be able to affirm the pre-existence of a "law" in the sense of the aforementioned provision, it is necessary that all criminal norms, whether of a written or unwritten nature, meet those two requirements and are enounced with sufficient precision so that everyone may foresee the consequences that are derived from their actions or from their omission.[17]

Article 7.1 makes no specific mention of the principle of the retroactivity of more favourable criminal law, in spite of it usually going hand in hand with the principle of non-retroactivity in the continental tradition of penal codes. However, whether it is or it is not considered part of the principle of legality in criminal law, the mandate of the retroactivity of more favourable subsequent law constitutes an unrenounceable tenet of criminal law, insofar as it is nothing but a necessary derivation of a correct understanding of the principle of non-retroactivity; and that is so even though both propositions certainly differ with regard to their foundation, because the first aims to guarantee individual freedom, while the second functions as a strict guarantee of legal certainty.

The omission of all references in article 7 ECHR to the aforementioned principle has, however, been no obstacle for the ECtHR to consider it within its area of protection. It did indeed do so in the ECtHR Judgement of 17 September 2009,

[14]Vid. the above-mentioned *Cantoni* judgement and also the ECtHR Judgement of 25 November 1997, c. Grigoriades v. Greece, and ECtHR Judgement of 8 July 1999, c. Erdogdu and Ince v. Turkey.

[15]ECtHR Judgement of 22 June 2000, c. Coeme and others v. Belgium. Vid., on the same point, among others, ECtHR Judgement of 15 November 1996, c. Cantoni v. France; ECtHR Judgement of 10 October 2006, c. Pessino v. France.

[16]Vid. a more careful analysis of the role that the ECtHR attributes to case-law in the context of art. 7 ECtHR in Huerta Tocildo (2014), pp. 530–533.

[17]Vid., among many others: the ECtHR Judgements of 24 May 1988, c. Müller and others v. Switzerland; ECtHR Judgements of 25 May 1993, c. Kokkinakis v. Greece; ECtHR Judgements of 15 November 1996, c. Cantoni v. France.

c. Scoppola v. Italy, in which it recalled that, in earlier decisions, it had adopted a contrary position to considering that the principle of the retroactivity of more favourable criminal law lay outside article 7.[18] It clearly distanced itself from those precedents, by considering that significant changes had come about since then—such as the entry into force of article 49.1 and the Court of Justice of the European Union Judgement of 3 May 2005, delivered in the Case of Berlusconi and others, in which it was recognized that the principle formed part of the constitutional traditions common to member States–. So its revision was convenient with a view to a correct interpretation of the principle of proportionality, because to impose a more severe penalty for the sole reason that it was the legally foreseen one at the time of the offence would be equal to ignoring all legislative change favourable to the accused that may have been introduced before the conviction. In consequence, it would amount to imposing a penalty on the defendant that both the State and the society have previously considered excessive and unnecessary. In consequence, the ECtHR, in this important decision, rectified its earlier point of view and concluded that, despite not having been explicitly covered in article 7 of the Convention, it had to be considered that the aforementioned provision guaranteed not only the non-retroactivity of the subsequent unfavourable law, but also the retroactivity of the more favourable subsequent law.

Finally, with regard to the concept of "penalty" that appears in article 7 ECHR, it was expressly stated in the ECtHR Judgement of 22 June 2000, c. Coeme v. France, that it has an autonomous scope that allows the Court, in order to make effective the protection offered in that article, to go further than appearances and to appreciate whether a specific measure is converted into a "penalty" in the sense of that clause, for which, regardless of the denomination that it may have received, the nature and final purpose of the measure, its qualification in internal Law, the procedures associated with its imposition and enforcement, and its severity will all have to be taken into account.[19]

[18] Vid. the Decision of the Commission of Human Rights of 6 March 1978, delivered in the Case of X v. Germany, in which the claim of the applicant that article 7 had been violated was declared inadmissible for not having applied a law subsequent to the time of committing the acts in which the conduct for which the applicant had been convicted was decriminalized. On that occasion, the Commission expressly concluded that the provision referred to in the Convention did not include the right to the retroactivity of the more favourable criminal law. Vid., in the same sense, ECtHR Judgement of 5 December 2000, c. Le Petit v. United Kingdom; ECtHR Judgement 6 March 2003, c. Zaprianov v. Bulgaria.

[19] Criteria previously proclaimed in the ECtHR Judgement of 9 February 1995, c. Welch v. the United Kingdom. In the same sense, ECtHR Judgement of 12 February 2008, c. Kafkaris v. Cyprus; ECtHR Judgement of 17 September 2009, c. Scoppola v. Italy.

3.3 *The Application of the Former Criteria in the ECtHR Judgement of 21 October 2013: Special Consideration of the Distinction Between Determination and Execution of the Penalty*

The application of the retroactive legal interpretation *in malam partem*, known as the Parot doctrine, of the criterion of foreseeability used to assess the compatibility of a criminal law—in the broad sense mentioned earlier—with the text of article 7 ECHR required a preliminary step from the ECtHR consisting of the incorporation in the concept of penalty mentioned in that provision of the particular result of jointly applying the norm in which the maximum limit of 30 years of execution was established and the norm that, up until 1995, had regulated the remission of sentence for prison work.

With this introduction of the joint interplay between the above-mentioned rules in the concept of the penalty, and not in the execution of the penalty—that is, in the phase of determining the maximum imposable penalty and not merely in the following phase of its enforcement—the ECtHR sought to resolve the principal argument advanced, among others, by the Spanish Constitutional Court to deny the application to this case of the guarantees arising from the principle of penal legality. The Court at Strasbourg had certainly been using this distinction, and continues to do so, between what is strictly the "penalty" and the "enforcement of the penalty", in order to make effective the demarcation between those cases that fall under the scope of protection of article 7 ECHR and those others that remain outside its coverage. But it is no less true that the Court had also previously noted that such a distinction is not always easy to establish in practice and that to do so, it will be necessary, beyond any appearances, to attend to whether or not a concrete measure substantially equates with a "penalty" in the sense of article 7 of the Convention.[20]

In its Judgement of 21 October 2013—in my opinion very correctly–, after highlighting the autonomous concept of "penalty" in the Convention and reiterating the distinction between those measures that "in substance" constitute a penalty and those others that uniquely refer to their enforcement or application, the ECtHR recalled that in effect, as it had said on other occasions, the distinction between one and the other might not always be clear. In consequence, the Court was not ready to "*rule out the possibility that measures taken by the legislature, the administrative authorities or the courts after the final sentence has been imposed or while the sentence is being served may result in the redefinition or modification of the scope of the "penalty" imposed by the trial court. When that happens, the Court considers that the measures concerned should fall within the scope of the prohibition of the retroactive application of penalties enshrined in Article 7 § 1* in fine *of the Convention*" (par. 89). So then: in this case, the ECtHR strictly concluded that, as the new interpretation advanced by the Spanish Supreme Court in 2006 involved

[20]Vid. Huerta Tocildo (2014), pp. 533–536.

the retroactive effect of extending the time in prison by almost 9 years "*this measure not only concerned the execution of the applicant's sentence, but also had a decisive impact on the scope of the "penalty" for the purposes of Article 7*" (par. 59).

With this first conclusion set down, the next one to reach was the response to the question of what the basis should be on which that reduction had to operate: whether on each of the sentences imposed—as STS 197/2006 of the Supreme Court maintained—or on the maximum limit of 30 years established at the time in PC73. In the opinion of the ECtHR, the response was clear in this last sense, given that the applicant could not have foreseen the interpretative variation introduced somewhat after the time of the facts by the Supreme Court, but that "*while she was serving her prison sentence [. . .] the applicant had every reason to believe that the penalty imposed was the thirty-year maximum term, from which any remissions of sentence for work done in detention would be deducted*" (par. 100); a belief that would, apart from anything else, be endorsed by the point that it was precisely the very existence of such a benefit that had systematically led the courts to consider that PC73 was more favourable than PC, which would make it meaningless to have arrived at the conclusion that the benefit lost all efficacy in the case of multiple prison sentences of extended duration in so far as, before it could be applied, the aforementioned maximum limit would have been exceeded.

It has been said—and the Kingdom of Spain claimed it to be so in its appeal before the ECtHR of 10 July 2012—that the inclusion of the effects of remission of sentence for work and its benefits in the concept of "penalty" of article 7 ECtHR contradicted what the ECtHR had decided earlier in its Judgement of 12 February 2008, c. Kafkaris v. Cyprus. In that case, it arrived at the conclusion that the benefit of conditional remission of the sentence and the mechanism of conditional freedom were not an integral part of that concept of penalty. Hence, the changes introduced in its regulation following the committal of the offense were not subject to the principle of non-retroactivity. It was in the circumstances of a conviction of life-imprisonment limited in reality to 20 years' imprisonment by the provision of a prison rule that would subsequently be annulled. The rule was substituted by a law that retroactively amended that maximum limit and that was applied to the applicant, notwithstanding which, without the ECtHR appreciating in this case a retroactive application of *reformatio in peius*, despite it supposing a substantial modification of his status as a prisoner by converting a prison term of a particular duration into a term of life imprisonment.

Such a criterion is to my mind more than debatable,[21] especially in view of that very decision in which it is expressly noted that the distinction between both measures "*is perhaps not always clear in practice*". Having taken account of this last affirmation, added to the scarce (if not to say inexistent) fundamental reasoning of the distinction under question, and in spite of the prison rule in existence, at the time of the acts, that restricted the penalty of life imprisonment to a maximum limit

[21]For a critical view of this ECtHR Judgement, vid. Cuerda Arnau (2013), pp. 65–66.

of twenty, the conclusion of considering that the subsequent repeal of that temporal limit implies no retroactive variation in the sentence that was imposed on the applicant appears surprising to me and quite frankly open to criticism. Especially if it is taken into account that this conclusion is accompanied by another that in my opinion comes to contradict it,[22] to wit: that there was in this case a violation of art. 7 ECtHR, given the lack of quality of the Cypriot law that was applicable to the applicant, which would have prevented him from discerning the scope of that penalty to a reasonable degree; an affirmation from which, however, no further conclusion was drawn because, according to the ECtHR, "*this matter relates to the execution of the sentence as opposed to the "penalty" imposed on him, which remains that of life imprisonment. Although the changes in the prison legislation and in the conditions of release may have rendered the applicant's imprisonment effectively harsher, these changes cannot be construed as imposing a heavier 'penalty' than that imposed by the trial court*".

I can therefore only partially share the positive assessment expressed in the sense that the decision in this case "*marks a cyclical change in the evolution of ECtHR case law in matters concerning the application of art. 7 ECtHR to questions, up until that time, relegated outside its area of control because they are considered pure execution of the penalties*".[23] It is true that, in the case of *Kafkaris*, the Court at Strasbourg proceeded to introduce the question debated in the sphere of the protection of article 7 of the Convention and, more specifically, in the concept of "penalty" employed in that provision, as the positive decision of the Court on its violation due to a lack of quality of the law may only be explained on those grounds. But this supposed advance is left in doubt when reaching the conclusion, hardly compatible with the above, that the inclusion of the case within the margins of article 7 ECHR does not entail the application of all the guarantees contained in that provision, present among which is, without any doubt, the right to the non-retroactivity of unfavourable criminal "laws".

In any case, and beyond these criticisms, some notable differences have to be observed between the case of *Kafkaris* and the case of *Del Río Prada*. In this respect, although it is recognized that the ECtHR, in its Judgement of 21 October 2013, recognizes that it had admitted on other occasions that a reform of the prison legislation applied retroactively, which would exclude offenders sentenced to life imprisonment from the eventual benefit of remissions of sentence for prison work, concerned the execution of the penalty and not the penalty that was imposed, the Court subsequently stated, with regard to the claims made by the Kingdom of

[22]Thus, it is expressly affirmed in the dissenting opinion of Judge Borrego that accompanies this Judgement, in the following terms: "*[...] the majority find a violation of Article 7 but at the same time observe that "there is no element of retrospective imposition of a heavier penalty involved in the present case". In other words, there is a breach of the principle "no punishment without law" and yet no heavier penalty was retrospectively imposed. What a superb contradiction!". Moreover, in their understanding, the same distinction "between a penalty breaching the Convention and its implementation being in conformity with the Convention is quite magnificent"*.

[23]Cfr. Landa Gorostiza (2012), p. 14.

Spain, that this case differed from those "*which clearly concerned the penalty as opposed to its execution*" in so far as the controversial measure in them "*concerned remissions of sentence or "early release", not the maximum term that could be served in respect of the sentences imposed, which had not changed*" (par. 72). Furthermore, it also pointed to the existence of another substantial difference with those cases that, in this case, meant "*remissions of sentence for work done in detention were expressly provided for by statutory law (Article 100 of the Criminal Code of 1973), and not by regulations*" (par. 101). Up until the STS 197/2006, Article 100 had usually been interpreted as directly applicable to the maximum limit of 30 years of serving the term of imprisonment established in article 70.2 PC73, a limit that was configured in that way as a new *"autonomous conviction"* giving rise to a clear distinction between *"a penalty that is imposed"* and *"a penalty to serve"*.[24] So then: having accounted for those differences in the "flexible" concept of the penalty that the ECtHR handled practically *ad casum* and the value that it conceded to the legal interpretation, it may, in short, be affirmed that the ECtHR Judgements of 10 July 2012 and of 21 October 2013 have not meant an unforeseeable and unmotivated departure of the ECtHR from its earlier line of case-law, but an application of its consolidated criteria on the matter since the ECtHR Judgement of 9 February 1955, c. Welch v. the United Kingdom.

Once having situated the question in the context of the concept of the "penalty" in article 7 ECtHR and not in its execution, the following step taken by the ECtHR consisted in testing whether or not the interpretative variation represented by the Parot doctrine was foreseeable for those whom it addressed.[25]

In this respect, a complex argument was developed in the Judgements that are commented on, in which, after a detailed study of the Spanish legislation in force at the time the acts were committed and their development in case-law, it was concluded that the change in the paradigm introduced through STS 197/2006 was unforeseeable for the applicant. In the first place, because, in view of judicial and administrative practice with regard to the calculation of the remission of sentence for work before the Parot doctrine, it could not be expected "*that the penalty imposed might turn into thirty years of actual imprisonment, with no reduction for the remissions of sentence for work done in detention provided for in Article 100 of the Criminal Code of 1973*" (par. 112). In second place, because this punitive text was applied to him precisely on the basis that it was the most favourable law, from which the ECtHR deduced that "*in opting, as a transitional measure, to maintain the effects of the rules concerning remissions of sentence for work done in detention and for the purposes of determining the most lenient criminal law, the*

[24]For a more careful development of this difference, vid. Alcácer Guirao (2012), pp. 940 and ff.

[25]Confirmation that was necessary given that, as Alcácer Guirao affirmed, in the "*[...] use of flexible standards that characterize the Court at Strasbourg, the application of the canon of non-retroactivity does not adopt a rigid chronological criteria, but makes the affectation of article 7 ECHR depend on the core guarantee of foreseeability*", in such a way that "*[...] only when the change introduced in case-law subsequent to the acts might be unforeseeable for the citizen will the right be violated*" (2012, p. 942).

Spanish legislature considered those rules to be part of substantive criminal law, that is to say of the provisions which affected the actual fixing of the sentence, not just its execution" (par. 102); unlike the *Kafkaris* case, without the possibility of speaking here of a problem of the quality of law, because the law in force, including the case-law, "*was formulated with sufficient precision to enable the applicant to discern, to a degree that was reasonable in the circumstances, the scope of the penalty imposed on her, regard being had to the maximum term of thirty years [. . .] and the remissions of sentence for work done in detention [. . .]. The penalty imposed on the applicant thus amounted to a maximum of thirty years' imprisonment, and any remissions of sentence for work done in detention would be deducted from that maximum penalty*" (par. 103). Finally, the ECtHR attributed importance to the fact that the controversial change in case-law came about 10 years after the law to which it referred had been repealed (par. 114). For all these reasons and circumstances, the conclusion that it reached was that the applicant "*had no reason to believe that the Supreme Court would depart from its previous case-law and that the Audiencia Nacional, as a result, would apply the remissions of sentence granted to her not in relation to the maximum thirty-year term of imprisonment to be served, but successively to each of the sentences she had received*" (par. 117).

In short: once the question had been introduced in the framework of the protection of article 7 ECHR, the application of the set of guarantees foreseen in the article for the right to legality in criminal law led the ECtHR to declare that those guarantees had been violated, both by reason of the unforeseeable nature, for those whom it affected, of the new legal interpretation known under the name of the "Parot doctrine", and by reason of the retroactivity of an unfavourable nature that its application implied.

3.4 On the Violation of the Right to Liberty

As could not be otherwise, the ECtHR of 21 October 2013 started its assessment of this motive by stating that the deprivation of liberty has to be "legal" (par. 125). It likewise indicated that the distinction between "penalty" and "execution of the penalty" for the effects of article 7 ECHR was not determinant for the application of article 5.1(a) ECHR, as the measures related with the execution of a sentence or its reduction can affect the right to freedom recognized in this latter provision (par. 127). In this way, as opposed to the attitude maintained by the SCC in the sense of not examining this claim in the numerous unfavourable Sentences it pronounced, the ECtHR clearly admitted its autonomy regardless of whether or not it could appreciate a violation of the right to legality or to effective judicial protection.[26]

---

[26]What is demonstrated in view of the Joint Partially Dissenting Opinions presented by Judges Mahoney and Vehabovic, in which, although they did not share the opinion of the majority with

That said, it is evident that the conclusion previously reached on the violation of article 7 ECHR by reason of the retroactive application *in malam partem* of the Parot doctrine necessarily led the Court to consider the period spent in prison beyond 2 July 2008 as illegal, which was the point when the applicant should have been released by application of the constant legal interpretation of articles 70.2 and 100 PC73 prior to STS 197/2006. Thus, in this case, as it could appreciate an intimate connection between the violation of the right to legality in criminal law and the violation of the right to personal freedom, the ECtHR was exempted from further reasoning with respect to that latter violation.

4 Final Conclusions

I think that, in conclusion, despite the political, media and social upheaval following the definitive annulment of the "Parot" doctrine by the ECtHR of 21 October of 2013, this decision was based on an impeccable legal argument and logically deducible from the posture maintained earlier by the ECtHR, in consolidated case-law, on the requirements for foreseeability and non-retroactivity of unfavourable criminal law as unrenounceable guarantees of the right to legality in criminal law contained in article 7 ECtHR, of the broad concept of "law", of the flexible concept of "penalty" and of the important role that is attributed to legal interpretation.

In view of these premises, the decision of the Court at Strasbourg in the Case of Del Río Prada was, unlike the Parot doctrine that it annulled, absolutely foreseeable. More so: I would dare to say that it was the only legally possible decision, if the wish is to prevent an unfavourable change in the legal interpretation of a criminal norm from being retroactively applied, thereby allowing the judges to do what the legislator is prohibited from doing.[27] It is on the contrary very clear, on the basis of the above-mentioned Judgement, that it is not appropriate to speak, in the scope of the right to legality in criminal law, of a retroactive application of unfavourable legal interpretations, unless those interpretations were, by reason of the concurrent circumstances, of a foreseeable nature for those they addressed or unless they referred to questions completely beyond that scope of protection.

The immediate effect of the ECtHR Judgement of 21 October 2013 has been the swift release of some of those affected, to whom the unfavourable legal interpretation, definitively abolished in the Judgement, would have been applied. It is worth hoping that it may also produce other more or less immediate effects: I refer, in particular, to the need of the Spanish Constitutional Court to review its doctrine on the fundamental right to legality in criminal law enshrined in article 25.1

regard to the violation of art.7 ECHR, they made clear however their agreement with regard to the breach of art.5.1 ECHR.

[27] Vid. this argument in Vives Antón (2006); likewise, in Alcácer Guirao (2012), p. 945.

Spanish Constitution, adapting it to the parameters established by the ECtHR in relation to the inclusion in its field of case-law and with the application of the principle of the non-retroactivity of unfavourable criminal law to the case-law of that same ilk.[28]

References

Alcácer Guirao R (2012) La Doctrina Parot ante Estrasburgo: Del Río Prada c. España (STEDH 10.7.2012, N° 42750/09). Consideraciones sobre la aplicación retroactiva de la Jurisprudencia y la ejecución de las Sentencias del TEDH. Revista de Derecho Comunitario Europeo 43: 929–952

Cuerda Arnau ML (2013) Cambios jurisprudenciales y retroactividad desfavorable (a propósito de la STEDH Del Río Prada c. España). Revista Penal 31:52–69

Cuerda Riezu A (2006) El concurso real y la acumulación de penas en la Sentencia del Tribunal Supremo 197/2006, de 28 de febrero, relativa al caso Henri Parot. Observaciones legales y constitucionales. Cuadernos de Derecho Judicial 7:215–296

Díaz Crego M (2013) Cuando Parot llegó a Estrasburgo. Teoría y Realidad Constitucional 31: 579–611

García-Pablos de Molina A (2006) Relevancia de los cambios de criterio de la doctrina jurisprudencial y los plenos no jurisdiccionales del Tribunal Supremo. Cuadernos de Derecho Judicial 7:181–214

Huerta Tocildo S (2014) El contenido debilitado del principio europeo de legalidad penal. In: García J, Santolaya P (eds) La Europa de los derechos, 3rd edn. Centro de Estudios Políticos y Constitucionales, Madrid, pp 399–427

Landa Gorostiza JM (2012) Ejecución de penas y principio de legalidad ante el TEDH. InDret 4:1–25

Llobet Anglí M (2011) Caso Parot. In: Sánchez-Ostiz Gutiérrez P (coord) Casos que hicieron doctrina en Derecho Penal. La Ley, Madrid, pp 895-910

Muñoz Clares J (2006) La "Doctrina Parot": comentario a la Sentencia del Tribunal Supremo (Sala 2.ª) 197/2006, de 20 de febrero. Revista General de Derecho Penal 5:1–10

Rodríguez Montañés T (2013) Doctrina Parot: ¿podemos pasar página?, eldiario.es, October 27

Vives Antón T (2006) Una sentencia discutible. El País, March 11

---

[28] Vid. a defence of the application of this principle to the case-law in Alcácer Guirao (2012), p. 945. In the opinion of that author, which I share fully, as I have had reason to make clear in earlier works (vid. Huerta Tocildo (2014), pp. 415–417), there are reasons that "*[...] endorse the correction of proscribing the unfavourable retroactivity of case-law [...] On the one hand, the Constitutional Court has been giving case-law enormous protagonism in the proper enforcement of the guarantee of certainty expected in the criminal norms [...] If that is so [...] it is nothing but coherent to conclude that the definition of criminal law by case-law should be subjected to the same requirement of foreseeability and non-retroactivity* in peius *as criminal law itself*".

Rise and Fall of the Parot Doctrine: Multi-Level Protection of the Rights to Legality and to Liberty

Teresa Rodríguez Montañés

1 The Development of the Parot Doctrine and Its Scope[1]

1.1 First Steps

Henri Parot was convicted of multiple crimes (murders, assaults, serious injuries, membership of a terrorist organisation, possession of weapons, possession of explosives, forgery. . .), committed between January 1979 and April 1990. Twenty-six prison sentences were passed between 1990 and 1996, comprising multiple terms of imprisonment (in all, they amounted to over 4000 years).

However, under Article 70.2 of the 1973 Penal Code, as in force at the time the acts were commited, the maximum term to be served by a convicted person was 30 years. A rule that was also applicable where multiple sentences had been imposed in different proceedings, if the offences in question could have been tried in a single case because of their legal and chronological links. Sentences were grouped together (*accumulation*), as provided for under article 988 of the Law on Criminal Procedure (LECrim), and then the maximum term to be served was fixed on the basis of that accumulation.

Once his convictions were all final judgements, Mr. Parot requested the accumulation of the sentences and the application of the maximum term of imprisonment established by article 70.2 of the 1973 Penal Code (a tripling of the heaviest penalty imposed or, in any event, 30 years).

Former Law Clerk at the Spanish Constitutional Court (2001–2013), Professor of Criminal Law at Universidad de Alcalá.

[1]Rodríguez Montañés (2014), p. 138ff.

T.R. Montañés (✉)
Universidad de Alcalá, 28801 Alcalá de Henares, Madrid, Spain
e-mail: teresa.rodriguez@uah.es

M. Pérez Manzano et al. (eds.), *Multilevel Protection of the Principle of Legality in Criminal Law*, DOI 10.1007/978-3-319-63865-2_9

On 26th April 2005, the *Audiencia Nacional*, Criminal Chamber[2] agreed on the accumulation of the sentences but not as had been requested. In accordance with the proposal of the Ministry of Public Prosecution, convictions were grouped into two blocks (the first one, from January 1979 to April 1982, and the second one from 1984 to 1990), for each one of which the maximum term of thirty years was set (30+30). Over the intervening period (from 1982 to 1984) the offender had interrupted his criminal activities. It is this interval that made it possible to form two blocks of penalties.

1.2 The Supreme Court Judgement

An appeal lodged by Mr. Parot against this decision was upheld by the Supreme Court (SC), Criminal Chamber, STS 197/2006 of 28 February 2006. The SC stated that the distinction made between time periods "*lacks any foundation*" and highlighted that this interpretation would mean that *"if Henri Parot had continued carrying out attacks without interruption, this criminal activity would paradoxically have been more favourable to him"*, as it would have been possible to accumulate the penalties and apply the limit of 30 years.

If the decision in STS 197/2006 had merely dismissed his appeal and upheld the accumulation of all the sentences, reduced to the maximum prison sentence of thirty years, the Parot doctrine would never have existed. However, the Supreme Court went somewhat further. By going beyond the purpose of the process and clearly showing incongruence *extra petitum*—that is, by pronouncing on a matter that nobody had asked of it to and that was not the object of the proceedings—it changed the method of applying remissions of sentences for work done while in detention (art. 100 of the 1973 Penal Code): they would no longer be subtracted from the maximum term to be served, as had been the case until then, but from each of the sentences imposed in the various convictions, considered on an individual basis and starting with the most serious ones; having served the first, the following would then begin (subtracting the relevant remissions) and so on, successively, up to the maximum limit in art 70.2 of the Penal Code (normally thirty years).

And so the Parot doctrine was conceived, that would henceforth be applied not only to the case decided upon in STS 197/2006, but to all prisoners convicted under the 1973 Penal Code. One of these prisoners was Ms. Del Río Prada, who had been granted remissions of sentences amounting 3282 days, that subtracted from the maximum term of 30 years, meant that she should have been released on 2nd July 2008, according to the calculations of the prison at which she was serving her sentence. However, applying the new doctrine, the *Audiencia Nacional* ordered the

[2]Court with jurisdiction in terrorist cases, sitting in Madrid, and responsible for the execution of sentences.

prison authorities to issue a new release date, thereby prolonging her imprisonment until the year 2017.

Earlier on and without exception up until that point,[3] the judicial and prison authorities in charge of the enforcement of sentences had been subtracting the number of days of remission for work done in detention from the upper limit of imprisonment, once the accumulation of sentences had taken place and the upper limit been fixed (art 70.2 of the Penal Code). That limit was considered a new sentence to which would be applicable not only the remissions of sentence for work but all other prison benefits. A criterion endorsed by more than one unequivocal pronouncements of the Supreme Court.[4]

Despite the forcefulness of the precedent, STS 197/2006 stated—on the contrary—that "the upper limit of 30 years does not become a new sentence, separate from those successively imposed on the offender (...) but that this limit represents the maximum time the offender may spend in prison", a limit referring to the total sentence to serve and not to the sentences that are imposed. A statement based on a series of grammatical and systematic reasons, and considerations of a political-criminal nature, without doubt with enormous weight in the departure from case-law.[5]

1.3 What Effects were Entailed in this Change of Doctrine?

The new doctrine introduced a new approach to the calculation of remissions, which was unfavourable to the prisoner, applied retroactively, and with a *de facto* invalidation of all previously granted remissions in practically all cases in which it was applied.[6] In essence, and through case-law interpretation, all those offenders who were in this situation were excluded from the benefit—with no legal foundation, as no type of crime or criminal was excluded from article 100.

In addition, that "*interpretation*" was made at a time when the interpreted rule had already been repealed; sentence remission for prison work having been abolished in the 1995 Penal Code, which establishes in article 78 an "*effective*

[3]This statement is not discussed by the Supreme Court itself even and is unanimously defended in the doctrine. Among many others, Alcacer (2012), p. 931; Gómez Benítez (2013); Manzanares Samaniego (2011), pp. 7/16; Sanz Morán (2006), pp. 32–33; Vives Antón (2006).

[4]Among others, and as recognised at the Judgement, the STS of 8 March 1994, and the SSTS of 15 September 2005 and 14 October 2005.

[5]As pointed out by Landa Gorostiza (2012), p. 3: "*the so-called Parot doctrine is a particular manifestation of the growing agitation which reigns in the criminal-legal treatment of the most serious criminality*", *and of the tension between the demands of the Rule of Law and "the growing punitive claims, which point to a trend towards longer prison sentences, in harsher regimes, and even to bringing back life imprisonment or the death penalty*".

[6]Nistal Burón (2013), p. 4.

serving of sentences". As pointed out by Vives Antón,[7] "*one may wonder whether judges (...) can adopt an interpretative norm that could not have been passed into law without incurring in unconstitutionality*". In fact, nobody disputes that if a law had established such a provision, it would not have been possible for it to be applied retroactively without breaching the prohibition of unfavourable retroactivity enshrined in the Constitution. "*As, according to the Spanish Constitution*", continues Vives, "*the judges are subject to the rule of law, it seems difficult to understand how they are able to regulate matters in a way that would be proscribed in law*".[8]

As a consequence, the expectations of the offender of release at a certain point in time were dashed (intervals up to eleven years between one calculation and another had been the norm). These expectations were founded on an incontrovertible and unanimous application of case-law and on equally unequivocal acts of the prison Administration, reflected in periodically prepared sentences reductions and, in many cases, even on proposals for definitive release. In essence, the *rules of the game* had changed in the calculation of the sentence served up until that point, extending the prison term in accordance with the rules applied to the enforcement of their sentences up until that point in time.

All these information—together with the existence of prison and judicial practices, endorsed by the Supreme Court itself, radically different and unequivocal throughout the period of validity of the 1973 Penal Code—was taken into account in the Judgements of the European Court and are the key to an understanding of them. This information had not, incidentally, been overlooked by at least three Supreme Court judges who prepared a decisive dissenting opinion on the Judgement.[9] An opinion that begins by affirming the discrepancy with the majority approach, because "*what is proposed as merely an innovative interpretation of article 70.2 of the 1973 Penal Code is, in reality, a drastic alteration of the meaning of the norm and of its prescriptive context*". After recalling that "*the non-retroactivity of less favourable criminal law provisions is an intangible dogma of the rule of law*", it literally affirms that this interpretation is "*an actual rewriting of the letter of article 70.2 of the 1973 Penal Code*", (...) "*which plainly and simply equates in a tacit way-prejudicing the offender retroactively- to the application of article 78 of the 1995 Penal Code, in its current redrafted form due to Organic Law 7/2003*".

[7] El País, 2006.

[8] El País, 2006.

[9] Those signing the separate dissenting opinion were Judges José Antonio Martín Pallín, Joaquín Giménez García and Perfecto Andrés Ibáñez.

2 The Evasive Response of the Spanish Constitutional Court as an Example of Lack of Protection of the Fundamental Rights at Stake

The *amparo* appeal against the STS 197/2006 had been held inadmissible by the Constitutional Court in 2010.[10] However, a significant number of *amparo* appeals lodged against the application of the doctrine in different cases meant a judgement on the constitutionality of the Parot doctrine was inevitable. On 29th March 2012, the Court in Plenary Session substantially endorsed its constitutionality, when simultaneously ruling on 31 *amparo* appeals, delivering 25 Judgements dismissing the appeal, three Judgements on their inadmissibility and three Judgements upholding them.[11]

The Judgements were not unanimous or even large majority decisions. Separate opinions were attached by 5 of the 11 judges in the Plenary Session.

The Constitutional Court appreciated no violation of the right to legality (article 25.1 of the Spanish Constitution, SC) in any of the SSTC of 29 March 2012, because the application of the Parot doctrine concerned only the execution of the prison sentence not its legal definition, and because the maximum term of imprisonment set down by law had not been exceeded. It referred to ECtHR case-law, according to which questions relating to the "*manner of execution*", in so far as they imply no harshed penalty than is provided for in law do not concern the right to criminal legalty, enshrined in article 7.1 ECHR, although they can affect the right to liberty and security.[12]

It likewise rejected any retroactive application of an unfavourable law (article 78 of the 1995 Penal Code), as the applicants contended,[13] and after stating that changes in case-law criteria and their consistency with the Constitution have to be analysed from other perspectives, among which the principle of equality (article 14 SC), it also rejected any violation of that principle.[14]

Having set out and after affirming that the object of the appeal was neither the STS 197/2006 of 28 February, nor the interpretation of ordinary legality established therein by the Supreme Court (which had previously been excluded when the Court rejected the violation of the principle of legality), the constitutional problem was redirected towards an analysis of the judicial decisions which, in each case, denied the official release under the application of the old system of working out the

---

[10] ATC 179/2010 of 29 November 2010.

[11] The first Constitutional Court Judgement, which served as a guide on the remaining cases, was STC 39/2012 of 29 March 2012. This Judgement and SSTC 57/2012 and 62/2012, upheld the applications for "amparo" (protection). On the other cases where the applications were held to be inadmissible or dismissed. Alcacer (2012), pp. 933–935; Ortega Carballo (2012), p. 305.

[12] STC 39/2012 of 29 March 2012, FJ 3.

[13] STC 39/2012 of 29 March 2012, FJ 3.

[14] STC 39/2012 of 29 March 2012, FJ 3.

remission of sentences, and ordered new release notifications, in accordance with the new doctrine.

At this point, one might have expected that the Constitutional Court—as it noted when it rejected any violation of the fundamental right to criminal legality and as it appeared to point out when it stated, quoting its own case-law, it stated that remission of sentence for the work done in prison directly affects the fundamental right to liberty enshrined in article 17.1 SC—would have at least put forward a rigorous analysis of the eventual violation of the right to liberty.

Indeed, the case-law of the Constitutional Court had explicitly stated that remissions of sentence for the work done while in prison directly affects the fundamental right to liberty (article 17 SC), because the period of imprisonment is, among other things, dependent upon its application in accordance with the provisions of article 100 of the 1973 Penal Code (SSTC 174/1989 of 30 October 1989; 31/1999 of 8 March 1999; 186/2003 of 27 October 2003; 76/2004 of 26 April 2004). And the inadmissibility had also been affirmed of subsequent modifications, brought in through changes in the criteria adopted by the Judge (STC 174/1989), of the total amount of the benefit. Furthermore, given that the right recognized in article 17.1 SC only allows deprivation of liberty "*in the cases and in the manner provided by the Law*", the Constitutional Court had affirmed that the violation of this right cannot be excluded as a consequence of the manner of sentence execution: whether in relation to the computation of the length of the stay in prison, due to inobservance of the legal provisions regarding consecutive sentences or, if applicable, revised sentences that may reduce the time spent in prison by the offender, in as much as they entail an unlawful lengthening of that stay in prison and, therefore, an unlawful loss of liberty (SSTC 147/1988 of 14 July 1988; 130/1996 of 9 July 1996).

However, such an analysis was never made and the constitutional issue of the case was completely blurred, by redirecting the analysis to the "*violation of the right to effective judicial protection (article 24.1 SC) as regards the right to liberty (article 17.1 SC) in its aspect concerning the right to the intangibility of final judicial decisions*". This excessively narrow approach to the question led to very unsatisfactory results.

Certainly, in some of the cases under analysis there was a problem of the intangibility of final judicial decisions, as there were judicial decisions declared *res iudicata* that had incorporated or taken into account the prior criterion (applying remissions to the maximum term of imprisonment). However, to limit the constitutional problem raised by the Parot doctrine to this issue and, consequently, to dismiss all the other *amparo* appeals, plainly and simply implies a wish not to confront the problem.[15]

By adopting this approach, the Court overlooked the fact that while the sentence is being served, the sentencing Court is not *de facto* in charge of its enforcement.

[15]In a similar sense, the individual concurring opinion of Judge Adela Asúa on STC 39/2012 of 29 March 2012.

Those in charge are the prison authorities and the judges responsible for the execution of sentences. Prison authorities forwarded the proposals for sentence remission (proposing the remission of the sentence for prison work to the judge) and the judge responsible for the execution approved or modified the proposal from the Administration. Once the remissions were approved, they became part of the "*prison property of the convict*": the prison administration recorded its concession and regularly computed provisional "*statements*" that recorded the time served and remaining to be served, taking into account not only the number of days effectively served, but also the number of days remitted for prison work, in all cases subtracted from the accumulation of sentences. This procedure did indeed take place in all cases and should be assessed, at least, from the perspective of the requirements of the right to liberty (article 17 SC, article 5 ECHR). But nothing was done, despite the awareness that some of those affected by the application of the doctrine had appealed to the European Court of Human Rights, whose case-law made it difficult to affirm that there were no problems here relating to the fundamental rights of those affected.

3 Was the Parot Doctrine in Accordance with the Constitution? Possible Approaches from the Spanish Constitution

The Parot doctrine had a lot to do with the Constitution, even though some sought to present it as a mere question of the interpretation of prison legality. It is true that the Supreme Court is the foremost interpreter of legality, but the Constitutional Court is the foremost interpreter of the Constitution. The Constitution enshrines the right to liberty, a right that may be denied to no-one other than "*in the cases and in the manner provided by law*" (article 17.1 SC), and the principle of penal legality (article 25.1 SC). The Constitution guarantees in article 9 not only this principle, but also the non-retroactivity of unfavourable penalty provisions, legal certainty and the prohibition of arbitrariness. The Constitution enshrines the division of powers and declares that judges and Courts are subjected to the rule of law and that their roles consist solely of the exercise of jurisdictional power (article 117 SC), not the design of criminal policy, which is exclusively the role of legislators.

With this starting point, there were, in my opinion, two constitutionally rigorous approaches to the problem, which correspond to what we could call the *ex ante* perspective and the *ex post delictum* perspective. The individual opinions of Judges Asúa and Pérez Tremps refer to these two approaches: the right to criminal legality (article 25.1 SC) and the right to liberty (article 17.1 SC). Both articles make reference to the law: the former, in relation to the requirements of the legal definition of the penalty to be imposed; the latter in relation to the legitimacy of the deprivation of liberty following the enforcement of a custodial sentence. If sentence remission for prison work (article 100 of the 1973 Penal Code), and its computation to the maximum term to be served form part of the legal definition of the sentence (as sustained by Judge Asúa), the constitutional problem was indisputably one of legality (article 25.1 SC). But if it were not so—and perhaps it was not incontrovertibly so–, then the constitutional issue does not simply vanish. It has to be relocated under the scope of constitutional protection in article 17.1 SC, which states that no one may be deprived of their liberty other than in the cases and in the manner provided so in law. A law that has the requirements of foreseeability, certainty and quality that are no less than those of article 25.1 SC, as highlighted in the express opinion of Judge Pérez Tremps and in the case-law of the ECtHR, because these are the requirements with which all laws that limit fundamental rights must comply. In both these cases, the change of criterion, unfavourable and unforeseeable for those affected undeniably so in the case of the Parot doctrine could not be applied retroactively without undermining the constitutional requirements enshrined in the above-mentioned articles.

3.1 The Principle of Legality and the Parot Doctrine

As stated earlier, I do not see the violation of the principle of legality as incontrovertible, at least according to the interpretation of article 25.1 SC that the Constitutional Court had up until then been applying and to which STC 39/2012, FJ 3, refers. Let us do not forget that we are not considering a change in the law but a departure from the case-law (in which the constitutional case-law was no longer applying the canon of article 25.1 SC, but that of article 14 SC). It is at least arguable whether the problem posed by the case is the definition of the length of the sentence (clearly a matter for article 25.1 SC) or merely of the form in which it is served (in which case it would not be a matter for article 25.1 SC but could affect the right to liberty enshrined in article 17 SC). This latter position is the one sustained in Constitutional Court case-law where it argues that the remission of sentence for prison work affected the right to liberty.

The basic scope of the principle of legality refers to the definition of offences and penalties in law not only of a formal, but also of a material dimension. That means, the mandate on specificity and the prohibition on the retroactive application of unfavourable decisions. All of this is connected with legal certainty, from an *ex ante* perspective with regard to the time at which the offence is committed. The principle of legality, from the political-constitutional perspective, is an essential guarantee of legal certainty: citizens know that only by using existing laws approved by Parliament may offences and their penalties be defined. In this way, they can foresee the consequences of their actions, which connect the principle of legality with the preventive efficacy of Criminal Law. Foreseeability of the penalty *ex ante* means that when an individual decides to commit an offence, he has to know the risks to which he is exposing himself.

The scope of article 25.1 SC includes the penalty established for each offence, and the rules for determining the penalty, the conditions of prison work, and the maximum term of imprisonment (30 years in these cases). So, whoever commits an offence can foresee the length of sentence to which he is exposing himself, in so far as those are the rules that the Judge will have to apply when sentencing. All this constitutes the penalty to be imposed in accordance with the law.

A first problematic issue is found here. Many authors argue that remission of sentences conformed the lawful penalty but this opinion is neither undisputed nor incontestable. Those authors state that the 30 years of imprisonment were not 30 but 20, because the Spanish system provides a remission of one day for every 2 days worked in detention (article 100 of the 1973 Penal Code), which reduces sentences by about one third. If this were the case, we would be within the area of protection of the right to criminal legality (article 25.1 SC) and the Court should have declared that the new interpretation of the Supreme Court violated this fundamental right. After all, it constituted an unfavourable change of interpretation, which could not be foreseen by those whom it addressed. Quality law should incorporate consistent case-law interpretation according to the ECtHR and its interpretation of article 7.1 of the Convention.

However, it must be taken into account that remissions might or might not be obtained. The letter of the law (art. 100 of the 1973 Penal Code) was: "*Once his judgement or conviction has become final, any person sentenced to imprisonment may be granted remission of sentence in exchange for work done while in detention*", excluding the possibility of obtaining remission for those who breach the terms of their sentence or who repeatedly engage in misconduct. Those who work and show good behaviour might, on an individual basis, have their sentences shortened. This possibility was in the system, but it was not automatic (it was necessary to work, even if in practice anything was deemed to be work, the law established that it was necessary to work), it admitted exceptions (cancellation of remissions for misconduct, for breach of rules), and it had to be approved by the judge responsible for the execution. The judge might or might not approve the remissions proposed by the prison authorities, or he might modify the proposal, and so on. It was of course an alternative that the law offered to the convict as a way of shortening the effective duration of the sentence that was imposed, and of course a fictional serving of the sentence was joined to the actual sentence, making it possible to deduct one day for every 2 days of work and so on. But all of this was granted individually, after the prisoner had worked and after the approval of the judge responsible for the execution of sentences and it might not even be granted at all. I therefore have many reservations over whether it is possible to affirm that Spanish criminal law provided for a maximum term of imprisonment of 20 years, because the 30 years mentioned in article 70.2 of the Penal Code became 20 through the remission arrangements. It could become 15 or 17 (if there were any extraordinary remissions), or remain at 30, if there was no entry into the remission system, or any other figure depending on the number of days worked and on conduct. All of this situates the matter in relation to the conditions of sentence enforcement rather than the area of its legal definition. In essence, the possibilities of shortening the sentence imposed in accordance with the law, even if they are provided for in the law—as incontrovertibly occurred with the remission of sentences for prison work—will not necessarily define the typical sentence.

In addition, Constitutional Court case-law neither extends the scope of article 25.1 SC to the enforcement or execution of the penalty in general, nor to prison privileges, nor in particular to the remission of sentences for work while in detention. Constitutional Court case-law had explicitly stated that the remission of sentences directly affects the fundamental right enshrined in article 17.1 SC, because the period of deprivation of liberty depends, among other factors, on its application in accordance with the provisions of article 100 of the 1973 Penal Code (SSTC 174/1989 of 30 October 1989, FJ 4; 31/1999 of 8 March 1999, FJ 3; 186/2003 of 27 October 2003, FJ 6; 76/2004 of 26 April 2003, FJ 5). And it had also stated that the inadmissibility of changes that may apply to privileges because of changes in the criteria adopted by the Judge (STC 174/1989, FJ 4). Furthermore, and given that the right recognized in article 17.1 SC allows the deprivation of liberty only "*in the cases and in the manner provided by the law*", the Constitutional Court had stated that it was not possible to exclude violations of this right, as a consequence of the way the sentence is served. Especially, in relation to the reckoning of the time spent in prison, due to non-compliance with the legal provisions regarding consecutive sentences or, if applicable, revised sentences that may reduce the time the offender spends in prision, in as much as those sentences entail an unlawful lengthening of the prison term and, therefore, an unlawful loss of freedom (SSTC 147/1988 of 14 July 1988, FJ 2; 130/1996 of 9 July 1996, FJ 2).

3.2 The Right to Liberty and the Parot Doctrine

There was, therefore, another possible approach to the case, one that was more in line with the Constitutional Court case-law itself and perfectly compatible with the ECtHR's case-law: the approach that considers the requirements of the right to liberty (article 17.1 SC, article 5 ECHR). The distinction between the sentence and the enforcement or execution of the sentence[16] is irrelevant in that approach; it would unmistakenly have had to lead to the affirmation of a violation of the right to liberty.

From the perspective of the right to liberty, I believe it is unsustainable to affirm that the prisoner only has the right to know when the sentence will end at the time of his official release and definitive discharge from prison. This view would lead to legal uncertainty and a lack of certainty that would be intolerable from the point of view of the right to liberty. My understanding is that this fundamental right gives the prisoner the right to know how much time he has served and how much time he

[16] As the Judgement of the ECtHR Grand Chamber recalls, for the purposes of article 5 of the Convention, it is irrelevant to make a distinction between the penalty and the execution of the penalty (which is likewise applicable to article 17.1 SC).

has still to serve, in accordance with the law that governs the enforcement of his sentence. And that law has to meet minimum standards of "*quality*" and "*foreseeability*" (in the terminology of the ECtHR) on the date on which the sentence is passed and throughout the subsequent period of deprivation of liberty. I, therefore, agree with the Grand Chamber of the ECtHR[17] on this point: the "*law*" authorizing the continued detention of the applicant beyond the date on which it should have ended using the traditional reckoning of sentence remission for prison work was not foreseeable and, therefore, its application violated the right to liberty.

4 The Protection of the European Court of Human Rights[18]

The Parot doctrine was finally declared contrary to the right to both legality and liberty enshrined in articles 7 and 5 ECHR by the European Court of Human Rights, not in a case known as *Parot v. Spain*, but in the case of *Del Río Prada v. Spain.*[19] And that declaration not in one but in two Judgements, passed by the Third Chamber and by the Grand Chamber of the Court.

The applicant (Inés del Río Prada) was one of the many ETA prisoners to whom the Parot doctrine had been applied, only a few weeks before the date on which she should have been released. Specifically, the authorities of the prison in which she was serving her sentence had proposed her definitive discharge on 2nd July 2008, taking the remissions of sentence for work (3282 days) as days to be subtracted from the upper limit of 30 years. The *Audiencia Nacional* did not, however, approve the proposed discharge, but ordered a new release notification applying the Parot doctrine established in STS 197/2006, and then, using the new calculation, and in its Order of 23rd June 2008, set the date for the final release for the applicant on 27th June 2017, almost 9 years later. With all national channels exhausted, and her *amparo* appeal declared inadmissible on the grounds of insufficient constitutional significance, the applicant lodged an appeal with the ECtHR.

4.1 The First Judgement of the ECtHR

On 10th July 2012 (just a few months after the Constitutional Court had endorsed the doctrine, as set out above), the Third Chamber of the ECtHR passed a Judgement condemning Spain for the violation of articles 5.1 and 7 of the Convention.

[17]Section 4.2.2.

[18]Rodríguez Montañés (2014), 146 ff.

[19]ECHR Judgement of 10 July 2012, c Del Río Prada v. Spain and ECHR (GC) Judgement of 21 October 2013.

The Chamber began its assessment related to article 7 of the Convention by recalling that it was an essential element of the rule of law, which occupies a prominent place in the Convention system of protection, as is underlined by the fact that no derogation is allowed even in times of war or other emergency (par. 45). In conformity with its case-law, the Court distinguished between measures that in substance constitute a penalty and measures that concern the application or enforcement of the penalty, recalling that only the former enjoy the protection of article 7, and recalling also that the distinction between the two is not always clear in practice (par. 48).

Secondly, the Judgement then analysed whether, in view of the circumstances of the case, the calculation of sentence remission for prison work is or is not part of the definition of the "*penalty*" imposed on the applicant or whether it only concerned its execution. After examining the letter of article 100 of the 1973 Penal Code—which contains no specific rule on this matter—and determining what the interpretative practice was (taking into account both the actions of the prison authorities in accordance with the judicial authorities and the previous case-law of the Supreme Court itself, par. 53–54), the Chamber concluded that "*at the time when the offences had been committed and at the time when the decision to combine the sentences had been adopted, Spanish law, taken as a whole, including the case-law, had been formulated with sufficient precision to enable the applicant to discern (...) the scope of the penalty imposed and the manner of its execution*", unlike what happened in the case of Kafkaris v. Cyprus (par. 55). And that the new method for calculating the remission of sentences set by the Supreme Court when it departed from its case-law not only concerned the execution of the penalty that was imposed but also the scope of the penalty for the purposes of Article 7. "*It was a measure which likewise had a decisive impact on the scope of the penalty imposed on the applicant, resulting in extending the applicant's prison term by almost nine years*" (par. 59).

With the matter within the scope of protection of article 7, the Chamber analysed whether the departure from case-law was or was not "*reasonably foreseeable*" for the applicant. The conclusion was that "*it was difficult, practically impossible*" to foresee the departure from the case-law of the Supreme Court either at the time of the offences, or at the time of sentence accumulation (par. 63). Hence, the ECtHR decided that there had been a violation of article 7 of the Convention (par. 64). It came to this conclusion after noting that there was no case-law before STS 197/2006 to the same effect; that the practice of the prison and judicial authorities consistently applied the criterion established earlier by the Supreme Court itself in a Judgement of 8th March 1994; that the new case-law "*deprived the remissions of sentences for prison work of any meaning*", implying that she had to serve an actual term of 30 years' imprisonment; that the departure from case law came after the enactment of the new Penal Code of 1995, which had abolished the remission of sentences for prison work and which, in article 78, established harsher rules for calculating prison benefits for prisoners who had received multiple prison sentences. And it recalled in this respect that "*the domestic courts must not, retroactively and to the detriment of the individual concerned, apply the criminal policy behind legislative changes brought in after the offence was committed*" (par. 60) The data was obvious and compelling and this much was pointed out by the ECtHR.

The Chamber then dealt with the alleged violation of article 5 of the Convention. And although the arguments made a prior reference to the contents of this precept and to the requirements of the "*legality of the detention*" and the "*quality of the law*" which authorizes the deprivation of liberty, none of this seemed to have any real effect on the case. The Judgement limits itself to stating that it has to examine whether the actual duration of the deprivation of liberty was sufficiently foreseeable for the applicant, and concluded that this was not the case. In the light of the same reasons that led it to state that article 7 had been violated, the Chamber stated "*that at the material time the applicant could not have foreseen to a reasonable degree that the effective duration of her term of imprisonment would be increased by almost nine years, and that following a departure from case-law a new method of applying remissions of sentence would be applied to her retroactively*" (par. 120) [...] "*she could not have foreseen to a reasonable degree that the method used to apply remissions of sentence for work done in detention would change as a result of a departure from case-law by the Supreme Court in 2006, and that the new approach would be applied to her.* (par. 130). In essence, as a consequence arising from the violation of article 7, the Chamber concluded that from 3rd June 2008 (the date on which she should have been released in accordance with the remission calculation system in use before STS 197/2006), the deprivation of liberty was not "*lawful*", and that article 5.1 of the Convention had likewise been violated.

For all these reasons, the Chamber held that the State was to pay the applicant 30,000 Euros in respect of non-pecuniary damage and "*that is was incumbent upon the respondent State to ensure that the applicant was released at the earliest possible date*" (par. 83).

4.2 The Grand Chamber Judgement

The Spanish Government requested the referral of the case to the Grand Chamber of the Court under article 43 of the Convention, and it was heard in the Grand Chamber on 22nd October 2012.

On 21st October 2013, the Grand Chamber of the European Court held that there had been a violation of articles 7 and 5 of the Convention. The statement on the violation of article 5.1 (the unlawful deprivation of the liberty of the applicant) was adopted unanimously, whereas the statement on the violation of article 7 of the Convention was adopted by 15 votes to two. Although the Grand Chamber accepted the declarations and, substantially accepted the reasoning in the Judgement of the Third Chamber, its construction is more solid and nuanced, and more clearly expressed. In addition, with regard to the violation of article 5.1, it is not seen to derive directly from the stated violation of the right to legality, but is constructed autonomously.

4.2.1 The Principle of Legality

The Grand Chamber built its discourse in relation to the principle of legality around three pillars: the scope of the principle of legality in general; the concept of the penalty and its scope and the foreseeability of criminal law (this including both statute law and case-law).

After recalling the importance and the scope of the principle of legality and the scope of the concept of penalty, the Court declared it possible *"that measures taken by the legislature, the administrative authorities and the courts after the final sentence has been imposed or while the sentence is being served may result in a redefinition or modification of the scope of the "penalty" imposed by the trial court"*. And that when this occurs, "*the measures concerned should fall within the scope of the prohibition of the retroactive application of penalties enshrined in article 7.1 in fine of the Convention. Otherwise, States would be free – by amending the law or reinterpreting the established regulations, for example – to adopt measures which retroactively redefined the scope of the penalty imposed, to the convicted person's detriment, when the latter could not have imagined such a development at the time when the offence was committed or the sentence was imposed. In such conditions, article 7.1 would be deprived of any useful effect for convicted persons, the scope of whose sentences was changed ex post facto to their disadvantage. The Court points out that such changes must be distinguished from changes made to the manner of execution of the sentence, which do not fall within the scope of article 7.1 in fine*" (par. 89). And in order to determine whether a measure taken during the enforcement of a sentence concerns only the manner of enforcement of the sentence or affects its scope, the Court deemed that it was necessary to examine the "*intrinsic nature*" of the penalty imposed, taking into account national law as a whole and the manner it is applied at such a time. It then recalls the essential role of case-law in the definition of the offences and penalties by means of the interpretation of criminal laws, it even being possible to declare that there is a violation of article 7 arising from the absence of any case-law interpretation that is accessible and reasonably foreseeable (par. 93).

The application of the above principles to the case led the Grand Chamber to look into the scope of the penalty imposed under domestic law, taking into account for this purpose not only the letter of the law, but also the case law and the interpretative practice and whether that scope was defined in conditions of accessibility and foreseeability. And on this point, it concluded, just like the Chamber, that despite the possible ambiguities in the law, applicable Spanish Law, as a whole, including case-law, had been formulated with sufficient precision to allow the applicant to comprehend the scope of her sentence: a sentence equivalent to a maximum term of thirty years established by article 70.2, from which any remissions of sentence for prison work would be deducted (par. 103). This conclusion was reached after it had been determined that the prison and judicial authorities consistently reckoned the remission of sentences for work in prison by taking the maximum length of sentence to be served established in article 70.2 of the 1973

Penal Code according to an interpretation endorsed by the Supreme Court itself in 1994; that it had been applied to the applicant by comparing the penalties provided for in 1973 Penal Code and in 1995 Penal Code, to determine which of the two laws was the most favourable to her; and that this practice had been applied to a large number of people convicted under 1973 Penal Code (par. 98). The Grand Chamber therefore affirmed that "*while she was serving her prison sentence –and in particular after the Audiencia Nacional decided on 30 November 2000 to combine her sentences and fix a maximum term of imprisonment– the applicant had every reason to believe that the penalty imposed was the thirty-year maximum term, from which any remissions of sentence for work done in detention would be deducted.*" (par. 100).

The Grand Chamber then went on to consider whether the application of the doctrine modified the scope of the enforcement or that of the penalty itself and concluded that it changed the scope of the penalty imposed, as it deprived the remissions granted under the law (3282 days in total) of any useful effect. The approach to calculating the remissions was therefore considered to go beyond mere prison policy and implied a redefinition of the scope of the penalty imposed, for which reason it fell within the scope of application of article 7 of the Convention.

Finally, the Court looked at whether the Parot doctrine was reasonably foreseeable, concluding that from its analysis of the case (among others, that the departure from case-law was adopted in a manner contrary to consistent prison and judicial practice, as the Government itself recognized; that it had been adopted in 2006, 10 years after the repeal of the interpreted law; that it had the effect of anulling the benefit of the remissions already granted), "*there was no indication of any perceptible line of case-law development in keeping with the Supreme Court's judgement of 28 February 2006. The applicant therefore had no reason to believe that the Supreme Court would depart from its previous case-law and that the Audiencia Nacional, as a result, would apply the remissions of sentence granted to her, not in relation to the maximum thirty-year term of imprisonment to be served, but successively to each of the sentences she had received. As the Court has noted above (§109 and 111), this departure from the case-law had the effect of modifying the scope of the penalty imposed, to the applicant's detriment*" (par. 117). And, therefore, had been a violation of article 7 of the Convention (par. 118).

4.2.2 The Right to Liberty

In relation to the alleged violation of article 5.1 of the Convention, the Court indicated—agreeing with the applicant and going against what was argued by the Chamber, which appeared to link the violation of article 5 exclusively with that of article 7—that the distinction between "*penalty*" and "*execution of the penalty*" for the purposes of article 7 is not relevant for the purposes of article 5 (par. 127).

It then went on to point out that the applicant did not dispute that her detention was legal until 2 July 2008, only her continued detention in prison after that date. The Court recognized that the prison sentences handed down to the applicant amounted to more than 3000 years and that the period of imprisonment actually served had not reached the maximum of 30 years established in article 70.2 of the 1973 Penal Code.

> However, the Court must examine whether the "law" authorising the applicant's continuing detention beyond 2 July 2008 was sufficiently foreseeable in its application. Compliance with the foreseeability requirement must be examined with regard to the "law" in force at the time of the initial conviction and throughout the subsequent period of detention. In the light of the considerations that led it to find a violation of Article 7 of the Convention, the Court considers that at the time when the applicant was convicted, when she worked in detention and when she was notified of the decision to combine the sentences and set a maximum term of imprisonment, she could not have foreseen to a reasonable degree that the method used to apply remissions of sentence for work done in detention would change as a result of a departure from case-law by the Supreme Court in 2006, and that the new approach would be applied to her" (par. 130). "The Court notes that the application of the new case law "effectively delayed the date of her release by almost nine years. She has therefore served a longer term of imprisonment than she should have served under the domestic legislation in force at the time of her conviction, taking into account the remissions of sentence she had already been granted in conformity with the law (see mutatis mutandis, Grava, cited above §45) (par. 131).

The Court concluded that from 3 July 2008, the applicant's detention had not been "*lawful*", in violation of Article 5 §1 of the Convention (par.132) and Spain was again urged to ensure that the applicant was released "*at the earliest possible date*".

5 Concluding Remarks

Fortunately, on this occasion, the Spanish judiciary reacted in the only way a judicial body could react to a ruling of an international court which declared that Spain had unlawfully held the applicant in prison since 2008. They complied with the ruling and executed it without delay, without turning to the excuse that there was no procedure for the execution of the European Court Judgements.[20]

The applicant was immediately released by the *Audiencia Nacional* and the Parot doctrine was annulled by the Supreme Court, the very organ that had created it. By an Agreement of the Supreme Court General Chamber on 12th November 2013, the Supreme Court itself—seeing that there were no appropriate procedural mechanisms for the execution of the rulings of the ECtHR—decided that remissions of sentence had to be deducted from the maximum term to be served established after the accumulation (former criterion) of all sentences currently being served, imposed before 28th February 2006 and to which 1973 Penal Code had applied before its repeal.

[20] Against those who fought for all types of delaying tactics, others clearly stated that it should be implemented immediately, and by the judges themselves. Among them, Gómez Benítez (2013).

A dark chapter in our democracy thus came to an end. The so-called Parot doctrine was unlawful, an excuse dressed up in legal arguments to force prisoners to remain in prison after they had served their sentences, by changing the rules which were in force until then, without any exceptions. As I have stated on other occasions, it should not have existed, "*which would have prevented the regrettable spectacle of large numbers of prisoners being released, most of them convicted for terrorism offences, and who can now say that they have been the victims of a State which does not respect their human rights as declared by an International Court. The Parot doctrine made it possible to keep them in prison [until now], but by breaching the basic rules of our Democracy and delegitimizing the State vis-à-vis terrorism and in the eyes of international bodies and public opinion. This, in my view, is too high a price to pay. In this matter, unfortunately, none of the Spanish institutions was able to live up to expectations. Perhaps it is now time for them to start doing so and to move on*".[21]

References

Alcacer Guirao R (2012) La Doctrina Parot ante Estrasburgo: Del Río Prada c. España (STEDH 10.7.2012, N° 42750/09). Consideraciones sobre la aplicación retroactiva de la Jurisprudencia y la ejecución de las Sentencias del TEDH. Revista de Derecho Comunitario Europeo 43:929–952

Gómez Benítez JM (2013) El final de la doctrina Parot. El País, October 21

Landa Gorostiza JM (2012) Ejecución de penas y principio de legalidad ante el TEDH. InDret 4:1–25

Manzanares Samaniego JL (2011) Reflexiones sobre el caso Troitiño, la doctrina Parot y los vaivenes jurisprudenciales en materia de terrorismo. Diario La Ley 7654

Nistal Burón J (2013) El controvertido periplo judicial de la "doctrina Parot" (De la Sección 1ª de la Sala de lo Penal de la Audiencia nacional al Tribunal de Estrasburgo). Diario La Ley 8068

Ortega Carballo C (2012) Doctrina del Tribunal Constitucional durante el primer cuatrimestre de 2012 (with Requejo JL, Duque JC, Fossas E). Revista Española de Derecho Constitucional 95:263–310 (303–310)

Rodríguez Montañés T (2013) Doctrina Parot: ¿Podemos pasar página? eldiario.es, October 27

Rodríguez Montañés T (2014) Doctrina Parot: claves para entender las sentencias del TEDH en el caso Del Río Prada c. España. Eunomía 6:137–152

Sanz Morán A (2006) Refundición de condenas e imputación de beneficios penitenciarios. Revista de Derecho Penal 18:11–43

Vives Antón T (2006) Una sentencia discutible. El País, March 11

[21] Rodríguez Montañés (2013).

On the Principle of Criminal Legality and Its Scope: Foreseeability as a Component of Legality

Juan Antonio García Amado

1 On the Foreseeability of Legal Consequences: Which Normative Provisions Are and Which Are Not Protected?

1.1 Which Expectations Are and Which Are Not Protected by Criminal Law?

Foreseeable, according to the Dictionary of the Spanish Royal Academy, is "*What may be foreseen or comes within normal foresight*". To foresee is "*To see in anticipation*" or "*To know, to conjecture by some signs or indications what has to happen*" or "*To have or to prepare resources against future contingencies*".

Human actions can also be classified as more or less foreseeable, with the support of the empirical data that may be available. If we offer a glass of wine to a heavily alcohol-dependent person, it is foreseeable that he will accept it; if a mother and father see a child of theirs in serious danger, it is foreseeable that they will do everything possible and even risk their own lives to save the child.

One would be adopting the perspective of an observer, a social point of view, in the above example. There is also the perspective of the individual who acts. In such a case, the question of the individual concerns the consequences of his own action on himself. An individual may wonder about how a friend may react, if he tells him a great lie involving a matter of importance to them both, and will conclude that it is foreseeable that he will get annoyed or will no longer see him as a loyal companion.

Professor of Philosophy of Law at Universidad de León.

J.A.G. Amado (✉)
Universidad de León, Campus Vegazana, 24071 León, Spain
e-mail: jagara@unileon.es

M. Pérez Manzano et al. (eds.), *Multilevel Protection of the Principle of Legality in Criminal Law*, DOI 10.1007/978-3-319-63865-2_10

An individual may also ask himself what might happen to him, if he fails to comply with a legal provision. In this case, his concern will be over the possibility and probability of the corresponding sanction that might be applied to him under Law. But the foreseeability of the sanction is variable and depends on several factors. We know that we are more likely to face the pertinent punishment, if we commit a murder than if we exceed the speed limit on a motorway.

The foreseeability of the legal consequences of our actions is one of the dimensions of legal certainty. With regard to afflictive penalties, modern legal systems and those of the State under the Rule of Law reinforce this dimension of legal certainty as the foreseeability of the legal consequences of our conduct, though not in its whole scope, but in no more than one aspect.

If I flagrantly exceed the permitted speed limits on a motorway, I do so knowing that I may be sanctioned and I am fully aware that I am taking this risk and even regard it as probable. But if, in the end, it is not detected or my infringement is not reported and I am not punished, what was to a large extent foreseeable to me does not in fact materialize. But we would never say that a right of ours has been violated, because our foresight or legal expectations have not been realized.

Let us compare that with another situation. I make a contract with a neighbour by which I lend him 20,000 Euros at an annual interest rate of 30%, without there being any type of established legal or case-law provision that forbids agreement on such a high rate of interest. But a court declares that this interest rate is abusive and that the other party is not obliged to pay it. I believed that our agreement was fully legal and binding as there were no provisions vetoing its clauses when we established them. With the ruling in question, what to me was completely foreseeable, as my legal right, becomes unrealizable and my expectation is completely dashed. I would not have lent the money that I lent, if I had known beforehand that this outcome was possible or in any way foreseeable.

As a general rule, we may therefore say that the Law supports legal expectations, but in a nuanced way:

(a) If it concerns afflictive penalties, the legal system does not support the expectation of being penalized, but that of not being penalized upon any legal grounds, or that of not being penalized to a greater degree than is legally foreseen. If I go through a red traffic light in front of a city policeman and he does nothing to fine me as prescribed by the regulation, the fact that, knowing the law, what I expected to happen did not in fact happen, is not seen as a legal problem.
(b) Outside this actual sanctioning context, if the judge, without any legal basis that could have been known to me in advance, decides, in the above example involving a contract, that the other party is not obliged to comply with the loan agreement, the opposite of what I expected will have happened and this will remain so, without any greater or subsequent protection for my expectation, even though the surprising legal ruling adversely affects me.

Legal certainty in terms of foreseeability is greater, the greater the degree of certainty or probability with which we are able to calculate the legal consequences of our actions in advance, in terms of the content of the reaction of the competent legal institutions in the case. This degree of foreseeability depends, among other things, on such items as:

(a) The level of specificity of the norm applicable to the case. Obviously, the greater the semantic indeterminacy of the applicable legal statement, the greater the uncertainty of the subjects, as a consequence of the fact that the decision-making institutions will have broader discretion when interpreting the words and expressions of the provision. Hence the importance attached in criminal law to the principle of specificity.
(b) The extent to which the legal controlling and sanctioning institutions strive to perform their role. If, for example, in my experience, traffic wardens always turn a blind eye to a certain infringement, I will expect them to act in the same way when I am the one who commits it. In such cases, my fact-based expectation will contradict my legal expectation: I know that the regulation prohibits my action and makes it punishable and I also know that in practice, it is highly unlikely that I will be given this punishment. It goes even further than that. If I am given a punishment in a way that is absolutely exceptional, I can allege discrimination against me, even for legal purposes.
(c) The particular practice of judges is linked to the understanding of the Law that they operate. Apart from other considerations, of little relevance here, a legal practice which is strongly legalistic or attached to the letter of the law and not prone to exceeding the limit of the possible interpretations of the provision, makes the results more foreseeable than case-law that leans towards principlism, or that prefers to seek justice in the specific case in question.

In this context, in criminal matters the foreseeability of the criminal consequences of our actions is strongly protected, but with the following peculiarity: the negative legal implications of our actions, in the form of criminal punishment, cannot be more negative than what we could, aware of the rules, reasonably foresee. However, there is no problem, nor is it considered a basic principle or a right of the affected person, if:

(a) The consequence is more favourable than that which he could reasonably foresee (for example, because he is given a lesser punishment or because he is acquitted) or because a legal change, which occurs after the time at which the action was performed, decriminalizes the behaviour or means that it warrants a lesser punishment and this new decision is retrospectively applied.
(b) The negative consequence applied to the individual is harsher than may reasonably be expected, but it is not a criminal punishment. It may be the case of civil liability, seen here as civil liability for an offence, and in particular when such uncertain factors as moral (or non-material) damage come into play. In matters of civil liability, (except in matters in which a scale is applied), the principle of specificity is not the same as in criminal matters, and the principle of full reparation for the harm becomes as imprecise, as if the criminal law judge were simply told that he is allowed to apply whatever penalty appears

proportional to the seriousness of the offence against the legal asset. It may be that this cannot be otherwise, but the effects are somewhat curious when we consider the foreseeability of the adverse legal consequences of our actions: a criminal sanction of 500 Euros should be "foreseeable" and the principle of the specificity of the penalty comes into play, but a sentence, from the same criminal court when the actions accumulate, to provide compensation of 100,000 Euros for damages, even non-material damages, has no need to be "foreseeable" in the same way.

In criminal matters, the relationship between the principle of legality and foreseeability is indisputable and is, therefore, delimited as follows: the punishment handed down for the offence cannot be harsher than what an average citizen may reasonably foresee, making use, as appropriate, of expert advice on the subject. On the other hand, there is no violation of a basic right associated with the principle of legality in criminal matters, when the penalty handed down is less severe than what could reasonably have been foreseen by this subject at the time of his action. This guarantee is for the offender, not for the victim. My calculation of the measure of the foreseeable punishment for the person who robbed me does not matter. What matters is my foresight regarding the limit of the penalty that I may face if I rob someone else.

A second element involves what the punishment is, what punishment is understood to mean. Let us suppose that N prescribes a punishment of several years imprisonment for the offence committed by S and that, in application of N, S is convicted. In T^1 a provision L^1 covering penitentiary issues was also in force. This stipulated that terms of imprisonment had to be served in individual cells of at least 20 m^2 in size. On a day between T^1 and T^2 or during period T^3, L^1 is replaced by a new provision L^2, under which terms of imprisonment should be served in cells for two people and of no less than 20 m^2. The big question here is whether, by virtue of the principle of legality in criminal matters, S should serve his sentence in the better conditions set by L^1 or whether the principle of legality in criminal matters is not incompatible with S spending his time in prison (or the remaining part of his sentence when L^2 comes into force) in the less favourable conditions of L^2, assuming that S prefers to be alone in his cell.

It is clear that if L^2 is applied to S, his hypothetical foresight or expectation of having a cell to himself and having greater privacy in prison[1] will be frustrated. But perhaps the decisive factor lies not merely in individual foresight or expectations, but in the sense that these expectations can reasonably be given as a justification of

[1]I have not failed to notice that in this example there is a change in the conditions under which the sentence is to be served, but not in its duration. I mention this to point to the need for general solutions rather than purely casuistic ones. On the unclear barrier between the punishment and its duration, Díaz Crego (2013), pp. 587–588, writes that "*If a clear difference can formally be established between the punishment and the modalities of its enforcement, that borderline loses clarity in those circumstances in which the modality of its enforcement implies a notable aggravation of the punishment, i.e. a significant lengthening of its duration*".

certain restrictions when applying current rules at any given time. In truth, to talk of foreseeability is not the same as to talk of effective foresight or expectations. It is a lot to expect each subject to operate in each aspect of his life by weighing up the foreseeable consequences of his actions. It seems absurd to think that, in general, a person who is going to commit an offence will reflect deeply on the scale of the punishment that he risks facing. Moreover, the occasional, "non-professional" criminal will sometimes know that his action constitutes an offence, but he will seldom be aware of the specific margins or the maximum limit of the punishment that he may have to face. And, obviously, it is almost approaching the realm of fantasy to suppose that certain criminals, such as terrorists or the perpetrators of certain crimes of a sexual nature, among many others, stop to think about whether it is really essentially worth it to them, given the type and duration of the punishment which may be applied to them.[2] And no matter how much we use the figure of expert advice, one cannot imagine that it is very normal for a person who is tempted to commit an offence or who finds himself compelled to do so in certain vital situations to consult a lawyer before making up his mind to go ahead, or to seek a well-commented case-law report.

1.2 Real Expectations or Foreseeability?

From what I have just said, it appears to me that what is protected by the principle of legality in criminal matters is not certain and real foresight but foreseeability as an abstract possibility. If the protection was for actual foresight, we would have to conclude that there is no reason why the principle of legality has to protect whoever was without it or whoever, to his own detriment, was guided by erroneous foresight. For example, for a person who has committed manslaughter, completely convinced that the sentence for manslaughter was between 20 and 30 years' imprisonment, there would be no difficulties in applying a subsequent provision to that person that would raise the punishment for manslaughter to such a term of imprisonment, because by doing so it would confirm rather than frustrate his foresight.

Thus, what is safeguarded is not the foresight but the possibility of foresight: the foreseeability. As in so many other areas of Law, there is a kind of standard reasonable individual subject. What in Tort Law and other fields of Private Law is the standard average man or what used to be called the good family man, or for economists is that mysterious figure of the *homo economicus*, is for Criminal Law what we could call the standard rational or dispassionately calculating, well informed criminal. It is not that we potential criminals are like that. Moreover,

[2]For the same or similar reasons to those set out by Hava García (2014), p. 155: *"As this stage now, it should appear an incontrovertible fact that both life imprisonment and the death penalty are senseless in the prevention of terrorist attacks, as these are usually committed by hardened criminals, who show themselves impervious to what is called positive general prevention"*.

few will be like that, and those who are (white collar offenders, rich fraudsters surrounded by good advisors) will not appear to us as the most pleasant, for us to wish that the guarantees and the protection of their foresight of the punishment of their conduct should be fully maximised. What is protected is the mere theoretical or hypothetical possibility that we may—if we wish and are able—foresee the criminal consequences of our actions. It does not mean that Criminal Law treats us all as if we were all very clever and, in addition, perfectly informed. It is more about not treating us as incapable, like pure objects; or only favouring the well-founded expectations of those who really have them and can have them without great effort.

If I am right about something in the above, it will not be out of leisure, when talking about foresight or expectations, that our analysis becomes a little complex. To begin with, let me repeat that non-compliance with negative expectations, as a general rule, is of no matter to Criminal Law; in other words, it is of no matter whether the result is better than expected or better than what could reasonably be expected, as occurs when a more favourable rule is applied retrospectively. Secondly, if what has to be safeguarded is foreseeability rather than the possible and often missing current foresight, it is important to clearly delimit the moment at which that foreseeability counts (in what counts). I believe that it only makes sense to take as a time reference for this moment, the time at which the offence is committed. But, then, if we talk of foresight we find ourselves with a slight paradox.

It is very possible that I will commit an offence one day without knowing that I am committing an offence, but in an inexcusable error (again *homo poenalis*, although not in the Lombrosian sense, but by analogy with *homo economicus*), or even suspecting with good reason that my conduct is punishable, but without having even a fairly clear idea of what punishment I may have to face. I will have an even poorer knowledge of any details of the prison regime and the possible ways in which my punishment may be applied. But once the legal process begins, I will seek out the information and, furthermore, I will have a lawyer to advise me. The true expectation, the calculation and the foresight arise at this point and, of course, before entering prison, if the punishment is of this type, and I will have procured all the information needed to give me detailed knowledge of what awaits me and what I may expect. The paradoxical aspect is that the protection of my expectation is greater when it is less likely that there is an expectation or one that is accurate or minimally detailed, while my expectation is no longer considered when this is more certain and precise. I will repeat that the expectation in itself is not defended but its possibility. And if this were not the case and it was a matter of supporting actual rule-based expectations, what should count should not be the moment at which the offence occurs, but the moment, any moment, at which the expectation arises, after the offence; and, above all, someone who at any time does not have expectations or has wrong and unfavourable expectations would not be protected.

1.3 What Norms Are Taken into Consideration to Protect the Foreseeability of Their Effects?

We have been discussing legal expectations, expectations regarding the possible (negative) consequences of our conduct. But we have still to discern which provisions are the ones that can feed into that (possibility of) expectation. Nobody now debates the principle of criminal legality in application to criminal law. The matter now under debate is whether this principle also extends to the case law that is used to interpret criminal law. Is foreseeability also protected here by the principle of legality? Should the theoretical or hypothetical possibility be safeguarded of someone knowing in advance how the provision applying to his case is going to be interpreted and knowing that this interpretation is not going to be more unpleasant for him, although it may be less unpleasant?

It is obvious and right that the principle of legality prevents judges from being able *motu proprio* to establish new offences or to increase the penalties for existing ones. Clearly, and adding the principle of linking the judge to the law, it should not be considered lawful either for judges to disregard substantive criminal provisions, in whatever respects they are clear and in those cases that clearly fit them, although one would not draw upon the dimension of the subjective right of the principle of legality in criminal matters and one could also analyse the possible liability of these judges for failing to adhere to their fundamental remit. Nor is there any doubt that the principle of legality radically vetoes the analogical application of the criminal norm that defines the criminal offence. The theoretical problem, discussed in the doctrine, leads back to whether the interpretations that the judges make of the criminal provisions that establish criminal offences are considered part of or an essential complement of those interpreted rules and whether, therefore, the prohibition of retroactivity with regard to unfavourable consequences also applies to those interpretations.

We have legal provision N which establishes a certain offence and its corresponding penalty. In the wording of N there is a term or expression, "X", which admits two possible interpretations, which we shall represent as I^1 and I^2. Neither of these two interpretations is unreasonable or openly incompatible with the usual or technical sense of "X" and it is possible to provide good, relevant arguments in favour of each of them. I^1 is a narrower interpretation and I^2 is wider, although without bordering on the limit with analogy. This implies that the universe of cases that come under N, interpreted in accordance with I^1 (N/I^1), is narrower than the universe of cases which come under N interpreted as per I^2 (N/I^2). There will therefore be at least one case (let us call it Z) that will not be penalized under N/I^1 and that will be penalized under N/I^2. The action of subject S is a case of Z. The interpretation of N is done in the light of case-law and it may be that:

(a) Case-law has so far been interpreted in accordance with N/I^2; it is chosen to interpret N in the way that makes Z punishable under N. If S wanted to create an expectation regarding the criminal consequences that could result from his

Z-type action and he only obtained information on N, he would be in doubt. If, in addition, he became aware that this is the interpretation that has been applied so far, he will expect to be penalized. If, when his action is judged, that interpretation is changed and the restrictive one, I^1, is applied, his negative expectation is frustrated on acquittal; if, on the other hand, in his case, the court maintains its previous interpretation, the extensive one (I^2), his foresight or expectation will be confirmed on his conviction. We know that there is no question of an attack on the principle of legality when case-law changes to an interpretation that is more favourable to the offender than the previous one, even when his foresight is invalidated, and even though that change was unforeseeable.

(b) The contrary alternative to the above: case-law interpretations have been more favourable to the offender, selecting the narrow interpretation. In the case of S, an interpretative change occurred and the option that is less favourable to him is now chosen. With the previous line of interpretation, he would have been acquitted, but with this one he is now convicted. If before deciding to carry out his action, S had obtained information on the case-law, he would have had the expectation of impunity, which now turns out to be negated.

There is nothing in the "nature of things" or any type of criminal "logic" that makes it necessary to protect case-law based legal expectations and not merely based on the norm. The truth is that it is a political or a political-legal decision. It could even be the legislator himself who elevates the maintenance of a favourable line of case-law, if and when established, into a mandatory item, as part of the principle of legality. Or this may be established by a court with the relevant power, or, for example and as appears to have happened in the case of the judgement of the ECtHR in the case of Del Río Prada, by an international court with competence in the subject and with the power to impose its case-law, one way or another, on the national courts. However, given that the decision is ultimately a legal-political one with significant effects on the criminal legal system and its system of sources or of relationships between powers and organs, the least that may be done is to take into account and consider, in an unhurried manner, the general consequences and to analyse some very relevant details.

(a) It will be extremely useful here to clarify what can or should be understood by case-law for these purposes. Does one single decision of any court in the first instance suffice? Does it require a certain consistent line from any courts? How many judgements and over what period of time? Could there be exceptions which do not undermine the overriding force of the majority line once it has been established, even with those exceptions, or has the case-law of those courts to be unanimous? Or is that case-law only established by the highest court or those judicial organs to whose decisions this faculty of creating binding case-law has been attributed? If this is the case, is a first favourable ruling sufficient or should there be two or more than two along the same lines?

(b) If, on the grounds of the principle of legality and the protection of the expectations of the defendant, such force or normative value commensurate with that of the law itself were assigned to the case-law of lower judicial organs, would their favourable interpretation be considered binding on the higher court too? This stance may be defended, but in that case we would have the interesting and atypical phenomenon of a higher judicial organ that is bound by the precedent set by courts below them on the judicial rungs of the ladder.

(c) In addition to introducing a "hetero-precedent" of special importance, an unusual power of "auto-precedent" would become a valid part of our system. Whichever judicial body is the body of reference, once the interpretation which is most favourable to the defendant has been chosen by it in the first case (or two), that interpretation could not be altered and changed for a less favourable one, except, at best, for future cases.

(d) It would not be out of place for the theory to take note of and calmly examine the possible perverse effects. The judicial body in question, when establishing this "hetero" and self-binding favourable case-law, will know that it is only pinning itself down when it chooses such an interpretation to the benefit of the defendant, yet if it chooses the other, it will always be allowed to alter it in the future, replacing it with a more favourable one. There is reason to fear a possible spur for the judges who wish to maintain their freedom in the future, choosing now the interpretation that is the harshest of those that are reasonably possible.

(e) Alert to the fear of perverse effects, the legislator may find an incentive there to toughen the law and to sever the effects of the favourable interpretation at the root when such effects do not please him or do not serve his political interests. At that point, the independence of the judges, in terms of interpretative autonomy[3] or discretion, may also be harmfully diminished. These effects would certainly be felt in the future, but not for those cases which have taken place under the rule and previous favourable interpretation. But the future criminal may end up paying for the broken crockery, if it can be put like that, and facing criminal laws which no longer leave any doubt over the legal interpretation at each time, but rather the certainty of harsher consequences. It is possible that this has already happened on some occasions.

---

[3]In the opinion of Díaz Gómez (2013), p. 27: *"a significant sector of the doctrine, which probably constitutes the majority, has considered that changes in case-law, even detrimental ones, should not be included in the guarantee of the non-retroactivity of unfavourable norms. In this way, the courts maintain their margin for interpretation, preventing the immobility entailed in the impossibility of modifying the previous exegesis of the norm"*.

2 Some Additional Considerations from the Ruling of the ECtHR in the Case of *Del Río Prada* and on the Relationship Between Foreseeability and the Principle of Legality in Criminal Matters

In 2014, I had an article published under the title "On some consequences of the ruling of the ECtHR in the case of Del Río Prada v. Spain: non-retroactivity of unfavourable criminal jurisprudence and changes in the sources of production of Criminal Law". The two theses that I supported in the article were that the ruling introduced serious changes in the system of Criminal Law sources and of the relationships between both the legislative and the judicial branches and within the hierarchy of the criminal courts, and that the Court, when referring to the expectation of Inés del Río with regard to the possible term of her sentence to be served, had not taken into account the point in time at which her offences were committed, but instead one that was even subsequent to the commencement of prison work that might lead to sentence reduction. I remain convinced of the first thesis, as will be seen below. As far as the second one is concerned, I also support it, although admitting that it may be more debatable, depending on how consolidated the favourable interpretations of articles 70 and 100 of the Penal Code of 1973 were from the first few years of its enactment, and on the type of judicial decisions we adopt as a valid basis for the emergence of that expectation; in other words, whether those of the lower courts (or even the decisions of the Prison Administration) suffice or whether it has to be based solely on the interpretation of the Spanish Supreme Court (SSC), which did not happen until 1994.

What I now seek to do is to put forward some new, complementary considerations on the subject of foreseeability, with regard to the above-mentioned ruling of the European Court of Human Rights.

2.1 *Possible Interpretations*

Some authors have maintained that STS 197/2006 of 28th February 2006, which created the so-called "Parot Doctrine", surpasses the possible interpretations of articles 70 and 100 of the Penal Code of 1973. Such is, for example, the recent and very well-argued opinion of Mariona Llobet Anglí.[4] Nevertheless, it does not appear that this is the clear opinion of all or most of the doctrine. At the heart of all this is the complex, theoretical question of what could be understood by "possible interpretation" of a normative text. The fact that there may be good

[4]Llobet Anglí (2015), pp. 7 ff. Previously, Cuerda Arnau (2013), p. 58, had also expressed valuable reasons to argue that the interpretation given by the Spanish Supreme Court in STS 167/2007 was not one of the possible interpretations of rule 2 of article 70 of the Penal Code of 1973.

systematic reasoning in favour of one interpretation will not necessarily imply that there can be no alternative interpretation that is not unreasonable. The alternative interpretation will not be unreasonable when, likewise in its favour, reasons or arguments may also be contributed that do not patently violate logic or semantics, without depriving the precept in question of sense or reason.

The arguments of Llobet Anglí seem quite convincing to me, but it appears to me that, if she is right, the ECtHR should have given a different and much more forceful rationale to its sentence condemning Spain, because we would have been dealing with a crude and flagrant breach of the principle of legality involving disregard of the legal provision, rather than with a change in case-law adversely affecting the defendant, resulting from the alteration of a previously established interpretation. Even conceding that Llobet Anglí may be on the right track with her assessment, I will continue to assume here, for analytical and dialectic purposes, that the interpretation given by the Supreme Court in 1994 and the one it adopted in 2006 were both possible and could be reasonably defended. I refer to the contents of the interpretations themselves, in purely theoretical terms, at the margin of other contextual data.

Reading the abundant and sound criminal law literature on the ruling of the ECtHR in the matter of Del Río Prada v. Spain convinces me that the interpretation of the above-mentioned precepts, invoked by the SSC in 1994 and modified by that Court in 2006, was in fact very firmly and unanimously established. This interpretation was the case both in legal practice and in prison administration practice. It does nothing to topple the theoretical problem of whether, in 1994, the SSC could not perhaps have altered the interpretative rationale of that practice with some retroactive effects.

2.2 *What (Possible) Knowledge Should Be Considered as Constituents of Protectable Foreseeability?*

Let us go back to the subject of foreseeability in relation to the principle of legality. My intention is not to combat the ruling of the ECtHR as such, which causes me no kind of moral or political concerns, but to analyse the consistency in the abstract of the argument of foreseeability and the effects on the conformation of the sources and the relationship between the judicial bodies in the penal system.

Among the items that were firmly established, as a result of the constant case-law of the Spanish Constitutional Court (SCC) and the SSC, was the doctrine that the prohibition of unfavourable retroactivity was not paramount for case-law; in other words, that the retroactive application of unfavourable or less favourable case-law than the one that had been previously applied was possible. If this is true, as it clearly appears to be, was this not a further component of those that constitute foreseeability? Specifically, and to the case in point, a prisoner in the situation of Inés del Río might be aware of two things:

(a) That the judges had been interpreting the rules in such a way that the reduction in the sentence through prison work was subtracted from the maximum prison sentence of 30 years. This possible knowledge gave rise to a favourable expectation for prisoners condemned to very long sentences for successive offences.
(b) That the highest jurisprudence and even the SCC were affirming that, among the possible interpretations of criminal norms and of the precepts on the enforcement of penalties, a new and more unfavourable interpretation than the previous one may be retroactively applied. With this information, also known to the defendant (or the defendant through counsel), there is an element of risk added to the earlier favourable expectation that is not separate from the expectation itself. Such a complex expectation has a structure of the following type: 'X' is reasonably foreseeable, but 'not X' cannot be ruled out.

Let us draw a comparison for the purposes of clarification, for what it is worth and bridging the distances. Suppose I have a friend who each year on his birthday invites me to a delicious meal at the most expensive and luxurious restaurant in town. He has been doing so for 25 years, year after year. But from the very beginning he told me that if he ever ended up jobless and, therefore, saw a reduction in his income, he would not invite me there, but to an ordinary fast-food take-away. After all those years, I have a solid expectation that yet again he will give me a splendid invitation on the occasion of his next birthday and, furthermore, I am convinced that the company in which he works is financially sound and that he, a professional in that firm, is highly valued. However the unexpected (but not discountable) happens and my friend is dismissed or his company closes. My well-founded expectation or foresight is frustrated, but I always knew that risk existed and was aware of it.

Let us now imagine, in the face of my indignation or disappointment and given that I insist on being invited another year to the best restaurant, a third friend offers to mediate and determines that my expectation, after so many years, is more than solid. Furthermore, I had already bought myself an elegant suit for the celebration this year. In consequence, that mediator concludes that the friend cannot let me down and must invite me to the expensive restaurant again. In deciding so, the element of risk that was known to me and incorporated in my overall expectations from the outset is not taken into account.

In a certain sense, the ECtHR has been doing something similar way to the above. What its decision imposes is the non-retroactivity of unfavourable jurisprudence. It has two basic consequences:

(a) Looking towards the future, it modifies the elements of possible expectations because, for the future, it eliminates that element of risk that existed previously: the risk (supported by the case-law of the SCC and the SSC opposed to the line that the ECtHR now maintains) that the current, more favourable interpretation may be replaced by a less favourable and retroactively applied interpretation.

(b) Looking towards the past, it means that component of risk that could be part of the whole, reasonable expectation may be ignored and disregarded. It is as if the expectation of Inés del Río could have and should have been merely the expectation that is based on favourable jurisprudence, without taking the high case-law into consideration that stated that beneficial penal expectations could be modified, applying the new and less convenient interpretation retroactively. In the comparison given above, it is as if I had never known or had to take the warning of my friend into consideration concerning what would happen to his invitations, if he became unemployed.

Let us reflect for a moment on an affirmation in which Llobet Anglí,[5] in her very well-reasoned article, summarises her position and that of a considerable part of the doctrine which has critically dealt with the "Parot doctrine": *"In consequence, in my opinion, once the interpretation taken was, unanimously, that of not distinguishing between penalty and sentence, the change was an unforeseeable punitive intervention in accordance with the available information known to the citizen assessed in her case by an "expert person". For this reason, the principle of legality was violated"*. If we take this approach to its logical conclusions (and, acknowledging, beyond this specific case, that we are talking about possible interpretations of a norm), it would mean that once there is an interpretation that has been unanimously adopted for a period of time, this possible interpretation will become the only possible one, if it is favourable, because the option of subsequently having another of the possible interpretations will violate the principle of legality in criminal proceedings. It is what we could call the inertia effect of the favourable interpretation. Due to this force of inertia, the established favourable interpretation excludes any subsequent alternative interpretation, even though the SSC or the SCC say that the prohibition of non-retroactivity is not extensible to judicial decisions, but only to the legal norm. The favourable interpretation unanimously accepted for some time by the judges becomes solid and acquires the same validity as the legal rule itself, and just as the SSC cannot alter the text of the law, nor will it be able, not even the Supreme Court, to alter that interpretation unfavourably.

The conclusion is that a 'hyper-protection' is consolidated, through the approach of the ECtHR, of the positive expectations or foresight of the offender, based on selecting only those elements that support the favourable foresight and without entering into the assessment of those that could also have been reasonably considered as a risk that those positive effects would not materialise, and without that non-compliance being anti-juridical. So, I insist, no matter what we may think, from the standpoint of our moral convictions or those concerning political-criminal matters, in the Spanish legal system, before the ruling of the ECtHR, the retroactivity of unfavourable case-law was neither anti-juridical nor operated as an anti-juridical practice in the courts.

---

[5] Llobet Anglí (2015), p. 13.

With regard to material criminal law, positive foreseeability or one of no unfavourable effects is full (within the limits not dependent on interpretations), because the retroactive application of a law that is both subsequent and detrimental to the act is normatively excluded. This prohibition is part of the principle of legality and is constitutionally prescribed. With respect to case-law, foreseeability will always be relative, if the retroactivity of changes to case-law has no normative obstacles. It would be so, if the Constitution were not to limit itself to guaranteeing (art. 9.3) "the non-retroactivity of punitive measures that are unfavourable", but instead said that the non-retroactivity of unfavourable provisions regarding penalties and of unfavourable case-law interpretations of the provisions regarding penalties is guaranteed. Given that no such thing is said in either the Constitution or the legislation, such foreseeability with respect to case-law is relative or conditional; or it was until the ruling of the ECtHR.

For this positive foreseeability to be full rather than relative, it has to be certain that a change in case-law is not going to be applied retrospectively to the detriment of the offender. In other words: (1) it is foreseeable that the beneficial interpretation will continue to be applied, because; (2) it is sure that a less beneficial subsequent interpretation will not be (validly) applied retrospectively. If this second element makes sense, it is because there is a binding legal basis: there is a norm that prohibits the retroactive application of subsequent unfavourable jurisprudence and contrary to the previous favourable one.

Did such a legal basis exist? Was that norm in the Spanish system before the ruling of the ECtHR in the case of Del Río Prada? Articles 9.3 and 25.1 of the Constitution and art. 7 of the European Convention on Human Rights did indeed exist. They do not expressly prevent the retroactivity of case-law which is less favourable to the offender, but there is one curious effect: the principle of criminal legality that these precepts enshrine is no obstacle to their more favourable interpretation for offenders, and herein is the interpretation found that makes less beneficial case-law non-retroactive. But a norm is not the same as one of the possible interpretations of that norm.

Let us assume then that article 7 of the European Convention admitted two possible interpretations. With its ruling on the case of Del Río Prada, the ECtHR opted for the interpretation that was more propitious to the offender and, in so doing, established the norm, which did not previously exist, that unfavourable case-law is non-retroactive. To the extent to which the case-law of the ECtHR turns out or appears to be binding in the future for national courts (and, at least, that is how it will in fact be understood for the purposes of avoiding future condemnations of the State), the normal effect of decisions that establish binding case-law will have occurred: they convert into a norm, into due and acceptable, that of the possible interpretations of the norm of reference for which they opt. With an additional effect: in future, the ECtHR will not be able to modify (judging past cases) its case-law on art. 7 of the Convention, favourable to offenders, if it is not at the expense of incurring in an absolute contradiction with what this judgement has affirmed: that retroactive modification of case-law in favour of the offender is not possible.

Furthermore, the ECtHR will have turned the criminal case-law of each State into a source of criminal Law of equal value as the law, in that which contains favourable interpretations and in accordance with the principle of legality: although the judges may alter their interpretation to move to a more favourable one that is applied to the case under the effect of a less beneficial one, it is not permitted to apply case-law retroactively that is less favourable than the one that was current at the time when the act occurred that is on trial (or, even, at a subsequent point in time). The courts are able to modify their "interpreted rule", but not to apply its unfavourable parts retroactively: exactly the same thing as happens with the criminal legislator and his product, criminal law. But with some specific points in mind:

(a) If the previous well consolidated case-law is from a lower court,[6] neither can a decision of the Supreme Court which alters it unfavourably be retroactively applied.
(b) If the previous case-law is from lower courts, but is unfavourable, and the later case-law of the Supreme Court is more favourable, it will be possible to apply it retroactively.

Conclusion: the offender always wins and the principle of legality in criminal matters becomes the principle of maximum favourability for the offender.[7] I do not comment on this and, therefore, I do not criticize it from a moral point of view or from a political or political-criminal point of view. I only submit the consequences that each reader will be able to judge from those perspectives. Having said that, the first demand is that we make such judgements with the appropriate coherency, that we make judgements of this type in a consistent manner, as this is the basic requirement of rationality.

---

[6]On this point and in the case involved in the ruling of the ECtHR, we should bear in mind what is well explained by Rodríguez Montañés (2014), p. 140: *"It has to be borne in mind that the full or partial discharge of sentences, computation of benefits and the definitive release of offenders (that is the time at which the computation of sentence reductions for prison work takes effect) are not questions of which the Supreme Court is cognizant, because the decision is made by the organ responsible for the enforcement of the sentence and the appeal that is legally foreseen against its decisions is a petition for appeal against that organ itself. The Parot case reached the Supreme Court because it was a case of the "recasting" or accumulation of sentences, an admissible question for cassation as expressly foreseen in art. 988 LECrim. In fact, the Supreme Court did not admit cassation against the decisions of the sentencing Courts regarding definitive release, until its criterion changed the Court Order of 7th April 2008"*.

[7]It has been said that the ECtHR in its judgement widened the concept of penalty for the effects of art. 7.1 of the Convention (Díaz Gómez (2013), p. 27). In truth, the widening extended to three questions: the concept of penalty, the concept of legality (with the inclusion of favourable case-law within the "legality" which is protected by the principle of legality) and the time at which the expectation that is favourable to the offender arises, which is not necessarily, it appears, the time at which the offence is committed. On this final question, see my article: García Amado (2014), pp. 61 and ff.

2.3 Do We Maintain Favourability and the Protection of Expectations in a Coherent Manner and in All Cases?

As what matters to me here is to test the coherency and the scope of the thesis of foreseeability as a component of the principle of legality, we shall do another test or propose another conceivable scenario. Suppose there is a criminal provision N. For years the courts have been making an interpretation of N that is rather stilted, not well argued and difficult to reconcile with certain basic principles. Furthermore, there is a very strong doctrinal agreement that it is an improper and very unreasonable interpretation of N. But it is an interpretation that is very clearly favourable to the offender.

The question that we pose is as follows. Is the expectation or foresight that this interpretation will not be modified and replaced by one that is unfavourable, but much more tenable, reasonable and should it be safeguarded in the same manner? Should this hypothetical expectation be likewise protected by the principle of legality in criminal matters, in such a way that any retrospective application of an interpretation that is less favourable, but more reasonable, is forbidden? If our answer is indeed 'Yes', we should assume that the courts of today or a certain period of time strongly bind the courts of tomorrow, even when the doctrine that those of today establish in favour of the offender is difficult to defend.

Example. In a country there is a norm in force that punishes the offence of rape, which in the corresponding norm is defined as non-consensual sexual relations. As the judges in that place are quite sexist, for 20 years the case-law has been unanimous in saying that marital rape is not possible, that the husband who forces his wife to enter into a sexual relation that she has rejected is not committing an offence. The husbands have a more than reliable expectation in this respect on how courts will continue to rule in these cases. But one day this confidence is overturned by a ruling that for the first time considers that the husband can also rape his spouse. This decision is argued with great care and in a more than acceptable manner. Should that expectation that the defendant had or could have had be protected and shall we take the view that the ruling which condemns him violates his basic right that arises from the principle of legality in criminal matters? Shall we apply the current doctrine of the ECtHR and would the ECtHR itself apply it in this case?

If our opinion is that what should count, in order to accept the compatibility of this new line of case-law with the principle of legality, is the reasonableness of the interpretation in question and that the new interpretation is more reasonable than the previous one, we are attacking the foundations of the decision of the ECtHR in the Del Río Prada case. This is because what the principle of legality of art. 7 of the European Convention would exclude is not the retroactivity of unfavourable case-law, but the retroactivity of the unreasonable or less reasonable unfavourable interpretation, and no more than that. But, therefore, in that case, what the Court should base its decision upon is not the mere principle of non-retroactivity, but it will have to argue why one interpretation is better than another. The principle of legality would not therefore give the person awaiting trial the right to have the previous interpretation on which his expectation is based applied to him, but the right to have the previous interpretation applied to him, if it is more reasonable and only if it is more reasonable than the following one.

References

Cuerda Arnau ML (2013) Cambios jurisprudenciales y retroactividad desfavorable (a propósito de la STEDH del Río Prada c. España). Revista Penal 1:52–69

Díaz Crego M (2013) Cuando Parot llegó a Estrasburgo. Teoría y realidad constitucional 31:573–612

Díaz Gómez A (2013) La «doctrina Parot» y sus aspectos formales y constitucionales: a propósito de la Sentencia de 21 de octubre de 2013 del TEDH. Revista General de Derecho Penal 20:1–29

García Amado JA (2014) Sobre algunas consecuencias de la sentencia del TEDH en el caso Del Río Prada contra España: irretroactividad de la jurisprudencia penal desfavorable y cambios en las fuentes de producción del Derecho penal. El Cronista del Estado Social y Democrático de Derecho 41:54–63

Hava García E (2014) Antes y después de la doctrina Parot: la refundición de condenas y sus consecuencias. Eunomia Revista en Cultura de la Legalidad 6:153–173

Llobet Anglí M (2015) No sólo imprevisible, también irrazonable: otra vez sobre la «doctrina Parot». Indret 2:1–32

Rodríguez Montañés T (2014) Doctrina Parot: claves para entender las sentencias del TEDH en el caso Del Río Prada c. España Eunomia Revista en Cultura de la Legalidad 6:137–152

Chronicle of an Enforcement Foretold: The Effectiveness of the Del Río Prada ECtHR Judgement in Spain

Argelia Queralt Jiménez

Many States of the European Council have incorporated measures in their legal orders to make it possible to enforce the judgements from the Court at Strasbourg. The solutions adopted by each State are quite heterogeneous; however, the review (*revisión*) of previously closed domestic proceedings may be highlighted as a common mechanism in many States. In particular, these States have established the review of a criminal proceeding that ended with a final judgement as the legal mechanism with which to enforce an ECtHR judgement in relation to some of the rights connected with the national criminal proceeding.[1]

It is true that the judicial review of previously closed domestic criminal proceedings is not the only path that exists to execute European judgements, but it is one that has been established in the National legal orders.[2] On this point, Spain has up until very recently been an exception to the general rule among the Member States of the European Convention, as we shall see later on. However, over recent months, two very relevant changes have been introduced on this matter. The first, in relation to case-law, is the decision of the non-jurisdictional Plenary of the Second Chamber of the Supreme Court, on 21 October 2014, to admit the appeal for judicial hearing as a procedure for the enforcement of ECtHR judgements. The second is of a normative type: the reform of the Organic Law of Judicial Power (LOPJ), through

These pages have been shared with my colleagues from the Project "El impacto de las decisiones del Tribunal Europeo de Derechos Humanos: una aproximación comparada" (DER2012-37637-C02-01) directed by J. García Roca.Professor of Constitutional Law at Universitat de Barcelona.

[1]On these questions, Arangüena Fanego (2009), pp. 289–325.

[2]As claimed by Irurzun Montoro (2013), pp. 131–162, who considers that the reading of the possibilities of enforcement of the ECtHR judgements and of real compliance with these judgements and their effects is often excessively strict.

A. Queralt Jiménez (✉)
Facultat de Dret, Universitat de Barcelona, 08034 Barcelona, Spain
e-mail: aqueralt@ub.edu

M. Pérez Manzano et al. (eds.), *Multilevel Protection of the Principle of Legality in Criminal Law*, DOI 10.1007/978-3-319-63865-2_11

which the review of final judgements before the Supreme Court has ultimately been incorporated as a means of enforcing sentences from the European Court of Human Rights (ECtHR) in relation to Spain.

1 The Position of the Judiciary Towards the Enforcement of ECtHR Judgements Up Until 2014

Up until October 2014, only one ECtHR judgement had been "enforced" (in the strict sense) in Spain: the extremely well-known judgement of the Spanish Constitutional Court (SCC) in the *Bultó* case. It involved a long and somewhat unclear journey through case-law relating to the possibility of enforcement of the decisions from Strasbourg through the SCC, in view of the lack of legally valid procedures to that end in the Spanish legal order.

Following the ECtHR Judgement of 6 December 1988, c. Barberà, Messegué and Jabardo v. Spain, upholding a breach of art. 6 ECHR, it was the SCC that, through an appeal for *amparo* (relief), enforced the European decision in its STC 245/1991 of 16 December of 1991.

The first step that the Constitutional Court took to decide on the appeal for a judicial review (*revisión*) lodged by Messrs. Barberà, Messegué and Jabardo was to clarify the object of the petition from the appellants. Despite what the *Audiencia Nacional* (National High Court) and the Supreme Court may have understood, it was not the enforcement of the ECtHR judgements in the Spanish order—ECtHR judgements are not executive in Spain, although in accordance with art. 96.1 and art. 10.2 Spanish Constitution (SC) they imply the existence of certain effects—, but "*what this Court has to examine in the present appeal for protection is whether the Judgement of the Supreme Court that is challenged, as an act of a Spanish public power has harmed fundamental rights recognized in the Constitution and whose protection in the last instance corresponds to this Constitutional Court*".

Beginning with this original way of reframing the object of the appeal, the SCC, after recognizing the technical correction of the original Supreme Court Judgement of 1990, finally declared the nullity of the judicial decisions challenged by the parties and ordered that the proceedings be rolled back to the time before the breach of the right to a fair trial (art. 6.1 ECHR), the counterpart in Spanish fundamental law to effective judicial protection (art. 24 SC), highlighted by the ECtHR.

The Constitutional Court applied the doctrine of present harm of a fundamental right, in order to hear the appeal for protection and to be able to rule in favour of the appellants; thus:

> The ECtHR is the qualified organ that has as its mission the interpretation of the Convention, and its decisions are in addition obligatory and binding for our State, when it is the respondent State. Hence, it follows that the adjudication of a breach of a right recognized by the European Convention, so declared in a Judgement from that Court, which likewise constitutes the actual breach of a fundamental right enshrined in our Constitution, corresponds to this court, as the supreme Judge of the Constitution and fundamental rights, with

> respect to which nothing that affects it can be irrelevant to it. It therefore has to be assessed, from the perspective of our internal Law, whether measures exist to be able to correct and to remedy the breach of that fundamental right satisfactorily, especially when it is a breach of the fundamental right to freedom of art. 17.1 SC, which remains relevant and will therefore not be redressed by its economic equivalent.

Subsequently, it went on to develop these ideas: "*the continuation of the effects of the convictions, which results from the judgement of the Supreme Court that is challenged here, implies the maintenance of that breach of the right recognized in the Convention*" and, if we take into account the obligatory nature of the ECtHR judgement and the mandate of art. 10.2 Spanish Constitution, the result is that "*the declaration of the breach of art. 6.1 of the European Convention declared by the ECtHR implies the factual existence and the continuance of a criminal conviction imposed for the breach of a right recognized in art. 24.2 SC, and, in addition, as it concerns a loss of freedom imposed without the observance of the formal requirements required by the Law, it is also harmful to the fundamental right to freedom of art. 17.1 SC*". Public powers are obliged by the SC and the democratic State under the rule of Law "*to protect and to redress a breach of a fundamental right that continues to be current in a satisfactory way*". Given these circumstances and "[having] *confirmed the persistence of a current breach of art. 24.2 SC (which implies at the same time the breach of art. 17.1 SC), it corresponds to this Court, in so far as the actors have not obtained adequate redress for the violation of that right, to declare on the supposed contravention of the right in proceedings with all due guarantees and to redress and to remedy the breach of the fundamental right, taking into account the characteristics of the conviction.*"

In short, although it is true that the violation of fundamental rights could not be directly imputed to the Supreme Court judgement of 1990, it led to the consolidation of a situation involving breaches of fundamental rights arising from earlier decisions that, in consequence, also had to be annulled.

In 1997, in the Court Order (*Providencia*) of 23 April, relating to the enforcement of ECtHR Judgement of 9 December 1994, c. Hiro Balani v. Spain, the SCC pointed out that until the Spanish legislator had incorporated the necessary mechanisms in the Spanish legal order to enforce the decisions of the ECtHR, the remedy that should serve that end was the appeal for *amparo*. That would of course be so, provided there was a series of concurrent conditions: in the first place, the breach of the European Convention declared by the ECtHR had to take place in the course of a criminal proceeding; in second place, it should entail a breach of everybody's right to a fair trial (art. 6 ECHR), which in turn highlights a breach of effective legal protection under art. 24 SC; in third place, the contravention of art. 24 SC should imply a real breach of the right to personal liberty of art. 17 SC. This last condition has to be understood in terms of a violation of some of the guarantees of art. 24 SC that would have implied the deprivation of personal freedom, due to a conviction, with any such a sanction in its enforcement phase.

Over the last decade, the SCC has adopted a series of decisions relating to the direct effectiveness of the judgements of the European Court that neither denied nor recognized the possibility of their enforcement. In STC 240/2005 of 10 October

2005, which involved the ECtHR judgement of 14 October 1999, c. Riera Blume v. Spain, although the SCC affirmed that the European judgement had already been enforced[3] and there was, therefore, no need to seek its internal enforcement, it added a new element to take into account when evaluating the direct effectiveness of the judgements of the European Court in the Spanish legal order: a "new fact" may be considered that authorizes the review foreseen in art. 954.4 Law on Criminal Procedure (LECrim), a judgement from Strasbourg that can *"affect different procedures from those in which that declaration has its origin [breach of the Convention]"*.[4]

STC 313/2005 of 12 December 2004 came a little later. This decision ruled on the *amparo* appeal for relief lodged by Mr. Perote, who sought the enforcement of the ECtHR judgement of 25 July 2002, c. Perote v. Spain, in which the European Court had declared that the right to an "independent and impartial tribunal" (art. 6.1 ECtHR) had been violated in the proceedings before the Spanish courts. So, the main conclusion worth drawing from this judgement was that the possibility of enforcing the judgements from Strasbourg through the *amparo* appeal opened by the STC 245/1991 of 16 December 1991 continued to exist, provided that there was an ongoing breach of the right.[5] Having said that much, the doctrine in STC 245/1991 was not applied in that specific case given that, according to the Court, the violation of the fundamental right was not, in the first place, current, because the term of imprisonment had already been served—although the matter of compensation for loss of employment remained and the name of the appellant was still on the List of Convicted Criminals—; and, in second place, because the ECtHR showed no evidence of causality between the breach of the right to an impartial judge and the conviction of Mr. Perote.

Later on, in STC 197/2006, the Constitutional Court ruled on the appeal for *amparo* lodged by Mr. Fuentes Bobo, who was seeking the execution of the ECtHR Judgement of 29 February of 2000, c. Fuentes Bobo v. Spain, that had been pronounced in his favour, essentially, through his readmission to the staff of RTVE, as well as full payment of any outstanding salary yet to be settled. In this circumstance, the Court rejected the possibility of applying the doctrine in STC 245/1991, basing its argument on the absence of present and real harm to the fundamental right, because the damage caused had been restored, having paid out the costs awarded by the ECtHR for pecuniary and non-pecuniary damages assessed for material and moral damages (art. 41 ECHR). In this judgement, it

---

[3]It referred to the Decision of the Council of Ministers.

[4]STC 240/2005 of 10 October 2005, FJ 6. This approach to enforcement in which the same value of the judgements delivered by the European Court in the same proceedings would not "necessarily" have to be recognized, is at the least paradoxical, as the Magistrate P. Pérez Tremps pointed out in this dissenting opinion in STC 197/2006 of 3 July 2006.

[5]In STC 313/2005 of 12 December 2005, FJ 3b, after considering that the alleged violation was not real, the Court affirmed: *"as there was no application of the specific doctrine emanating from STC 245/1991 [...]"*, which meant recognizing that it would be worth applying it under other circumstances.

may be highlighted that the SCC appeared to recognize that the fundamental right with respect to which the actual breach could be asserted is not necessarily limited to freedom. So, the *amparo* appeal could be lodged as a means of enforcement of the ECtHR judgements with regard to fundamental rights other than liberty provided that their violation was present.

Less positive was the recognition of the interpretation offered by the Supreme Court with which the door was closed, for so long as there was no reform of procedural law, to having recourse to civil review as a mechanism for the enforcement of judgements from Strasbourg; specifically, the Court affirmed that in relation to civil procedural norms, of subsidiary application in labour procedure, a subsequent ECtHR judgement cannot be considered as a "retrieved document" that authorizes a review of the proceedings.

Later on, STC 70/2007 of 16 April 2007 was delivered. This decision spelt the end of criminal proceedings for drug trafficking in which the conversations recorded by telephone tapping were obtained and used as incriminatory evidence. Following the ordinary procedure, the prisoner convicted by the court of first instance sought the protection of the SCC, alleging that the telephone surveillance to which he had been subjected, had not been done with due respect for the preceptive constitutional and legal guarantees. The Court, in STC 236/1999, of 20 December 1999, had rejected the claim of the appellant, reasoning that the surveillance had been carried out in accordance with the constitutionally recognized standard for this type of investigative measure. The case came to Strasbourg where in the ECtHR Judgement of 18 May 2003, c. Prado Bugallo v. Spain, the Court declared a breach of art. 8 of the European Convention, because the authorized telephone surveillance was not in accordance with the standard of legal foreseeability set down in European case-law.

Mr. Prado then lodged an appeal for a judicial hearing with the Supreme Court, arguing that the judgement from the European Court implied that one of the incriminating pieces of evidence used in his conviction had clearly been obtained in contravention of the right to the secrecy of communication and, in consequence, in breach of the right to the presumption of innocence. According to the appellant, this situation was sufficient motive for a review. Although the Supreme Court denied the petition for review, considering that the presumption of innocence of the appellant had not been affected, as the information obtained through the surveillance was not the only and the most relevant of the probative elements that had led to the conviction of Mr. Prado, in ATS 5417/2004 of 29 of April 2004, a series of affirmations of great transcendence were advanced in relation to the enforcement of judgements from the European Court:

> an appropiate interpretation of article 954.4 of the LECrim is one that considers that the suppression of evidence, validly declared unlwaful, that has been used in the conviction as a probative element against the presumption of innocence of the accused, is a new fact that might suppose his innocence, revitalizing the presumption that initially protected him, if there is no other valid and sufficient evidence against him. The impossibility of taking into account the probative material evaluated for the conviction is, in these cases, taken from the

> Judgement of the ECtHR, in so far as it declares that the contravention of conventional right that has the status of a fundamental right by our Constitution has been breached.[6]

Mr. Prado then lodged an *amparo* appeal before the SCC that resulted in the aforementioned ruling (STC 70/2007 of 16 of April 2007). In so far as this decision affects us now, it offers a new reading of the question relating to the enforcement of the ECtHR judgement. In the first place, the judgement says nothing about the appropriateness of using the appeal for a judicial review as a mechanism for the enforcement of judgements from Strasbourg, but it did, in contrast, evaluate the reasonability of the reasoning delivered by the Supreme Court in its Ruling with regard to the harm that may have been caused to Mr. Prado's right to the presumption of innocence, as a consequence of what the ECtHR expressed with regard to the secrecy of the communications. In other words, it avoided referring—either directly or indirectly—to the executive nature of the European judgements in the Spanish legal order. The doubt that therefore arises is the following: in the case that the SCC considered that the reasoning of the Supreme Court on the non-affectation of the right to be presumed innocent was unreasonable, would it have proceeded, as it did in STC 245/1991 of 16 of December 1991 to enforce the ECtHR Judgement of 18 May 2003, c. Prado Bugallo v. Spain? The question is pertinent, if it is taken into account that in this case the decision of the ECtHR highlighted evidence of the violation of art. 24 of the Constitution on the guarantees of due process in a criminal proceeding that had concluded with a prison sentence that had yet to be served, which implied ongoing harm to the right to liberty.[7] Once again, the answer was left in the air.

Although there have, subsequently, been other occasions in which the SCC has pronounced on the enforcement of judgements from the Court of Strasbourg, what has been expressed is enough to form an idea of the position of the SCC in this respect:

1. In principle, ECtHR judgements are not executive and there is no European Convention mandate stating that they have to be enforced (on this point, it should be said that the ECtHR remains silent, but that the Council of Ministers of the Council of Europe has been at pains to ask States to establish mechanisms to do so, and that in all the debates on the future of the European system, it has been presented as a priority to safeguard the subsidiarity and the subsistence of the system.
2. However, the Constitutional Court cannot remain impassive before the declaration of the breach of rights by the ECtHR, above all, in situations where a current breach of the fundamental right to liberty concurs, as a minimum. The SCC will be responsible for the enforcement of ECtHR judgements that have their origin in criminal proceedings, in which the breach of rights declared by the European Court entails a breach of the right to personal liberty.

---

[6]ATS 5417/2004 of 29 April 2004, FJ 7.

[7]ATS 5417/2004 of 29 April 2004, FJ 6.

3. The SCC maintains that if the ECtHR has recognized a just satisfaction for material and moral damages, then the European judgement will be seen as having been enforced and, therefore, there is no point in seeking its enforcement through the courts in Spain.

2 The Interpretative Effects of ECtHR Judgements in Spain

The impact of the interpretative effects of ECtHR judgements has been more regular thanks to the existence in the Spanish legal order of art. 10.2 SC. This constitutional provision has been the object of multiple studies, as it is one of the key pieces in the relation between international Law and the national legal order. It is not a provision that determines the position that one international treaty or another ratified by Spain should take in the Spanish legal order, but it is more a question of the constitutionalization of a particular function that international treaties play in matters of fundamental rights in the Spanish system: the interpretation of rights and liberties enshrined in the SC.

Art. 10.2 SC imposes an interpretative canon on those applying and interpreting the Law, which means that the Courts, including the Spanish Constitutional Court will not necessarily have the obligation, when reasoning their judgements, to explain the conformity of their arguments with those of the relevant international treaties. Instead, the relevance of the obligation imposed by art. 10.2 SC is that, in practice, the Courts have to ensure the compatibility of their reasoning on fundamental rights with the treaties and the decisions taken by their supervisory organs in matters of human rights.

And, as has been said, the follow up of ECtHR case-law by the Spanish courts and, especially by the SCC, is in terms of the empirical study of its judgements very notable.[8] In addition, it is a fact that the interpretative references that the Constitutional Court used with greater regularity are the European Convention and the case-law of the European Court. The reason is simple: the European standard of guarantees arises today as the minimum and common standard for all the States that constitute the Council of Europe, in great measure, due to the credibility that the system generates, because of the jurisdictional nature of the highest court that guarantees respect for their rights.

[8] A detailed study may be found in Queralt Jiménez (2008), pp. 193 and ff.

3 The Enforcement of the ECtHR Judgement in the Río Prada Case and Its Implications

3.1 The ECtHR Judgement in the Del Río Prada Case: An Uncomfortable Judgement for Spain

On 21 October 2013, the Grand Chamber of the ECtHR ratified the decision taken by the Chamber on 10 July 2012 in the case of *Del Río Prada v. Spain*, which had ruled on the claim presented by a convicted terrorist to whom the so-called *Parot doctrine* had been applied.[9] Through these decisions, the ECtHR placed a damper on a doctrine that is not easily intermeshed with the principle of legality foreseen in art. 25 SC. All of it because the Criminal Chamber of the Supreme Court, in its STS 197/2006 of 28 February, changed its earlier case-law—and the most widespread judicial practice under this sort of circumstance—and came around to defending that the prison benefits foreseen in the Penal Code of 1973—an applicable norm in those cases—should be calculated in relation to each of the convictions that had been imposed and not in relation to the maximum applicable prison term of 30 years imprisonment foreseen in the aforementioned Criminal Code. With this formula, the Supreme Court ensured that ETA prisoners who were on the point of release after having served the maximum term of imprisonment—from which the prison benefits had been subtracted—, had to remain in prison until they had served the complete prison term of 30 years.

The Supreme Court, with this realignment of its case-law, converted the dangerous maxim that the end justifies the means, into a judicial criterion. All the repulsion that terrorist acts may produce in us will never justify that the legal actors renounce a consolidated position with no legal justification and arrive at a new interpretation of the norm that implies lengthening the real sentences of the inmates: the foreseeability of the norms and legal certainty are two pillars of the Spanish constitutional system that we cannot allow to be brought down.

The Court of Strasbourg concluded in 2013, as it had done in 2012, that the prison authorities changed the effective duration of the sentence when they applied the new case-law criteria of the Supreme Court, given that the real duration of the prison term was modified, which in practice implied a retroactive interpretation of a more restrictive criminal norm. As a consequence of this conclusion, the European judges of the Grand Chamber, as the Chamber had already done, declared that the Spanish State should release the appellant immediately.

[9]On the scope of this doctrine, see Díaz Crego (2013), especially pp. 579–599.

3.2 The Audiencia Nacional Before the ECtHR Judgement in the Del Río Prada Case: Its Direct and Indirect Effects

In AAN 61/2013 of 22 October 2013, the Plenary of the Criminal Chamber of the Spanish *Audiencia Nacional* signalled the "enforcement" of the ECtHR judgement in the case of *Del Río Prada v. Spain*. It meant the release of the appellant, Ms. Inés del Río, and caused immense commotion in both scientific circles and the media. On the contrary, it is argued here that the *Audiencia Nacional* did no more than apply the legal norms that were binding upon it: on the one hand, those of the ECHR and the case-law of the ECtHR and, on the other, the case-law of the SCC. The *Audiencia Nacional* itself argued as much in its Court Decision expressly recognizing that if it did not enforce the ECtHR Judgement, then the SCC would do so. Therefore, it fell to the *Audiencia Nacional* to execute it, in order not to waste the time of institutions and individuals. And the *Audiencia Nacional* could make this affirmation, because it had the case-law of the SSC in mind relating to the enforcement of the ECtHR Judgement from which, as has been seen, it is worth noting that in view of the current harm to the right to liberty, there could be no other response to the judgements of the ECtHR than their enforcement and, in the absence of another pathway, through the *amparo* appeal.

And the fact is that the *Del Río Prada* case presents all the particularities to be enforced in the strictest of terms, as:

1. The Court, using an exceptional instrument in the judgement of the ECtHR pointed out by sixteen votes in favour and one against, that Spain should guarantee that the appellant be released from prison at the earliest possible date.
2. The mandate set in the operative part of the decision is direct, clear and unconditional, unopen to any interpretation at all, such that, in conformity with the most basic norms of International Law, it places a specific obligation on the State for compliance.
3. It is true that in this case, the Court awarded just satisfaction, but only for moral damages, it being understood that material damages can only be satisfied through the release of the appellant.

Thus, the combined interpretation of the synthesis of the position of the SCC with regard to the enforcement of ECtHR judgements and the summary of the operative part of the ECtHR judgement in the *Del Río Prada* case allow us to affirm that this supposition coincides with the criteria advanced by the SCC to set itself up as the body that enforces the judgements of the ECtHR. Thus, the breach of the ECHR noted by the ECtHR occurred in the course of a criminal proceeding; in second place, a breach of a right occurred that provoked an lengthening of her sentence; and, the most relevant point, in third place, the breach of a right of the ECHR implies ongoing harm to the right to personal liberty of art. 17 SC.

In fact, the 2012 Judgement of the Chamber of the European Court[10] would have deserved to have been enforced, at least provisionally, despite the statements that

[10]ECtHR judgement of 10 July 2012, c. Del Río Prada v. Spain.

were somewhat out of kilter with the Law issued by some Spanish authorities, following the publication of the 2012 judgement of the Chamber, affirming that in general they are not binding on the institutions of the signatory States.[11] As I defended at the time, although the judgement of the Chamber might be re-examined,[12] as the Spanish Government has requested, neither should it be forgotten here that, contrary to the general rule of this judicial instance, the European Court ordered the State to guarantee the release of the appellant in the shortest possible time[13]: in the face of this demand, the Spanish institutions could hardly remain impassive. So, while recognizing the lack of a final judgement, as some sectors of the judiciary argued, the obligatory nature of the decisions of Strasbourg—aside from their enforcement-related issues—required the release of Ms. del Río Prada. In this circumstance, the *Audiencia Nacional,* the *de officio* court trying the case, could have decreed the release of the convicted prisoner. As it did not do so, the counsel for the appellant requested her release in conformity with the principles and through the channels foreseen in Spanish criminal procedural Law.

In any case, the response of the judicial power was indeed immediate after the Judgement of the Grand Chamber, complying with the mandate contained in the European judgement, and that it was based on:

1. The binding nature of ECtHR judgements, as established in art. 46 ECHR.
2. The character of a legal norm with which compliance is obligatory from the ECHR, given that it has formed part of the Spanish legal order ever since it was ratified by Spain.
3. The mandate incumbent on Spanish public powers of interpretation in accordance with international treaties on matters of fundamental rights envisaged in art. 10.2 SCC.
4. The subjection of Spanish courts to the Law, which in this context means *"linkage to the Convention and the decisions and doctrine of its organ and jurisdictional guarantee [the ECtHR]"*.
5. The "clear and conclusive" nature of the mandate of the ECtHR for the release of Ms. Del Río Prada.
6. Finally, returning to the conclusions in the judgement of the Constitutional Court (STC 245/1991 of 16 December 1991) that have been expounded above: at the very least, that the conviction had been arrived at following a violation of the guarantees of due process, in this case, the illegitimate retroactive application of the law, and that this was provoking present harm to the right to liberty. It is worth recalling a sentence from the decision of the *Audiencia Nacional* in 1991 that highlighted that: "*the European Court is an obligatory jurisdiction to which our State has voluntarily submitted*".

[11] As highlighted in Queralt Jiménez (2012), *Esperando a Parot*, El Diario, available at http://www.eldiario.es/zonacritica/Esperando-Parot_6_52204785.html (last accessed 09/11/2016).

[12] As is foreseen in art. 43 ECHR.

[13] Particularly, in its judgement, the ECHR maintained that "*the respondent State is to ensure that the applicant is released at the earliest possible date (see paragraph 83 above)*".

In view of these conditions, the *Audiencia Nacional* is conclusive:

> In our constitutional system, the declaration by the European Court that the European Convention has been breached, due to a contradiction with the principle of criminal legality and the right to liberty, implies (according to art. 10.2 SC, in relation with arts. 5 and 7 of the Convention) the verification of the existence of a breach of the right to freedom of art. 17.7 SC, in the context of serving a term of imprisonment. Having identified the existence of a present violation of a fundamental right, the jurisdiction should act.

To end its argumentation with a summary of the constitutional doctrine relating to the enforcement of the ECtHR judgements:

> Which cannot in itself prevent the Constitutional Court, in the ambit of its area of control and provided that the competent courts had not complied with the judgement of the European Court, from proceeding to quash the judicial decisions, in an exceptional way, something that it will undertake when the following requirements concur: a) the ECtHR has declared a breach of a right of the Convention that is correlative to a fundamental right that is constitutionally recognized and can be included in an appeal for amparo, b) the breach has occurred as a consequence of a decision in the criminal jurisdictional order, c) the effects of that breach persist over time and remain current at the time of seeking the enforcement of the judgement of the European Court, and d) that individual liberty is affected.

Clear and well balanced.

After this decision, only 2 days later, the same Plenary of the Criminal Chamber of the *Audiencia Nacional* in AAN 62/2013 of 25 October 2013, ordered the release and expunged the criminal responsibility of Mr. J. M. Piriz, to whom the *Parot doctrine* had been applied before his imminent release from prison in June 2008, on account of his having served his sentence.

In this Decision, the *Audiencia Nacional* reiterated its thoughts on the binding nature of the ECHR and the judgements of the ECtHR, in order to take a further step forwards; on this occasion, to recognize that these decisions generate effects beyond their own verdicts and beyond the sections of a specific case. The paragraphs of this decision are transcribed below because of their clear and pedagogic positioning, in a way that few courts have done so to date in Spain:

> The pronouncements that the ECtHR delivers clearly transcend the appellant and are of general application to all cases in which similar situations emerge and it is so expressed in certain passages of the judgement [...].
>
> In short, beyond the case of Inés del Río, with a general nature, the ECtHR highlights the incompatibility with the ECHR of the retroactive application of the criteria for reckoning prison benefits introduced by STS 197/2006. But more so, the European Court, as the organ of the Convention in charge not only of decisions over specific situations, but also of their interpretation, has fixed a criteria in this Judgement to which the value of "final interpretation" should be recognized, binding for all States. Therefore, this pronouncement, as well as due to the conventional obligations assumed by Spain with the ratification of the Convention, which implies submission to the decisions and case-law of the ECtHR, has necessarily to be taken into account by this court when resolving the situation that is now set before it, also because our own constitutional text orders it to be so, when in its art. 10.2, it establishes that the interpretation of the norms relating to the fundamental rights and the liberties that the Constitution recognizes will be done in accordance with the international treaties and agreements on the same matters that are ratified by Spain.

Without a doubt, at this time, the case-law of the ECtHR marks the canon or the international standard in the recognition and protection of fundamental human rights in Europe, with its projection to other continents, and it also constitutes the marker on the scales that serves as the reference to calibrate the quality of the "Rule of Law" in the states of its member countries. The acceptance and linkage of all the States of the Council of Europe to its case-law, and not only to those directly affected by its decisions, does not only serve for the homogenization of European law that we share, but it especially constitutes one of our signs of cultural identity and of common European civilization. Separation from it not only implies an infringement of international legal obligations, but also a distancing from Europe and the meaning of its civilization.

If we reread the section in these pages dedicated to explaining the effect of a final interpretation of the ECtHR judgements, it may be seen how the AAN 62/2013 of 25 October 2013 in the *Piriz case* is in accordance with its demands. It is, moreover, in a case against the same State and with respect to which the European decision has already warned that there were others affected by the retroactive application of the new reckoning of the sentence with regard to prison benefits. The ECtHR had already delivered its judgement, on two occasions, and, therefore, its position with regard to the compatibility of the *Parot doctrine* with the European canon is clear.

3.3 The Supreme Court Before the ECtHR Judgement in the Del Río Prada Case: The Extension of Its Effects

The Decision of the Plenary of the *Audiencia Nacional* in the *Piriz case* was validated a little after by the Second Chamber of the Supreme Court that, in accordance with the Agreement of its General Chamber, of 12 November 2013, extended the effects of the *Del Río Prada* judgement to those convictions that were enforced under the old Penal Code repealed in 1973, and it agreed that "*in the cases of condemnatory judgements currently being enforced, delivered before 28 February 2006, in which the former Penal Code repealed in 1973 is applied, because the Penal Code of 1995 was no more favourable, the ordinary and extraordinary remissions that ensue will be made effective upon the maximum limit of sentence compliance established in accordance with article 70 of the aforementioned Code of 1973, in the way in which has been done prior to judgement num. 197/2006, 28 of February, of this Chamber*."

Without explaining it all, it is evident that the Supreme Court adopted this common criterion for all circumstances coincident with those of Inés del Río Prada and J. M. Piriz as a response to the mandate of the ECtHR, and of the Committee of Ministers, in that full compliance with an ECtHR judgement implies, as mentioned above, the avoidance of any repetition of the same breach of a conventional right. Thus, as a consequence of the ECtHR (Grand Chamber) judgement in the case of *Del Río Prada v. Spain*, it had to follow that the criterion applied by the *Audiencia Nacional* to this appellant should be applied to other prisoners to whom the *Parot* doctrine would have been applied, who were not only imprisoned for terrorism. In addition, this obligation is reinforced by the effect of a ‘final interpretation’. However, in this chain of cases in which there is a clear precedent that gives the specific pattern of how the principle of criminal legality should be interpreted in similar cases: whoever applies the Law has no margin for error. And, finally, and as a constitutional reinforcement, the SCC had to comply with the constitutional mandate of interpretation contained in art. 10.2 SC. So, as in all good Law, little margin was left for an alternative.

3.4 And So Too Subsidiarity

Lastly, it is worth mentioning a final argument to applaud the attitude of the Spanish courts in this chain of cases: the principle of subsidiarity of the European system for the protection of fundamental rights.

Subsidiarity is established in art. 1 ECHR in which it says that the States are before anyone else responsible for overseeing guarantees and respect for the rights and liberties contained in the Convention. Thus, the ECtHR is a jurisdiction of international and subsidiary protection and every day hundreds of claims are brought before it. Subsidiarity is understood, within a system of international protection, that should respect the sovereignty of the participant States that exercise it, in this case, selecting and establishing the system of safeguards that they consider opportune. Thus, this clause ensures the independence and autonomy of the internal jurisdictional organs, and the decision-making capacity of the political powers and the public administration. Finally, it respects the scope of action of democratically elected national legislators in which popular sovereignty is represented. All of them will imbue the rights and liberties recognized in their own categories and in the ECHR with form and content.

Having set that down, it should be remembered that both the conventional and the constitutional categories usually present the rights in vague precepts with little detail that are in need of development and adaption to the needs and requirements of societies, a function that by virtue of the principle of subsidiarity, should be carried out by national authorities, because they are better positioned to value the needs of society at any moment in time due to their direct and continuous contact with it.[14]

Likewise, subsidiarity, as a principle by which respect for the sovereignty of the participant States is made effective, justifies their margin of appreciation to make free choices over the means of implementing the rights and freedoms recognized in the ECHR in an effective way. As the ECtHR has always argued, the purpose of the ECHR is not to seek the uniformity of a response in the face of similar situations, but compatibility between the measures adopted by national authorities and the *acquis conventionnel*, making the harmonization process effective, as said above, in

[14]ECtHR Judgement of 7 December 1976, c. Handyside v. the United Kingdom.

matters of rights and liberties. The States should therefore search for responses that are compatible with conventional demands understood in the light of European case-law.[15] The States enjoy freedom to determine the manner in which that minimum standard established by the ECHR will be reached, and the instruments which should be implemented to achieve it, but, in so far as it is an inexcusable minimum, the margin is quite narrow in this phase of consolidation of the rights. It is also true that the more the guarantee of a right is developed, the more we distance ourselves from the essential to enter into a complementary phase, and the greater, in principle, the freedom of action of the State.

As things stand, it appears obvious that once the Court has determined that a specific measure is contrary to the ECHR, the subsidiarity of the system demands that the State take the relevant measures so that the violation is no longer upheld or is withdrawn and, by doing so, prevent the case returning to Strasbourg. It appears convenient now to recall the words of the (former) President of the ECtHR, Mr. - Jean-Paul Costa, on the principle of subsidiarity:

> [. . .] subsidiarity. It is perhaps more appropriate to refer to the sharing of responsibility for the protection of human rights between national authorities and the Court.[16]

The follow up of the interpretative effects is an effective instrument of respect for the principle of subsidiarity in the European system of guarantees and the assumption that the protection of rights is a shared responsibility freely assumed between both the States and the ECtHR.

4 The Judicial Review as a Means of Internal Enforcement of the Judgements of the ECtHR

The Second Chamber of the Supreme Court concluded the Agreement of 12 November of 2013 with the following desideratum:

> The Court considers it necessary that the legislative power regulate the appropriate procedural channel with the necessary clarity and precision in connection with the effectiveness of the decisions of the ECtHR.

The Supreme Court has been complaining in a more or less explicit way over recent years of the lack of legal prevision of the instrument of enforcement of ECtHR judgements against Spain in which the ECHR was declared to be breached. At the start of the 2000, the Supreme Court insinuated that a judicial review (*revisión*) could perhaps be the appropriate mechanism, but it soon discarded that possibility and clung to the impossibility of compliance with the judgements of the ECtHR through the aforementioned review foreseen in procedural laws in which

[15]ECtHR Judgement of 6 December 1980, c. Guzzardi v. Italy.

[16]Memorandum of the president of the European Court of Human Rights to the states with a view to preparing the Interlaken conference, 03.07.2009, p. 4.

nothing was expressly said nor was it said what the procedural consequence of a ECtHR judgement has to be.[17]

However, certainly motivated by the lack of support that the *Audiencia Nacional* felt at the time of releasing Ms. Inés del Río and other courts at the time of implementing the judgement of the Grand Chamber of the ECtHR in the case of this appellant, the Supreme Court 1 year later adopted the Agreement of 21 October 2014 in which the following was succinctly announced:

> Single point: the viability of the Appeal for a Judicial Review as a procedural means of compliance with the decisions of the ECtHR in which a violation of fundamental rights has been declared that affects the innocence of the person concerned.
>
> Agreement: In so far as there is no express judicial review in the legal order for the effectiveness of the judgements delivered by the ECtHR that discern the breach of a fundamental right of the convicted person by the Spanish Courts, the appeal for a review of art. 954 LECrim serves this function.

As may be seen, in view of the criticism flowing from certain sectors of the decisions adopted by the *Audiencia Nacional*, accused by some of acting against current legality, despite what has been said above, the Supreme Court decided to habilitate the appeal for a judicial review as a means of requesting the enforcement of ECtHR judgements in criminal matters. That is of course, as could not be otherwise, for so long as the legislator foresees nothing in that respect. Attention should be paid to the fact that the Supreme Court refrains from going so far as to determine whether the review, due to the pronouncement of an ECtHR judgement, should be understood as a form of expressing the causes that already exist in art. 954 LECrim or whether it is rather more a question of incorporating a new habilitating circumstance into case-law.

What is certain is that, since the adoption of the Agreement, the Criminal Chamber of the Supreme Court has already had the opportunity to admit an appeal for a review and, recently, of ruling on it.

In effect, after the ECtHR Judgement of 21 February 2012, c. Serrano Contreras v. Spain, the appellant before the Court of Strasbourg petitioned to the Supreme Court and requested authorization to lodge an appeal for a review of the judgements handed down by the *Audiencia Provincial* of Cordoba that had convicted him and the other accused, a decision that was in part confirmed in a subsequent Judgement of the Supreme Court. In ATS of 24 November 2014, the Supreme Court admitted this petition, in accordance with the agreement adopted in October of the same year. Finallythe Criminal Chamber of the Supreme Court delivered STS 330/2015 of 19 May 2015 partially in favour of the appeal for a judicial hearing.

In this decision, the Magistrates took the opportunity of limiting the scope of the review in circumstances where the enforcement of an ECtHR judgement was sought:

> This possibility is not to be interpreted in the sense that in all cases, if the ECtHR has appreciated the breach of a right recognized in the ECHR, it has to uphold the demand

[17] Arangüena Fanego (2009), pp. 301 and ff.

directly and it should automatically and inevitably agree on the nullity of the judgement for which a judicial review is sought. As the favourable judgement of the ECtHR does not grant the nullity or the repeal of an internal judgement, but limits itself to declaring the breach of a right recognized in the Convention, although it may contain, as happens with increasing frequency, a concrete modality of reparation or just satisfaction, as foreseen in article 41 of the Convention.

On the contrary, what permits the so-called appeal for a judicial review, reather more of a review process, is precisely the examination or re-opening of the case, which had been closed in a final judgement, with a view to the precision of the effects that the declaration of the ECtHR necessarily has to produce in the specific circumstance that is examined. So it is clear that the declaration of an existing breach of a right recognized in the Convention, either in the course of the proceedings, or in the acquisition or submission of a particular piece of evidence for the prosecution, will not always determine the nullity of the condemnatory judgement delivered against whoever appeals to the Court of Strasbourg, as it may be that the whole process has not been affected or that the declaration is not in reference to all the evidence, and that sufficient material persists, regardless of the breach that is declared, which justifies the continuance of the sentence, either totally or partially. It will therefore be necessary in each case, to determine the scope of the declaration issued by that Court, with regard to the content of its sentence and the sentence that is to be reviewed. And at present, when proceeding towards such a determination through the judicial review, the competence corresponds to this Supreme Court.

The Supreme Court stands, finally, and by its own decision, as the court entrusted with judicial enforcement of ECtHR judgements. Without doubt, the General Agreement of October 2014 is good news for people who, once an internal criminal procedure is over (even including the Supreme Court), appeal to Strasbourg and receive a judgement in their favour that declares the violation of a convention-related right, with constitutional parallels. These people know that they may bring the decision of the ECtHR before the Supreme Court and request a judicial review of their proceedings. We have in all probability gained greater legal certainty.

5 Legal Changes Towards the End of 2015 and the Incorporation of a Legal Mechanism of Enforcement of the Judgements of the ECtHR

On 21 July 2015, Organic Law LO 7/2015 in reform of the Organic Law of Judicial Power was passed, in which, finally, the review of a final judgement before the Supreme Court was incorporated as a means of enforcement of ECtHR judgements against Spain. Thus, the Explanatory Memorandum of the above-mentioned Organic Law explained that:

A provision is included [...] with respect to the judgements of the European Court of Human Rights that declare the breach of some of the rights recognized in the European Convention for the protection of Human Rights and Fundamental Freedoms and in their Protocols, establishing that it will be sufficient reason for filing the appeal for a judicial review exclusively of the final judgement handed down in the proceedings 'a quo'. With it, legal safety in such a sensitive sector is increased, with no room for doubt, as well as the

> protection of fundamental rights, the foundation of political order and social peace, as proclaimed in article 10.1 of our Constitution.

Organic Law LO 7/2015, in the first place, has meant the addition of a new art. 5 *bis* in the Organic Law on Judicial Power that establishes the general norm that incorporates the judicial review as an internal procedure to enforce the judgements of the ECtHR:

> An appeal for a judicial review may be lodged with the Supreme Court against a firm judicial decision, in accordance with the procedural norms of each jurisdictional order, when the European Court of Human Rights has declared that such a decision has been delivered in violation of some of the rights recognized in the European Convention for the Protection of Human Rights and Fundamental Freedoms and their Protocols, provided that the breach, in view of its nature and seriousness, involves effects that persist and that cannot cease in any other way that is not through this review.

In the course of developing this general provision, the Law on Civil Procedure (LEC; Ley 1/2000, de Enjuiciamiento Civil, arts. 510, 511 and 512), the Organic Law on Military Procedure (Ley Orgánica 2/1989, de Procedimiento Militar, arts. 328 and 504), and the Law on Contentious-Administrative Jurisdiction (Ley 29/1998, de la Jurisdicción Contencioso-Administrativa, art. 102) have all been amended, in such a way that in the three main jurisdictions the review procedure is foreseen as a means of enforcing ECtHR judgements. This new procedural possibility entered into force for the three jurisdictional orders on 1 October 2015.

With regard to the criminal order, it was Law 41/2015, of 5 October, in amendment of the Law on Criminal Procedure for speeding up criminal justice and the strengthening of procedural guarantees, which has incorporated a new reason for the request for a review in art. 954 LECrim: the pronouncement of an ECtHR judgement on the same proceedings.

Finally, the Law on Criminal Procedure is applied in a subsidiary way in the labour proceedings, in accordance with art. 236 of Law 36/2011 on the regulation of Social Jurisdiction, in matters concerning the review of firm judgements. The new art. 510 LEC will therefore be applied and the ECtHR judgements against Spain may also be enforced in the social order through the review procedure.

There are various questions that remain to be analyzed with regard to the new procedural channel for the enforcement of ECtHR judgements in Spain because, as may be seen in the reading of the aforementioned provisions, the review will take place if there is a series of concurrent conditions, on which there will be time to work and to write over coming months. I will limit myself to pointing out only one, but a relevant one: unlike what other European countries (Germany, France, Austria, for example) in the European scenario have done, in which the judicial review for the enforcement of ECtHR judgements has been limited to the criminal field, in Spain, as has been seen, it is recognized for the five jurisdictional orders (Civil, Penal, Contentious-Administrative, Social, and Military) into which the Spanish judiciary is divided. It remains to be seen what the motives of judicial policy are that have led the legislator to lend support to this breadth and generosity in the enforcement of ECtHR judgements. But that will be the subject of another article.

References

Arangüena Fanego C (2009) El cumplimiento de las sentencias del Tribunal Europeo de Derechos Humanos y la revisión de sentencias firmes. In: García Roca J, Fernández Sánchez, PA (eds) Integración europea a través de derechos fundamentales: de un sistema binario a otro integrado. Centro de Estudios Políticos y Constitucionales, Madrid, pp 289–325

Díaz Crego M (2013) Cuando Parot llegó a Estrasburgo. Teoría y Realidad Constitucional 31:573–612

Irurzun Montoro F (2013) La ejecución de las sentencias del Tribunal Europeo de Derechos Humanos. In: Queralt Jiménez A (dir) El Tribunal de Estrasburgo en el espacio judicial europeo. Aranzadi, Cizur Menor, pp 131–161

Queralt Jiménez A (2008) La Interpretación de los derechos: del Tribunal de Estrasburgo al Tribunal Constitucional. Centro de Estudios Políticos y Constitucionales, Madrid

Queralt Jiménez A (2012) Esperando a Parot, El Diario.es. http://www.eldiario.es/zonacritica/Esperando-Parot_6_52204785.html

The "Del Río Prada" Judgements and the Problem of the Enforcement of ECtHR Decisions

Carlos Ruiz Miguel

The European Court of Human Rights (ECtHR) Grand Chamber judgement of October 21st 2013 upholding the previous Court Chamber judgement of July 10th 2012 on the case *Del Río Prada* presents two sets of problems. The first is related to the substantial discussion on whether the Spanish State violated articles 5 and 7 of the European Convention on Human Rights. The second is related with the procedural features of the case. Although the first one has a clear interest, the procedural questions raised by this case are even more important. In this contribution, after (1) considering the content of the operative part of the judgement, (2) I suggest how convenient would have been to refer the case to the Court for a question of interpretation of this operative part. Then, I will argue the thesis of the lack of executive enforcement of the ECtHR judgements in (3) the European Law and (4) the Spanish Law. Afterwards I will examine (5) the irregular enforcement of this ECtHR judgement in Spain, and finally, (6) the evolution of the Spanish Law to enforce ECtHR judgements.

Professor of Constitutional Law at Universidade de Santiago de Compostela.

C. Ruiz Miguel (✉)
Universidade de Santiago de Compostela, Campus Sur USC, 15782 Santiago de Compostela, A Coruña, Spain
e-mail: carlos.ruiz@usc.es

M. Pérez Manzano et al. (eds.), *Multilevel Protection of the Principle of Legality in Criminal Law*, DOI 10.1007/978-3-319-63865-2_12

1 The Operative Part of the ECtHR Judgements from 10th July 2012 (Chamber) and 21st October 2013 (Grand Chamber)

1.1 The ECtHR judgements are not enforceable according to the Convention

The operative parts of the two ECtHR judgements on the *Del Río Prada* case raise the debate about the nature and especially the effects of the ECtHR judgements. The Court makes reference to two Articles of the European Convention on Human Rights that say:

> Article 46.1: "*The High Contracting Parties undertake to abide by the final judgement of the Court in any case to which they are parties*".
>
> Article 41: "*If the Court finds that there has been a violation of the Convention or the Protocols thereto, and if the internal law of the High Contracting Party concerned allows only partial reparation to be made, the Court shall, if necessary, afford just satisfaction to the injured party*".

There is no doubt that the ECtHR through its judgements (1) interprets the Convention and declares if the rights proclaimed in this text have been respected or violated; and (2) if the Court finds a violation of any of those rights, it may "afford just satisfaction" to the injured party "if the internal law of the High Contracting Party concerned allows only partial reparation to be made". The obvious consequence is that the accession of a certain State to the Convention will not oblige it to grant "full" reparation if a violation of the Convention is found. And despite the non-existence of such an obligation, the ECtHR may still afford a "just satisfaction". The conclusion is crystal clear: the ECtHR judgements may have a declarative and a partial reparatory effect, but not a nullifying one and ECtHR judgements alone are not in themselves enforceable according to the Convention.

1.2 The Del Río Prada judgement blurs the nature of the ECtHR judgements

Despite the clear text of the Convention, the ECtHR has pretended to give to its judgements a force not foreseen in the Convention, going "*ultra vires*" as happened in the *Del Río Prada* case in its (Chamber and of the Grand Chamber) judgements, as I will explain in this contribution.

These ECtHR judgements contain three important paragraphs (although not exactly the same) that deserve to be reproduced. The judgement of the Grand Chamber (done in English and French) says[1]:

[1]ECtHR (GC) Judgement of 21st October 2013, c. Del Río Prada v. Spain, par. 137–139. The judgement of the Chamber (ECtHR Judgement of 10th July 2012, c. Del Río Prada v. Spain, par. 81–83) has a similar but not the same content:

137. By virtue of Article 46 of the Convention, the High Contracting Parties undertake to abide by the final judgement of the Court in any case to which they are parties, execution being supervised by the Committee of Ministers. This means that when the Court finds a violation, the respondent State is under a legal obligation not just to pay those concerned the sums awarded by way of just satisfaction under Article 41, but also to take individual and/or, if appropriate, general measures in its domestic legal order to put an end to the violation found by the Court and to redress the effects, the aim being to put the applicant, as far as possible, in the position he would have been in had the requirements of the Convention not been disregarded (see, among many other authorities, Scozzari and Giunta v. Italy [GC], nos. 39,221/98 and 41,963/98, § 249, ECtHR 2000-VIII; Verein gegen Tierfabriken Schweiz (VgT) v. Switzerland (no. 2) [GC], no. 32772/02, § 85, ECtHR 2009; and Scoppola (no. 2), cited above, § 147).

138. It is true that in principle the respondent State remains free to choose the means by which it will discharge its legal obligation under Article 46 of the Convention, provided that such means are compatible with the conclusions set out in the Court's judgement (see Scozzari and Giunta, cited above, § 249). However, in certain particular situations, with a view to assisting the respondent State in fulfilling its obligations under Article 46, the Court may seek to indicate the type of individual and/or general measures that might be taken in order to put an end to the situation that gave rise to the finding of a violation (see Broniowski v. Poland [GC], no. 31443/96, § 194, ECtHR 2004-V, and Stanev v. Bulgaria [GC], no. 36760/06, §§ 255–58, ECtHR 2012). In other exceptional cases, the nature of the violation found may be such as to leave no real choice as to the measures required to remedy it and the Court may decide to indicate only one such measure (see Assanidze v. Georgia [GC], no. 71503/01, §§ 202–03, ECtHR 2004-II; Aleksanyan v. Russia, no. 46468/06, §§ 239–40, 22 December 2008; and Fatullayev v. Azerbaijan, no. 40984/07, §§ 176–77, 22 April 2010).

139. The Grand Chamber agrees with the Chamber's finding and considers that the present case belongs to this last-mentioned category. Having regard to the particular

---

81. (...) the respondent State is under a legal obligation not just to pay those concerned the sums awarded by way of just satisfaction under Article 41, but also to take the necessary general and/or, if appropriate, individual measures. The Court's judgements being essentially declaratory in nature, the respondent State remains free, subject to monitoring by the Committee of Ministers, to choose the means by which it will discharge its legal obligation under Article 46 of the Convention, provided that such means are compatible with the conclusions set out in the Court's judgement (see Scozzari and Giunta v. Italy [GC], (...), and Scoppola v. Italy (no. 2) [GC], (...).

82. Nevertheless, exceptionally, with a view to assisting the respondent State in fulfilling its obligations under Article 46, the Court has sought to indicate the type of measure that might be taken to put an end to the situation identified (see, for example, Broniowski v. Poland [GC], (...). In other exceptional cases, the nature of the violation found may be such as to leave no real choice as to the measures required to remedy it and the Court may decide to indicate only one such measure (see Assanidze v. Georgia [GC], (...), Alexanian v. Russia, (...), and Fatullayev v. Azerbaijan, (...).

83. The Court considers that the present case belongs to this last-mentioned category. Having regard to the particular circumstances of the case and to the urgent need to put an end to the violation of Articles 7 and 5.1 of the Convention (...), the Court considers it incumbent on the respondent State to ensure that the applicant is released at the earliest possible date.

The judgement of the Chamber was done in French and then translated into English. The French text of the last sentence of paragraph 83 says *"(la Cour) estime qu'il incombe à l'État défendeur d'assurer la remise en liberté de la requérante dans les plus brefs délais"*.

> circumstances of the case and to the urgent need to put an end to the violations of the Convention it has found, it considers it incumbent on the respondent State to ensure that the applicant is released at the earliest possible date.[2]

Having regard of these considerations we may understand the several contents of the operative part of the judgements. As far as this contribution is concerned, the most relevant part is:

> 3. Holds, by sixteen votes to one, that the respondent State is to ensure that the applicant is released at the earliest possible date.[3]

1.3 *Questions raised by the Del Río Prada judgement*

The texts of the reasoning and the operative parts of these judgements, as well as the official Spanish translation (from the French text) raise some important questions.

The first, is that some words of the 2012 Chamber judgement (par. 81) have disappeared in the 2013 Grand Chamber judgement: *"The Court's judgements being essentially declaratory in nature"*. While certainly omitted in the Grand Chamber judgement, the Grand Chamber itself could not have failed to recognize, when developing its reasoning, that the ECtHR judgements are declarative, because despite its omission, the Court takes care to say that what the court does is "to indicate" a measure with a view "to assisting" the respondent State, and an "indication" is not clearly an order.

The second question, related to the first, is that the "indication" of the Court is to release Del Río Prada "*at the earliest possible date*". And here we find a very important difference between the official versions in English and French, because in the French version the judgement says "*dans les plus brefs délais*". The word "possible" is omitted in the reasoning and in the operative part of the French versions of the judgements. We can leave aside the question of whether the Court has the power to "indicate" a measure and, what is more, to add that it is the "only one". The main point is that the English version says that this "only one" measure should be taken if "possible" "*at the earliest possible date*", but the French version merely says that the Court finds it is incumbent upon the respondent State to ensure the release of the applicant "without delay". Whith the word "possible" the Court

---

[2] The last sentence of par. 139 in the French version says *"(La Cour) estime qu'il incombe à l'État défendeur d'assurer la remise en liberté de la requérante dans les plus brefs délais"*.

[3] French text: *"qu'il incombe à l'État défendeur d'assurer la remise en liberté de la requérante dans les plus brefs délais"*. The operative part of the judgement of the Chamber says that the Court "5. Holds *that the respondent State is to ensure that the applicant is released at the earliest possible date (see paragraph 83 above)"*. French text: "5. Dit *qu'il incombe à l'État défendeur d'assurer la remise en liberté de la requérante dans les plus brefs délais (paragraphe 83 ci-dessus)"*.

explicitly leaves the decision over the possibility of enforcing its judgement to the respondent State.

2 The Convenience of a Request for an Interpretation or a Revision of the "Del Río Prada" Judgment

The judgements in the *Del Río Prada* case contain some statements that we could consider contradictory to the Convention or, at least, ambiguous and in need of a clarification. The Grand Chamber judgement could have been the subject of a request from any party to the case for an interpretation by the ECtHR (Rule 79 ECtHR), a referral from the Committee of Ministers for a ruling (Article 46.3 of the Convention), and a request for a revision of the judgement (pertaining to new facts) (Rule 80 ECtHR).

2.1 Eventual Request for an Interpretation from the Respondent State

The Convention does not foresee any challenge to the final judgements by the respondent. However, any party to an ECtHR case may, under Rule 79 of the ECtHR Rules of Court (1st January 2016) request on interpretation of the operative part of the judgements. This Rule says that (§79.1 and 79.2).

> A party may request the interpretation of a judgement within a period of one year following the delivery of that judgement.
>
> (...) it shall state precisely the point or points in the operative provisions of the judgement on which interpretation is required.

It is clear that no such request for an interpretation was filed by Spain, but did it have any basis to do so? Number 3 of the operative part of the Grand Chamber judgement (number 5 of Chamber judgement) says that *"the respondent State is to ensure that the applicant is released at the earliest possible date"* (English)/*"il incombe à l'État défendeur d'assurer la remise en liberté de la requérante dans les plus brefs délais"* (French). In justification of this statement, the ECtHR included several paragraphs in the two judgements (pars. 137–139 of the Grand Chamber Judgement and pars. 81–83 of the Chamber judgement).

In my opinion there are several grounds for such a request. First of all, being considered the "nature of the violation" of the Convention found in this case, where there are several sentences (none of them questioned before the ECtHR) that amount to more than 3000 years of imprisonment, it could be argued if the release of Del Río Prada should be preceded by an audience with the victims. Secondly, it may be directly asked if the ECtHR considered that point of the operative part of its judgement as "enforceable". And finally, the respondent State might have expressed its interest in the key sentence of the judgement and the consequences of its linguistic divergence. In my view the English version seems consistent with the declaratory nature of the ECtHR judgements, but the French version appears to be "*ultra vires*". According to Article 33.4 of the Vienna Convention on the Law of Treaties "*when a comparison of the authentic texts discloses a difference of meaning which the application of articles 31 and 32 does not remove, the meaning which best reconciles the texts, having regard to the object and purpose of the treaty, shall be adopted*". In this case it appears to my mind quite clear that neither the object nor the purpose of the treaty (the European Convention in this regard) justifies presumptive attachment of an enforceable aspect to ECtHR judgements.

2.2 Eventual Request from the Committee of Ministers for an ECtHR Interpretation

The "request for an interpretation" from the Committee of Ministers has a wider purpose than the request that a State party may introduce. Whilst the request by a Member State should only aim at the operative part of a judgement, the request for an interpretation from the Committee of Ministers might be aimed at "*a problem of interpretation of the judgement*" (Article 46.3 of the Convention). Article 46 of the Convention was amended by the Protocol no. 14 (entering into force on June 1st 2010) that added paragraphs 3 to 5 of this Article. Article 46.3 says that.

> If the Committee of Ministers considers that the supervision of the execution of a final judgement is hindered by a problem of interpretation of the judgement, it may refer the matter to the Court for a ruling on the question of interpretation. A referral decision shall require a majority vote of two thirds of the representatives entitled to sit on the committee.

Can we find such a "problem of interpretation" in the judgements of the *Del Río Prada* case? I think so.

First of all, it could be asked whether the omission in the Grand chamber judgement of the sentence *"The Court's judgements being essentially declaratory in nature"* (par. 81) included in the Chamber judgement, means that the Grand Chamber does not consider that its judgements are *"essentially declaratory in nature"*.

Secondly, it might be asked whether the Convention allows the ECtHR to "indicate" to the respondent State that the defendant should be released *"dans les plus brefs délais"* (at the earliest date), according to the French (but not the English) version. It might be questioned whether a sentence of that kind in the operative part is consistent with Articles 41 and 46 of the Convention that let the State to choose the means to fulfil its legal obligations.

Thirdly, social commotion over similar cases was evident in Spain, following the Grand Chamber judgement in the *Del Río Prada* case, when the Spanish courts, in cases other than this, ordered the immediate release of inmates who remained in prison according to the doctrine held by the Supreme Court to decide the *Del Río Prada* case. As we will see, the ECtHR clearly appears not to have initiated a "pilot-judgement-procedure", as foreseen in Rule 61 of the Rules of the ECtHR (introduced in 2011). The Spanish Government in its communication to the Committee of Ministers, dated November 19th 2013, on the following given to the judgement,[4] informed the Committee (paragraph 21 of the communication) that several orders had been dictated by the criminal courts extending the criterion set in the ECtHR judgement to other cases (the Government cites six decisions adopted between October 24th and November 14th). In my view, the Government of Spain should perhaps have raised a "problem of interpretation" with the ECtHR judgement, insofar as it was understood to be a "pilot judgement" affecting the measures in those orders, for the Committee of Ministers to submit to the ECtHR.

2.3 *Request by the State Respondent for Revision of the Judgement*

The Rules of the ECtHR also introduce another procedure not included in the text of the Convention: a request for revision. According to the Rule 80.1:

> A party may, in the event of the discovery of a fact which might by its nature have a decisive influence and which, when a judgement was delivered, was unknown to the Court and could not reasonably have been known to that party, request the Court, within a period of six months after that party acquired knowledge of the fact, to revise that judgement.

Are there any grounds for such a request in the case *Del Río Prada*? I think so. Reports in two Spanish mainstream communications media, on February 12th 2006, informed the public that Inés del Río Prada had received by fraudulent means from the system of sentence remission for work done in prison, established in Spanish law.[5] According to this information, Inés Del Río had enrolled on a regular course at the University of the Basque Country...while she remained in prison. No further information was provided on these allegations. One might, if suspicious, think that the Government indirectly censured the information, which was at that time in secret negotiation with the terrorist organization of which Del Río Prada was a member. Future governments, if minded to do so, might one day release information on this situation. Were it true, the ECtHR judgement might have to be

[4]See Communication de l'Espagne relative à l'affaire Del Río Prada contre Espagne (Requête n° 42,750/09)—Informations mises à disposition en vertu de la Règle 8.2.a des Règles du Comité des Ministres pour la surveillance de l'exécution des arrêts et des termes des règlements amiables [DH-DD (2013)1248].

[5]*Europa Press* (12-II-2006) and *El Mundo* (12-II-2016). http://www.elmundo.es/elmundo/2006/02/12/espana/1139745259.html [Accessed October 6th 2016].

revised, insofar it was considered that Del Río Prada followed legitimate "remission" activities that might turn out to be illegitimate.

3 The Non-Enforceability of the ECtHR Judgements in the European Law

The enforceability of ECtHR judgements may be considered from two different perspectives: the international and the domestic one.[6] Under the first perspective we may consider whether the ECtHR judgements are enforceable according to the Convention; under the second, even if these judgements are not enforceable *ex conventione*, they may become so *ex lege*, that is, under the domestic law.

3.1 The Convention established an obligation "to abide to", but not "to enforce" the ECtHR judgements

The Chamber judgement in the case *Del Río Prada* sustained that ECtHR judgements are "*essentially declaratory in nature*" and that "*the respondent State remains free, subject to monitoring by the Committee of Ministers, to choose the means by which it will discharge its legal obligation under Article 46 of the Convention, provided that such means are compatible with the conclusions set out in the Court's judgement*" (par. 81). In the Grand Chamber judgement, although omitted the references "*essentially declaratory nature*" and "*subject to monitoring by the Committee of Ministers*" were omitted the principle that the State remains free to choose the means is acknowledged (par. 138). This a statement may also be found in previous ECtHR judgements[7]

Previously, in the *Castillo Algar* judgement, the Court said

> The Court recalls that a judgement in which it finds a breach imposes on the respondent State a legal obligation under the Convention to put an end to such breach and make reparation for its consequences in such a way as to restore as far as possible the situation existing before the breach (restitutio in integrum). However, if restitutio in integrum is impossible the respondent States are free to choose the means whereby they will comply with a judgement in which the Court has found a breach. It falls to the Committee of Ministers acting under Article 54 of the Convention to supervise compliance in this respect (see, mutatis mutandis, the Akdivar and Others v. Turkey judgement of 1 April 1998

[6]There is a wide bibliography on this issue as well in Spain as in the European literature. The two main books in the Spanish literature are Ruiz Miguel (1997) and Bujosa Vadell (1997). Many articles have been written on this question too: Liñán Nogueras (1985), Morenilla Rodríguez (1989), Escobar Hernández (1992), Soria Jiménez (1992, 1995), Izquierdo Sans (1997), Rodríguez (2001–2002), De Juan Casadevall (2005), Torralba Mendiola (2007) and Ripol Carulla (2010).

[7]ECtHR (GC) Judgement of 13 July 2000, c. Scozzari and Giunta v. Italy par. 249; and ECtHR (GC) Judgement of 17 September 2009, c. Scoppola v. Italy (no. 2), par. 147.

> (Article 50), Reports 1998–II, pp. 723–24, § 47). Consequently, the applicant's claims under this head must be dismissed.[8]

It is worth noting that the ECtHR made this consideration following the petition from the applicant who *"sought an order quashing his conviction by the Central Military Court on 25 May 1994"* (par. 58).

The above implies that the ECtHR judgements are not enforceable, that is, they are not self-executing. However, according to Article 46 ECHR the State undertakes to "abide" by the final judgement of the Court. This wording is quite different to the one used in late similar Conventions as the American (Article 68.1 of the American Convention on Human Rights) and the African (Article 30 of the Protocol to the African Charter on Human and Peoples' Rights on the establishment of an African Court of Human and Peoples' Rights) treaties who say that the States undertake "to comply" with the judgments. On the contrary, to "abide" implies that is the State itself who chooses the way to try to enforce the judgement. If there is "good faith", if it is possible to abide by the judgement, i.e., if the domestic legal order has the means to enforce the ECtHR judgement, the State makes use of them. Otherwise, if the State lacks of "good faith", it will not enforce the judgement even if it has the means to do so. But it is essential to note that the Convention does not (and cannot) impose on the State the use of means that are not foreseen in the domestic legal order because the State is a "rule of law". Precisely because the Member-States live under the rule of law, state bodies should act according to the domestic law in force and are not allowed to violate the domestic legal order.

3.2 The pretended "precedents" to the Del Río Prada case

There is no doubt that no self-executing effect (enforceability) is attached to ECtHR judgements in the Convention. And it is a fact that the ECtHR case law has reiterated this doctrine.[9] However, to justify its "indication" to release the applicant in the case *Del Río Prada*, the ECtHR seeks to mention some pretended precedents:

> In other exceptional cases, the nature of the violation found may be such as to leave no real choice as to the measures required to remedy it and the Court may decide to indicate only one such measure (see Assanidze v. Georgia [GC], no. 71503/01, §§ 202-03, ECtHR 2004-II; Aleksanyan v. Russia, no. 46468/06, §§ 239-40, 22 December 2008; and Fatullayev v. Azerbaijan, no. 40984/07, §§ 176-77, 22 April 2010).[10]

However this consideration made by the ECtHR in the *Del Río Prada* case must be nuanced because one of the cases cited (*Aleksanyan*) does not fit with this case

---

[8]ECtHR Judgement of 28 October 1998, c. Castillo Algar v. Spain, par. 60.

[9]ECtHR Judgement of 13 June 1979, c. Marckx v. Belgium, para. 58. The Court has never explicitely overruled this doctrine.

[10]ECtHR (GC) Judgement of 21 October 2013, c. Del Río Prada v. Spain, par. 138; ECtHR Judgement of 10 July 2012, c. Del Río Prada v. Spain, par. 82.

and the other two (*Assanidze* and *Fattulayev*) are quite different among themselves and cannot be comparable to the case *Del Río Prada*.

In *Assanidze*, the ECtHR dealt with a person who was deprived of his liberty despite of his acquittal. The ECtHR held that *"the respondent State must secure the applicant's release at the earliest possible date"* (*"dans les plus brefs délais"* in the French version).[11]

In *Fatullayev*, the applicant (previously sued for the exact same statements in the civil proceedings and, as a consequence, having paid a substantial amount in damages) was sentenced to 2 years and 6 months' imprisonment. The Court considered that the circumstances of the case disclosed no justification for the imposition of a prison sentence on the applicant.[12] So, *"having regard to the particular circumstances of the case and the urgent need to put an end to the violations of Article 10 of the Convention"* the ECtHR considered *"that, as one of the means to discharge its obligation under Article 46 of the Convention, the respondent State shall secure the applicant's immediate release"* which was in fact the means foreseen in the operative part.[13]

Finally, the *Aleksanyan* case hardly appears comparable to this case insofar as the Court considered that "the Russian Government, in order to discharge its legal obligation under Article 46 of the Convention, must replace detention on remand with other, reasonable and less stringent, measure of restraint, or with a combination of such measures, provided by Russian law".[14] So the applicant was not sentenced. The *Aleksanyan* case cites as a precedent the ruling on *Abbasov*. However, the "*indication*" of the Court in the *Abbasov* case was the re-trial (not the release) of the applicant[15] an "indication" that was not included in the operative part of the judgement.

In conclusion, none of the abovementioned cases alleged by the ECtHR as precedents to *Del Río Prada* are really comparable. In *Aleksanyan* the Court did not indicate only one means. In *Fatullayev* a press offence, not a crime was the motive for sentencing the applicant who, moreover had already satisfied civil damages. In *Assanidze* the Court ruled that *"the respondent State shall secure the applicant's immediate release"*, but unlike to Del Río Prada, was acquitted in the proceedings. Having regard to these substantial differences, we cannot share the view that *Del Río Prada* does not *"introduce anything new"* and *"rests on a consolidated case law"*.[16] By the way, it is worth noting that up until today, the *Fatullayev* judgement (like many others) has not been executed.[17]

---

[11] ECtHR (GC) Judgement of 8 April 2004, c. Assanidze v. Georgia, par. 202–03 and § 14(a) of the operative part of the judgement.

[12] ECtHR Judgement of 22 April 2010, c. Fatullayev v. Azerbaijan, par. 103.

[13] ECtHR Judgement of 22 April 2010, c. Fatullayev v. Azerbaijan, par. 176–77, and 6 of the operative part of the judgement.

[14] ECtHR Judgement of 22 December 2008, c. Aleksanyan v. Russia, par. § 40.

[15] ECtHR Judgement of 17 January 2008, c. Abbasov v. Azerbaijan, par. 35 and ff.

[16] Alcácer Guirao (2012), p. 938; Andrés Sáenz De Santamaría (2014), p. 212.

[17] Committee of Ministers, 1265 meeting (DH), 20–21 September 2016, CM/Del/Dec (2016)1265, 22 September 2016.

3.3 The nature of the ECtHR judgements according to the ECJ of the European Union

The question whether the ECtHR judgements are or are not enforceable has also been examined by the European Court of Justice of the European Union (ECJ) in December 2014. This examination was pursuant to the request of the European Commission to the ECJ for an Opinion on Access of the EU to the ECtHR, where 24 of 28 EU Member States presented observations. At the time, one of the EU Member States, the UK, observed that

> As regards the procedure for the prior involvement of the Court of Justice, it is, first of all, maintained by the United Kingdom Government that that procedure is not necessary in order for the draft agreement to be considered compatible with the Treaties: given their declaratory nature, decisions of the ECtHR have no effect on the validity of EU law.

This view was shared by the ECJ that made the following clear statement on whether the ECtHR judgements are enforceable and self-executing:

> Proceedings before the ECtHR culminate either in a decision or judgement by which the ECtHR finds that the application is inadmissible or that the ECHR has not been violated, or in a judgement finding a violation of the ECHR. That judgement is declaratory and does not affect the validity of the relevant acts of the Contracting Party.[18]

4 The Non-Enforceability of the ECtHR Judgements in the Spanish Law

4.1 Constitutional Analysis

4.1.1 Constitutional provisions concerning the judiciary and the treaties

The Convention and all its Protocols to which Spain adhered have been ratified following the procedure established in the Article 94.1 of the Constitution, a different to procedure to the one (Article 93) used to adhere to the EU Treaties according to which "By means of an organic law, authorisation may be granted for concluding treaties by which powers derived from the Constitution shall be vested in an international organisation or institution". This means that powers derived from the Constitution to exercise jurisdiction have not been transferred to the Council of Europe or its judicial organs (i.e. ECtHR).

In the Spanish constitutional system, the judicial branch is bound by the statute law (Article 117.1 of the Constitution and Article 1 of the Organic Law of the Judicial Power). The consequence is that the judicial bodies may within the boundaries of statutory law allows them to do. The judiciary has no authority to enact norms of

[18]ECJ (Full Court) Opinion 2/13, of 18 December 2014, par. 20.

statutory level. Procedural rules are a matter of the "statutory law" of the central State, according to Article 149.1.6° of the Constitution. One author has suggested that the "treaties" should be considered as the "statutes" regarding the Article 117.1. As a consequence, Spanish judicial power should also be bound *"by the Convention and the decisions and doctrine of its judicial body"*.[19] However, this argument, used to justify the enforceability of the ECtHR judgements in Spain is a sophism because the premise it sets still needs to be demonstrated. Nobody denies that Spain is bound by the Convention. However, if the enforceability of ECtHR judgements is not established in the Convention, it is self-evident that such a binding effect cannot be in any case form the basis of the enforceability of ECtHR judgements in Spanish Law. In conclusion, it is clear that even accepting the non-problematic assumption that Spanish courts are bound to the "statutory law" and that includes the treaties, it is not acceptable to argue that a State is subject to more obligations than those explicitly established in the Treaty.

The enforceability of the ECtHR judgements has also been argued with a clearly incorrect interpretation of an unfortunate statement made obiter dictum by the Spanish Constitutional Court (SCC). Figueruela says *"Spanish law acknowledges the 'direct effect'* (efecto directo) *of the judgements from the Court at Strasbourt"* (STC 303/1993 of 21 October 1993). However, neither the SCC employs such words, nor are the words the Court uses quite right. What the SCC said, regarding ECtHR doctrine on the evidence of witnesses is that *"this recent doctrine of the European Court is not only self-executing* (de aplicación inmediata) *in our legal order by virtue of the Article 10.2 of the Constitution, but has always been recognized by Article 297.2° of the Criminal Procedure Statute"*.[20]

As we see, first, the SCC did not use the words quoted by Figueruela; and second, the SCC made reference to the ECtHR "doctrine", not to the operative part of its judgements. Hence the reference of the SCC to the Article 10.2 of the Spanish Constitution (which is an interpretative rule). A different question is whether it could be more fortunate to use the expression "interpretation" instead of "self-executing". In any case it is crystal clear, in my view, that STC 303/1993 of 21st October 1993 cannot be invoked to justify a pressumptive enforceability of ECtHR judgements in the Spanish law.

4.1.2 Spain did not vest the ECtHR to enforce its judgements

The ECtHR judgement that condemns Spain in the case *Del Río Prada* dramatically raised the question of the enforceability of ECtHR judgements that are "binding" but not "enforceable". According to Article 46 of the Convention Spain is then obliged "to abide" by the judgement. However, "to abide" is neither "to enforce" nor "to comply". "To abide" means that the State should take, in good faith, all the possible measures to give effect to the judgement in the domestic order. Article 46.2 of the Convention says

[19] Figueruelo Burrieza (2014), p. 121.

[20] STC 303/1993 of 25 October 1993 (FJ 8).

that "The final judgement of the Court shall be transmitted to the Committee of Ministers, which shall supervise its execution". However, Article 41 says that "*the Court shall, if necessary, afford just satisfaction to the injured party* (...) *if the internal law of the High Contracting Party concerned allows only partial reparation to be made*". In other words: according to the Convention, it is considered lawful that a Member State might not make "*perfect*" reparation, that is, a full enforcement of the ECtHR judgement. This stance will, of course, never allow the Member State to waive the obligation to communicate the Committee of Ministers the measures it has taken or plans to take in order to abide by the judgement as much as possible and to justify why a "perfect" reparation was not or is not possible. The communication to the Committee is therefore a test of the good faith of the Member State.

Spain has an obligation to abide by ECtHR judgements. However, careful examination of the Spanish legal order will confirm that at the time of the Del Río Prada case, ECtHR judgements were not enforceable in Spain. Their enforceablility is, moreover, not established in most domestic legal orders of the Member States. In fact, Spain never acceded to the Convention and its Protocols through the procedure detailed in Article 93 of its Constitution. So, the Council of Europe and its judicial organs (such as the ECtHR) were never vested with "*powers derived from the Constitution*" by Spain. Hence, the powers to annul statutes or to quash Spanish judgements were never transferred to the ECtHR.[21]

4.2 *The Question of the Enforceability of ECtHR Judgements Enforceability in the Constitutional Case Law*

The question of the enforceability of the ECtHR judgements has been raised in numerous cases before the SCC since 1991 up until 2006.

4.2.1 The first time where the question was raised: the Barberà case

In the first of these cases, *Barberá* (where the ECtHR found a violation of Article 6 ECHR, but not of Article 5 as in *Del Río Prada*), the applicants petitioned to annul the Spanish criminal judgements that had condemned them to prison sentences. The SSC dismissed their application with pertinent considerations,[22] but the applicants presented an appeal for (constitutional) *amparo* to the SCC that returned a confusing

[21]Even the above mentioned author who presumes to recognize the enforceability of ECtHR judgements by virtue of Article 117.1 of the Constitution acknowledges this fact. See Figueruelo Burrieza (2014), p. 121.

[22]STS (Chamber 2) 4th April 1990, Aranzadi 3157. This judgement upholds the earlier considerations exposed before (15th February 1990) presented by Morenilla, Supreme Court Justice and later Spanish ECtHR Justice (Morenilla Rodríguez 1989).

and contradictory judgement.[23] On the one hand, it sets out some unquestionable premises: (a) that the ECtHR jurisdiction is international and not supranational with the consequence that its judgements are not enforceable (FJ 2) and (b) that the ordinary courts are not allowed to annul its previous judgements (FJ 2). However, on the other hand, some highly questionable consequences arise from the SCC judgement: (a) it misinterprets the constitutional interpretation clause of the Article 10.2 of the Constitution and considers that a violation of a right contained in the Convention becomes *ex* Article 10.2 a violation of a constitutional right and therefore there is a "present violation"; and (b) although the right to liberty (Article 17 of the Constitution) was not invoked by the applicants of the *amparo*, the Constitutional Court considered that the case was a violation of such a right and deserved the *amparo* (FFJJ 4 and 5).

4.2.2 The SCC contradicts its previous judgment in the seconde time that deals with the issue: the Ruiz-Mateos case

However, the SCC changed its view in the second case where it had to deal with the question of the enforceability of the ECtHR judgements. In the *Ruiz Mateos* case,[24] the ECtHR found, as in *Barberá*, that Spain had violated Article 6 of the Convention. Mr. Ruiz Mateos asked for a constitutional *amparo* invoking the doctrine set up by the TC in the previous *Barberá* case. However, the SCC, in contradiction with its previous judgement, denied the admission of the *amparo* appeal and reasoned, unlike in its previous ruling,[25] that: (a) a violation of the Convention is not a violation of the Constitution, which is the supreme norm; (b) that the resolutions of the SCC have the force of *res iudicata*; and (c) that the SCC is only subordinated to the Constitution and to the Organic Statute of the Constitutional Court. The SCC ignored completely its doctrine on the "present violation" and sought to justify the different response given to Ruiz Mateos arguing that in Barberá there was a criminal procedure that had delivered prison sentences, which was not the case of *Ruiz Mateos*.

4.2.3 The Supreme Court denies the revision of a case despite an ECtHR ruling: the Castillo Algar case

Even more interesting is the case of *Castillo Algar* where the ECtHR condemned Spain for a violation of Article 6.1 of the Convention,[26] in the same way as in both

[23]STC 245/1991 of 16 December 1991, related to ECtHR Judgement of 6 December 1988, c. Barberà, Messegué and Jabardo v. Spain.

[24]ECtHR Judgement of 23 June 1993, c. Ruiz-Mateos v. Spain, 23 June 1993.

[25]Orders (Providencias) of the Constitutional Court, 31 January 1994 (applications for amparo 2291/93 and 2292/93). The text of those orders is not public, but I reproduced them, see Ruiz Miguel (1997), pp. 180–183. For a commentary on those orders, see Ruiz Miguel (1997), pp. 152–153.

[26]ECtHR Judgement of 28 October 1998, c. Castillo Algar v. Spain.

Barberá and *Ruiz Mateos*. As in the *Barberá* case, the applicant Castillo Algar was sentenced by a criminal court (although here a military-criminal court). It is worth noting that the applicant asked the ECtHR to annul the Spanish sentence at the origin of the violation of his right, but the ECtHR rejected this claim. Having noted that the ECtHR judgement was not enforceable *ex conventione*, Castillo Algar took steps to enforce it through the domestic law invoking the judgement of the SCC in the *Barberá* case. The applicant first sought *amparo* before the SCC which was refused because, according to the SCC, he had been afforded a "just satisfaction" and in this way it could be understood that the ECtHR judgement had been enforced.[27] Then, he requested the revision of the Spanish judgements considered by the ECtHR to have violated the Convention, but the Military Chamber of the SSC dismissed his application.[28] A further appeal for constitutional amparo followed against this new dismissal.[29]

4.2.4 The Supreme Court denies again a revision of a Spanish judgement: the Riera Blume case

After the ECtHR had condemned Spain for a violation of the right to liberty (Article 5.1 of the Convention) in the case *Riera Blume*,[30] the applicants applied for a revision of their sentence to the SSC the revision of their sentence, in line with the arguments advanced by the applicant in *Castillo Algar*. However, the SSC again denied the request.[31] Against that decision they then sought for *amparo* before the SCC. The latter examined the case but dismissed the application because it found sufficient evidence, in addition to evidence declared by the ECtHR as contrary to the Convention, to uphold the validity of the Spanish judgement that had sentenced the applicants to prison.[32]

4.2.5 The Supreme Court refuses to annul a judgement that the ECtHR declared in violation of the Convention: the Perote case

In the *Perote* case the ECtHR also found that Spain had violated Article 6.1 of the Convention.[33] The legal counsel of Perote petitioned the SSC for the anulment of his client's sentence (Article 240 of the Statute of the Judicial Power). Something similar was intended in the *Barberá* case, but the Court denied this possibility

[27] Order of the Constitutional Court, 11 March 1999.

[28] STS (Chamber 5), 27 January 2000.

[29] ATC 96/2001, of 24 April 2001.

[30] ECtHR Judgement of 14 October 1999, c. Riera Blume and Others v. Spain.

[31] ATS (Chamber 2), of 27 July 2000.

[32] STC 240/2005 of 10 October 2005 (FJ 8).

[33] ECtHR Judgement of 25 July 2002, c. Perote Pellon v. Spain.

reasoning in a similar way to the Constitutional Court in the *Barberá* case. The decision was again the subject of a constitutional *amparo*, though the Constitutional Court dismissed the application saying that the *Barberá* doctrine was not applicable because the *Perote* case lacked a "present" violation of the right that had been considered violated by the ECtHR.[34]

4.2.6 An ordinary court refuses the revision of a case despite an ECtHR ruling: the Fuentes Bobo case

The Spanish applicant in *Fuentes Bobo* followed alternative channels to try to enforce the ECtHR judgement.[35] He simply applied to the Spanish Court that had pronounced the judgement in the first instance for the enforcement of the ECtHR judgement. The court of the first instance denied the petition recalling that the applicant had petitioned the ECtHR for a "just satisfaction", which it understood as an alternative to the *restitutio in integrum* for which the applicant was now petitioning. Later on, Mr. Fuentes petitioned the SSC for the revision of the judgement (as both *Castillo Algar* and *Riera Blume* had previously done), but the SSC again dismissed the application.[36] Finally he turned to the SCC for a constitutional *amparo*, but the SCC dismissed his application with the argument that the violation of his right was not "present", a very questionable argument insofar as the applicant sacked from his job for expressing his opinions, had not been rehired.[37] Finally, the SCC appeared to close the door to any request for a revision of the (Spanish) judgements to enforce the ECtHR decisions.[38]

5 The Irregular (Partial) Enforcement of the ECtHR *Del Río Prada*

The day after the ECtHR (Grand Chamber) pronounced its judgement, the *Audiencia Nacional* approved a resolution enforcing the ECtHR judgement,[39] *even if the applicant did not ask the Spanish court to enforce the European decision.*

---

[34]STC 313/2005 of 12 December 2005 (FJ 3).

[35]ECtHR Judgement of 29 February 2000, c. Fuentes Bobo v. Spain.

[36]STS (Chamber 4), 20 November 2001.

[37]STC 197/2006 of 3 July 2006 (FJ 4). In his dissenting opinion Justice Pérez Tremps pointed this argument.

[38]STC 197/2006 of 3 July 2006 (FJ 6).

[39]Auto (Order) 61/2013, 22 October 2013, Criminal Chamber of the Audiencia Nacional (en banc).

5.1 *An Incorrect Understanding of the Convention and the ECtHR Judgement*

The order of the Audiencia Nacional enforcing the ECtHR judgement in *Del Río Prada* starts from a questionable premise as it states (FJ 3) that according to Article 46 of the Convention the obligation "to abide *by the judgement*" carries the obligation "to enforce *the judgements of the Court*" (emphasis added). However, as I have tried to make clear, accession to the Convention involves no obligation "to enforce" the judgements because these are not enforceable, but declaratory, as the European Union Court of Justice reminds us in the abovementioned Opinion from 18 December 2014.

Moreover, the order of the Audiencia Nacional emphasized that the *Del Río Prada* judgement held *"that the respondent State is to ensure that the applicant is released at the earliest date"* (*"en el plazo más breve"*) choosing the French version of the judgement (*"dans les plus brefs rélais"*) instead of the English one (*"at the earliest possible date"*). Based on theses premises, the Audiencia Nacional ordered the enforcement of the ECtHR judgement and, hence, the revision of the decisions ordering the continued imprisonment of the sentenced Del Río Prada.

However, as I have said both versions are quite different, but only the English one is the one which best reconciles the texts, having regard to "the object and purpose" of the treaty (Article 33.4 of the Vienna Convention on the Law of Treaties and, what is more, it is the only one consistent with the domestic Law at that moment because, as it has been seen, neither the statutory law nor the Constitutional Court case law allowed such "enforcement".

5.2 *Enforcement Without Official Translation of the Judgement*

In Spain, Castilian (or Spanish) is the official language, according to Article 3 of the Constitution. As a consequence, no official body may dispatch a document in another language that has not been officially translated. The Spanish Government told the Committee of Ministers that it *"immediately translated into Spanish"* the judgement on 23rd October 2013. However, the Audiencia Nacional met to discuss the issue and rendered its order one day before, on 22nd October 2013, in absence of any official translation.

5.3 *Enforcement in the Absence of Any Legal Provision Allowing Revision or Annulment*

I have shown that the ECtHR judgements are not "enforceable" according to the Convention. Notwithstanding, the domestic law may establish the enforceability to those judgements. The Audiencia Nacional acknowledges that there were no procedure established in the Spanish statutory law to enforce the ECtHR judgements.[40] However, it invoked the SCC doctrine contained in the cases *Barberá*, *Castillo Algar*, *Perote* and *Fuentes Bobo* (not to mention to case *Ruiz Mateos*), establishing that only the SCC, and the SCC alone, could annul by means of the constitutional *amparo* the domestic judgement that had violated the Convention. Amazingly, the Audiencia Nacional appears to be vested itself with the power of the SCC to do so.

5.4 The Denial of the Payment of the "Just Satisfaction" and "Costs and Expenses"

The operative part of the judgement *Del Río Prada* also stated that the Court:

> 4. Holds, by ten votes to seven, that the respondent State is to pay the applicant, within three months, EUR 30,000 (thirty thousand euros), plus any tax that may be chargeable, in respect of non-pecuniary damage;
>
> 5. Holds, unanimously, that the respondent State is to pay the applicant, within three months, EUR 1,500 (one thousand five hundred euros), plus any tax that may be chargeable to the applicant, in respect of costs and expenses

As far as the payment of the "non-pecuniary damage" is concerned, it was not enforced by the order of the Audiencia Nacional because it contradicted the domestic law that obliged Del Río Prada to compensate her victims for the harm they had suffered and because a resolution of the Committee of Ministers allowed not to enforce such payment to compensate the damages established by the domestic courts but not satisfied. This was also the position of the Spanish Government.[41] Concerning the payment of "costs and expenses", the Audiencia Nacional simply ignored it, but the Spanish Government said that the Committee of Ministers gave the national Governments the choice to compensate such "costs" with the pending obligations.[42] The decision of the Committee of Ministers on the execution of *Del Río Prada* case endorsed the compensation made by Spain.[43]

This decision clearly shows that the enforcement of an ECtHR judgement may yield to the domestic law. So, if the ECtHR judgement yielded to domestic law

---

[40]See Alcácer Guirao (2012), pp. 946–947; Ripol Carulla (2010), p. 93.

[41]Communication de l'Espagne relative à l'affaire Del Río Prada contre Espagne (Requête n° 42,750/09)—Informations mises à disposition en vertu de la Règle 8.2.a des Règles du Comité des Ministres pour la surveillance de l'exécution des arrêts et des termes des règlements amiables [DH-DD (2013) 1248].

[42]Monitoring of the payment of sums awarded by way of just satisfaction: an overview of the Committee of Ministers' present practice [CM/Inf/DH(2008)7 final, 15 January 2009].

[43]Decision of the Committee of Ministers, of 5 December 2013, on the case No. 19, against Spain, [CM/Del/OJ/DH(2013)1186/19].

concerning "damages" and "costs and expenses" there is evidence that it was not "enforceable" against the provisions of the domestic law.

5.5 *The Misenforcement of Del Río Prada as a Pilot-Judgement*

The wide sense given to the concept of "victim" led the ECtHR to permit individual applications against general norms.[44] The modifications of the Protocol paid no attention to this issue, but the Rules of the Court did pay some. On 21st February 2011, a new Rule was introduced (Rule 61) to give a differentiate treatment to the cases where violations were caused by a general norm (an "structural problem"). In those cases, the Court may initiate a "pilot-judgement procedure" adopting a "pilot judgement".

There is no doubt that at any moment of the procedure the *Del Río Prada* case was examined to rend a "pilot judgement". It was not in fact that kind of judgement. However, in the days following the *Del Río Prada* judgement, the Spanish courts annulled several decisions (*without a request by the parties concerned*) and released as many as 77 prisoners (mainly ETA terrorists), by applying the doctrine contained in *Del Río Prada*.

6 The Unconstitutional Agreement of the Supreme Court of 21 October 2014 and the New Organic Statute 7/2015 and Statute 41/2015

Before the *Del Río Prada* case, there had been several unsuccesful attempts to pass a legislation allowing the enforcement of ECtHR judgements in Spain (Bill sponsored by the Parliamentary group Izquierda Unida,[45] Report of the Council of State,[46] Government proposals in February 2013, Bill of Organic Statute announced on 3 April 2014), but all of them failed.

[44]See Ruiz Miguel (1997), pp. 39–41.

[45]*Boletín Oficial de las Cortes Generales. Congreso de los Diputados* (VII legislatura), Serie D: general, 7 June 2002, núm. 365, p. 26.

[46]http://www.consejo-estado.es/pdf/Europa.pdf.

6.1 The Unconstitutional Agreement of the Supreme Court of 21st October 2014

After the *Del Río Prada* case, the Criminal Chamber of the SSC (en banc) approved on 13 November 2013 an "Agreement" asking the legislative branch to regulate with the necessary clarity and precision a proper procedure to enforce the resolutions of the ECtHR... and overruling its judgement of 28 February 2006!!!.[47] This move raised a simple question: can an "agreement" of the Criminal Chamber of the SSC overrule a doctrine established in a judgement in a criminal procedure? But this was not the most surprising initiative taken by this Chamber of the SSC. One year later, the SSC took a new and questionable and dangerous step when on 21st October 2014 it passed a new "agreement" of the Criminal Chamber of the SSC (en banc) adding a new procedural track for the revision of judgements delivered by national courts, in which an ECtHR judgement appreciates a violation of fundamental rights, "*as long as it did not exist in the legal order an explicit legal provision about the enforcement of ECtHR judgements*".[48] It is worth noting that neither of these two "agreements" (specially the second one) has been published in the State Official Journal, although the latter has modified a legal provision (which is a blatant violation of the constitutional principle of the publicity of the norms proclaimed in Article 9.3 of the Constitution). The "Agreement" of 21st October 2014 was soon implemented when the SSC dictated an order (*Auto*) on 5th November 2014[49] authorizing a revision of a domestic judgement that the ECtHR considered as a violation of the Convention by the ECtHR. It was astonishing to read this argument in the FJ 2 of the Order supporting the enforcement of the ECtHR judgements: "*the doctrine has been surpassed that holds onto the declarative nature of ECtHR judgements*" because after the entry into force of Protocol 14 "*the binding nature of the ECtHR judgements in our legal order is beyond doubt*". Just one month later, in December 2014, the European Court of Justice stated...exactly the opposite, i.e., that the judgements of the ECtHR are of declaratory nature.

The "agreement" of 21st October 2014 is clearly inconsistent with the Spanish Constitution where the judicial branch is entitled to do only what a statute allows it to do it (Article 117.1 of the Constitution). No statute grants the Criminal Chamber of the SSC the authority to pass any kind of "agreements" which may be considered as a general norm and even less so of presumptive legal force. The norms enacted by State bodies of the Spanish system have to be published in the State Official Journal ("Boletín Oficial del Estado"). None of these requirements have been

---

[47]http://www.poderjudicial.es/cgpj/es/Poder_Judicial/Noticias_Judiciales/ci.Acuerdo_de_la_Sala_General_de_lo_Penal_del_Supremo_sobre_la__Doctrina_Parot__tras_la_sentencia_del_TEDH.formato3.

[48]http://www.poderjudicial.es/cgpj/es/Poder-Judicial/En-Portada/El-TS-establece-el-recurso-de-revision-como-cauce-para-ejecutar-las-sentencias-del-Tribunal-Europeo-de-Derechos-Humanos.

[49]ATS (2nd Chamber), of 5 November 2014 (in the procedure n° 20,321/2013).

respected. Unfortunately, it is not the first time that the SSC has assumed that it can modify the procedures established in the statutes.[50]

6.2 *The New Organic Statute 7/2015 and Statute 41/2015*

The enforcement of ECtHR judgements had finally received a regular treatment with the Organic Statute 7/2015, of 21st July 2015, and the Statute 41/2015 of 5 October 2015.

The first modifies the Organic Statute of the Judicial Power with the addition of a new Article 5 bis allowing the revision before the Supreme Court of any final judgement when the ECtHR had declared a violation of any right of the Convention provided that the effects of such a violation persist and no other means could end them. This Article 5 bis is a general provision ruling on all the procedures, but the Organic Statute 7/2015 also modifies other procedural statutes allowing this kind of revision in the Military (new Articles 328.2 and 504.2 of the Organic Statute 2/1989), Administrative-Contentious procedures (new Articles 102.2 of the Statute 29/1998), and Civil (new Article 510.2 of the Statute 1/2000) procedures. As far as Statute 41/2015 is concerned, it modifies the Statute on Criminal procedure to allow a revision in such cases (new Article 954.3). However, no provision has been passed to modify the Statute on the Labor Procedures, despite one of the prominent cases of failure to enforce an ECtHR judgement having originated in this kind of procedure (*Fuentes Bobo*).

References

Alcácer Guirao R (2012) La 'doctrina Parot' ante Estrasburgo: Del Río Prada c. España (STEDH 10.7.2012 n° 42750709). Consideraciones sobre la aplicación retroactiva de la jurisprudencia y la ejecución de las sentencias del TEDH. Revista de Derecho Comunitario Europeo 43:929–952

Andrés Sáenz De Santamaría P (2014) Acerca del Tribunal Europeo de Derechos Humanos y de la tentación de desacreditar al mensajero [a propósito de la STEDH (Gran Sala) en el asunto Del Río Prada c. España]. Teoría y Realidad Constitucional 33:199–218

Bujosa Vadell L (1997) Las sentencias del Tribunal Europeo de Derechos Humanos y el ordenamiento español. Tecnos, Madrid

De Juan Casadevall J (2005) La problemática ejecución de sentencias del TEDH en el Derecho español. Revista de las Cortes Generales 66:93–136

Escobar Hernández C (1992) Problemas planteados por la aplicación en el ordenamiento español de la sentencia Bultó. Revista de Instituciones Europeas 19-1:139–164

[50]Some time ago, the SSC introduced the "in camera" examination of certain evidences of the intelligence service, a practice not covered by any statute. See Ruiz Miguel (2002), pp. 260–265, for a critique on this practice.

Figueruelo Burrieza A (2014) Diálogo entre tribunales: la sentencia del Tribunal Europeo de Derechos Humanos de 21-X-2013 (Caso Sra. Del Río Prada contra el Reino de España). Revista Europea de Derechos Fundamentales 23:107–125

Izquierdo Sans C (1997) El carácter no ejecutivo de las Sentencias del Tribunal Europeo de Derechos Humanos. Derecho Privado y Constitución 11:351–378

Liñán Nogueras DJ (1985) Los efectos de las sentencias del Tribunal Europeo de derechos Humanos en Derecho español. REDI Revista española de Derecho Internacional 37-2:355–376

Morenilla Rodríguez JM (1989) La ejecución de las sentencias del Tribunal Europeo de Derechos Humanos. Poder Judicial 15:53–92 [also in (1990) BIMJ Boletín Informativo del Ministerio de Justicia 1554:935–969]

Ripol Carulla S (2010) La ejecución de las sentencias del Tribunal Europeo de Derechos Humanos en el ordenamiento español. Revista Europea de Derechos Fundamentales 15:75–112

Rodríguez A (2001–2002) Los efectos internos de las resoluciones del Tribunal Europeo de Derechos Humanos y la vinculación del juez español a su jurisprudencia. Teoría y Realidad Constitucional 8-9:201–216

Ruiz Miguel C (1997) La ejecución de las sentencias del Tribunal Europeo de Derechos Humanos. Un estudio sobre la relación entre el Derecho nacional y el internacional. Tecnos, Madrid

Ruiz Miguel C (2002) Servicios de inteligencia y seguridad del Estado constitucional. Tecnos, Madrid

Soria Jiménez A (1992) La problemática ejecución de las sentencias del Tribunal Europeo de Derechos Humanos. Revista Española de Derecho Constitucional 36:313–358

Soria Jiménez A (1995) Algunas reflexiones en torno a la ejecución de las Sentencias de Tribunal Europeo de Derechos Humanos. Anuario Español de Derecho Internacional 11:327–352

Torralba Mendiola EC (2007) Sobre la eficacia en España de las resoluciones del Tribunal Europeo de Derechos Humanos. Derecho Privado y Constitución 21:313–330